WASHINGTON
A MODERN GUIDE
TO THE NATION'S
CAPITAL

by Michael Frome

MAPS AND ILLUSTRATIONS BY
STEPHEN KRAFT

D1484937

DOUBLEDAY & COMPANY, INC.
GARDEN CITY, NEW YORK
1960

The American Scene, Henry James—Copyright 1907 by Harper & Brothers, copyright renewed 1935 by Henry James. Reprinted by permission of Harper & Brothers and Paul R. Reynolds & Son.

Advise and Consent, Allen Drury—Permission granted by Doubleday & Company, Inc. and William Collins Sons & Co., Ltd.

Guide to Washington Architecture, Carl Feiss—Carl Feiss, Washington Metropolitan Chapter American Institute of Architects. *A Guide to Washington Architecture, 1791–1957.* Reinhold Publishing Corporation.

Washington without Oratory, Roger Angell—Permission granted by Roger Angell.

"Washington Awaiting", by David C. Mearns in the *Wilson Library Bulletin,* June 1959—Permission granted by David C. Mearns and the H. W. Wilson Company.

The Potomac, Frederick Gutheim—Copyright 1949 by Frederick Gutheim. Reprinted by permission of Rinehart and Company, Inc.

Library of Congress Catalog Card Number 60-9477
Copyright © 1960 by Michael Frome
All Rights Reserved
Printed in the United States of America
First Edition

Contents

6   *Contents*

WASHINGTON
A Modern Guide to the Nation's Capital

The Washington skyline, looking across the
Potomac River from Columbia Island...

I *This Is the New Washington*

Washington, the way you see it now, is in the midst of the most dramatic transformation since George Washington and Pierre Charles L'Enfant raised it out of a mud puddle 160 years ago.

Two billion dollars' worth of public buildings are either newly opened or under construction. You'll find signs of an emerging new Mall, new waterfront, new bridges, new museums. Everything is changing—there is even a threat to redevelop the antiquated downtown business district.

Today's Washington is no longer a provincial Southern town. It is a booming metropolis, a mid-twentieth-century creature complete with freeways leading to suburbs deeper and deeper into the Maryland and Virginia countryside.

These and other roads enable you to reach exceptional scenic, historic, and recreational areas within three hours' drive of Washington. In one direction, the Shenandoah and Blue Ridge Mountains. In another, Chesapeake Bay and the Atlantic seacoast. We are surrounded by classic battlefields of the Civil War.

Culture deserves a word at the outset, because Washington periodically is the object of criticism from New York as a cultureless capital. This may once have been true. Today we can only invite our critics, learned and unlearned, to witness and enjoy the rise of the arts in Washington.

In short, the time has come to take a new, modern look at what we have here. Six million or more visitors come this way yearly, yet there is so much they never get to see or realize about this wonderful town that belongs to all Americans, and really to all the world. For example: you can park a trailer two blocks from the Jefferson Memorial, watch a baseball game a little more than a home run's length from the White House, walk in wilderness in the heart of the city, board a submarine at harbor, hear superb chamber music at the Library of Congress.

Washington, of course, is fundamentally a monumental city fashioned out of the dream of democracy. Here is where Lincoln walked and Washington before him; here were the focal dramas of the Civil War and the War of 1812 (when the British burned many of the public buildings), the joyous inaugurals and the solemn funeral processions down Pennsylvania Avenue.

Most important of all, here is where history is written every day of the year by a nation that insists free men and women, human error and disagreement notwithstanding, can govern themselves. You can follow the enactment of law in Congress, the administration of law in the executive departments, the interpretation of law in the Supreme Court.

Washington is everybody's city. The door is open to you at public buildings, museums, churches, and art galleries. Even the White House has its hours when the public is invited. And in many private places—the right restaurants, hotels, and bistros—you're likely to get the sense of public affairs that is paramount in the capital. (*Note:* if you pick up any rumors thirdhand or better, feel free to pass them along with embellishment.)

In Washington, you're at the crossroads of the modern world, rubbing shoulders with Indians from India and the Western plains, with Britons, Russians, and Latin Americans, as well as streaming high-school seniors, conventioneers, businessmen, generals, and GIs. And this is all their city, too.

I love these parts, and Virginia across the Potomac River where I live. Forgive me, however, for restraint in the use of superlatives, but after reading through a collection of guidebooks I am drenched with the downpour of grandeur and the endless representation of our capital city as a flawless shrine. Frankly, it just isn't built that way.

Washington is subject to criticism, which it often deserves. There are deep sociological problems. In architecture, we suffer the pains of changing, and sometimes poor, taste. As the late Senator John W. Daniel of Virginia observed, "If it be true that architecture is frozen music, then the Post Office Department is a shudder in stone." More recent was *Architectural Forum*'s gentle compliment to the new Senate Office Building: "It shows a state of architectural illness attended by extreme confusion, threatening to become chronic in Washington."

As you look over the scene, judge for yourself. The wider the public interest the more attractive our national capital will become. Especially in this period of boom, public alertness and concern are desirable to insure orderly, planned development. Don't be afraid to absorb a little of architecture; it will help you to appreciate Washington more.

Get out of character while you're here and do something different. You can enjoy any of our major points of interest and learn something from it. If you're an artist, try the FBI tour. And if you're a policeman, visit the National or Phillips Galleries. I've never heard of a dissatisfied customer at any of these places.

*George Washington took a deep interest in
Major L'Enfant's plans for the new capital...*

II *Birth of a Capital*

The new capital was derided as a "Serbonian bog" and "mud-puddle place," and Congress wondered why it ever agreed to move to the banks of the Potomac when Philadelphia had been so civilized, polite, and comfortable.

This was the shabby, inauspicious start of things for Washington in 1800. From then on, it grew so slowly and uncertainly that almost one third of its original 100 square miles was returned to Virginia in 1846. And it was really not until after the Civil War that its critics stopped trying to move the capital elsewhere.

Captain John Smith had been the first white man to explore the area, when he sailed up the Potomac from Jamestown in 1608.

In those days the tribal councils of the Manahoacs, battling the Powhatans, were held near the site where the Capitol stands now. But in time it was pre-empted by a company of Scotch-Irish settlers who called it New Scotland, later Carrollburg. Their tracts bore such names as Rome, Scotland Yard, Widow's Mite, Father's Gift, and the meandering stream below the hill was called the Tiber.

But before 1800 there simply was no city in the area Washington occupies now. There was a thriving town of Georgetown, then known as George Town, linked to Virginia with a small ferry, and the rural Carrollburg—but nothing in between.

How did our capital settle here? By 1787 the seat of government of the tiny republic had been much moved, from Philadelphia to New York, Baltimore, Lancaster, York, Annapolis, Princeton, Trenton, first one step ahead of the British, then of Continental troops demanding to get paid. For three years there had been proposals to select a permanent capital, but at the moment the Continental Congress was sitting in Philadelphia. There it was revising the form of government from Confederation to Constitution when it turned to seriously discuss establishing a "Federal Town, a Federal House for Congress and for the Executive Officers."

This discussion among friends and patriots lasted three years and almost wrecked the nation. Northerners nominated Germantown, in the city of Philadelphia, which was really the cradle of liberty. Southerners favored a site along the Potomac. A Georgia member warned that if the North persisted in its position it would "blow the coals of sedition and endanger the Union." James Madison grimly added that if Virginia had known what was coming "it would not be a part of the Union at this moment."

Ultimately, the decision on location of the capital was reached by Alexander Hamilton and Thomas Jefferson in a back room, or rather at a quiet sociable dinner. Hamilton, advocate of a strong central government, wanted Jefferson's support for the Assumption Bill, under which the federal government would pick up $20,000,000 worth of debts incurred by the states during the Revolution. Jefferson and his Southern friends opposed it as an invasion of states rights; besides, the Northern states, then called the Eastern, were the ones in substantial debt. Jefferson at this tête-à-tête indicated he might swing a couple of votes for the Assumption Bill if Hamilton could "sweeten it a little." The result: an agreement that the capital would stay in Philadelphia until 1800, then move south.

Once this decision was made, four men, four of taste and talent who knew what they were doing, were responsible for the basic design of the city. Much of the best of it today we still owe to:

George Washington, who, as a committee of one appointed by Congress, chose the site from along a designated 105-mile section of the Potomac. He had surveyed the country as a youth, encamped in it when he served under General Braddock, quaffed many a brew at taverns in Alexandria and Georgetown. With all his other qualities, Washington was a dreamer and idealist. He chose a romantic site, bordered by the winding river and wooded heights. It was practical, too, at the head of tidewater navigation (Alexandria and Georgetown already were port cities), an ideal location for a water trade route west along the Potomac.

Soon after, Congress lost interest in development of the capital. In 1791, it honored Washington by designating his name for the new city, but then told him to raise the money locally to buy land and construct public buildings. Maryland and Virginia had already provided some funds, but only enough for a start. Now Washington went to the 19 original landowners in the District of Columbia and proposed an amazing real estate transaction.

They were to transfer, without compensation, he suggested, portions of their land required for streets, and to sell land for public buildings at $67 an acre. Their remaining holdings within the city plan would be divided into lots and offered for sale, with the proceeds split equally between the government and property owners. The theory was that land values would soar and on this basis they agreed. The capital would never have materialized here had Washington not been, among other things, the master realtor of his day.

Pierre Charles L'Enfant, French-born artist, architect, and military engineer, who had served on Washington's staff during the Revolution and now became the first important city planner in

America. "No nation," he wrote Washington, "had ever before the opportunity offered of deciding on the spot where the capital city should be fixed, or of combining every necessary consideration in the choice of situation." He looked out across the bogs and farmlands and envisioned an ageless city as beautiful as Versailles. "The plan," he felt, "should be drawn on such a scale as to leave room for that aggrandizement and embellishment which the increase of the wealth of the nation will permit it to pursue at any period however remote."

L'Enfant designed broad, transverse streets and avenues, open squares, parks and circles, marking places for government buildings and even for the Washington Monument. To appease the rival communities of Georgetown and Carrollburg, it was decided to place the House of Congress near Carrollburg and the President's Palace near Georgetown. L'Enfant, however, was a poor appeaser. He was obdurate, temperamental, single-minded and, of course, he was right.

Thomas Jefferson, who, as Secretary of State, issued the order to L'Enfant to design a city and public buildings amidst the "hills, valleys, morasses and waters," then met twice weekly with him (Wednesday and Saturday evenings). As a classicist in architecture, he adapted the design of the Maison Carrée, the ancient Roman temple, which he had visited in Nîmes, France, for the Virginia Capitol at Richmond. He and Washington felt an affinity with Roman social institutions such as law and citizenship, and believed the setting of columns, pediments, porticoes, and domes would be a symbol of strength for the young republic.

Andrew Ellicott, the young Pennsylvania surveyor who actually laid out the city. First he placed boundary stones one mile apart. The cornerstone of the city was placed at Jones Point, south of Alexandria, on April 15, 1791, and a line run ten miles northwest. Of Ellicott's original 40 boundary stones, several are still in place. Then he fixed the "central point" by nightly observations from a perfectly level platform on the hill where the Capitol would be built, keeping the records of the north star and the moon until midnight to establish a line due east and west, then sighting another straight line due north and south. The center of the Capitol dome was marked at the point of intersection and from there he charted the Mall axis and symmetrical street layout. Later, when L'Enfant was fired, Ellicott, as his principal assistant and confidant, carried on, and improved the original plan.

Construction moved very slowly for lack of funds. Washington hesitated to ask Congress for help, fearful the capital would still go elsewhere. The property owners grew restless, apprehensive—and speculative. The most prominent was Daniel Carroll, whom Washington had appointed one of three commissioners to select building sites. He owned lands covering the major portion of Capitol Hill, which he proceeded to subdivide at prohibitive prices. Another was David Burns, a choleric, contentious Scotsman, who cultivated a plantation where the White House now stands. For some time he opposed transferring land to the government, and the President and the three city commissioners held several conferences with him in his cottage. In his testy way he delighted in defying Washington and once provoked the President to lose his well-known tact. "Had not the Federal City been laid out here," the President told Burns, "you would have died a poor tobacco planter." "Aye, mon," retorted Burns, "and had ye nae married the widow Custis ye would be a land surveyor today— and a dom poor one at that!"

Collision between L'Enfant and the property owners was inevitable. He was using *their* land for streets as wide as 160 feet and one grand avenue 400 feet wide. There was nothing like it anywhere. If Philadelphia was content with its narrow streets, why should anything else be needed here?

L'Enfant crossed with Daniel Carroll, who started to build his mansion, Duddington House, in the middle of New Jersey Avenue, near the Capitol. L'Enfant protested that it would close the avenue and destroy the general city plan. He prepared to have it torn down but Carroll blocked him with a magistrate's warrant. L'Enfant tried another way. He organized a gang of laborers who dismantled it completely by night, leaving not a single brick in place. Carroll in fury protested to Washington, who placated him by ordering the house rebuilt—though not in the middle of New Jersey Avenue.

The property owners demanded that L'Enfant publish his plan to promote the government sale of lots. He refused, claiming that if his maps were made public before the principal buildings were located, unsightly structures would be built on the best locations. Consequently, the sale of lots failed, the commissioners held L'Enfant responsible and the President was forced to dismiss him in 1792.

L'Enfant was offered $2500 for his enduring design of the national capital, which he haughtily refused. From then on, he was passed over as a federal architect and became an obscure landscaper, with one last opportunity in 1814. Secretary of War James Monroe placed him in charge of rebuilding Fort Washington south of the city when it was feared the British might try to attack by moving up the Potomac. L'Enfant cleared away the debris, demolished the old brick and began to construct a great fortress with 200,000 bricks, large supplies of stone and lumber. But the war ended before it was complete and the War Department began wondering about the cost and why portions of the old fort were not saved. L'Enfant refused to submit reports and detailed plans and was dismissed. Yet today his work still stands there, too, as an historic example of military engineering.

In his old age, L'Enfant was disbelieved as the designer of the Federal City. He haunted the committee rooms of Congress, asking for recognition and compensation; courtly but feeble, he was a figure for mockery and derision. He died unmourned in 1825 and was buried in obscurity until 1909; his grave now overlooks the city from an honored vantage point in Arlington National Cemetery.

President Washington, to return to the early period, was not faring too well either. He recoiled from the "land sharks" and "boomers," who took over the city after publication of the L'Enfant-Ellicott Plan. Lots were sold at high prices, but few homes were built.

Into this curious swampy mudhole, the government of the United States arrived in 1800. A packet sloop brought furniture and records. President John Adams came overland by stage on June 13, but was obliged to take quarters at the Union Tavern in Georgetown. Personnel on the government payroll numbered between 125 and 150.

The city looked "mean and disgusting." Pennsylvania Avenue, the best road, was a morass covered with elderbushes. The only two commodious homes belonged to Daniel Carroll and Notley Young. Near Georgetown a block of houses had been erected, which bore the name of the "Six Buildings." There were a few other dwellings, but the city was mostly covered with scrub oak on the high ground, marsh in the lowland.

Population: 3000. "The people are poor," wrote Secretary of the Treasury Oliver Wolcott, "and, as far as I can judge, live like fishes, by eating each other."

This sorry place was an object of satire throughout the fifteen states, and a very poor advertisement to the world. When Congress met that autumn, one year after the death of George Washington, twenty-four years after the birth of the new republic, there was a general desire to move the capital to some other, more civilized, place.

The status quo tried to claim the future, but a motion to move lost by two votes.

In this desolation, a sidewalk was attempted with a covering of chips left from hewing for the Capitol Building. But the trouble was that in dry weather sharp fragments cut the shoes and in wet weather it covered them with white mortar.

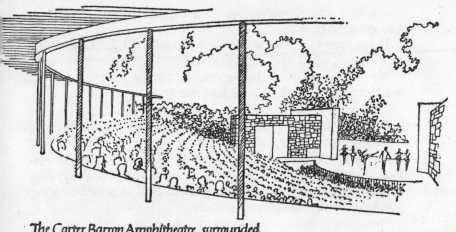

The Carter Barron Amphitheatre, surrounded
by the trees of Rock Creek Park...

III *The Weather, the Seasons, and What Happens When*

The weather in Washington reminds me of a winning candidate who promises everything and delivers, but you never know just when to expect it.

Sometimes it's April in January, and March is apt to behave like December—or May.

Or as Mark Twain found it here: "When you arrived (at the station at night) it was snowing. When you reached the hotel it was sleeting. When you went to bed it was raining. During the night it froze hard, and the wind blew some chimneys down. When you got up in the morning it was foggy. When you finished your breakfast at ten o'clock and went out, the sunshine was brilliant, the weather balmy and delicious, and the mud and slush deep and all-pervading. You will like the climate—when you get used to it."

If you care to follow Mark Twain's advice, "Take an umbrella, an overcoat, and a fan, and go forth."

My advice on what to expect, season by season, regarding weather, principal attractions and events, is:

SPRING—It's wonderful, most attractive, liveliest time of year. Mild weather usually arrives earlier than it does in most Northern cities (prepare for possible 80 degrees in March), flowers burst into bloom starting with magnolia, then followed by cherry blossoms, azalea, dogwood, wisteria, pansies. Lots of crowds; be sure you have hotel or motel reservation.

EVENTS

April (or late March), Easter Sunrise services, Arlington National Cemetery, Walter Reed General Hospital, Carter Barron Amphitheatre.

Easter Monday, egg rolling, White House lawn (adults admitted with children only; you bring the eggs).

Cherry blossoms, greatest sight of spring, usually reach their peak around the Tidal Basin (pink and white Yoshino and Akebono single blossoms) for about ten days in early April, followed by deep-pink Kwanzan double blossoms at Hains Point later in the month. Weather is the determining factor; sometimes they're early, sometimes late. Cherry trees were presented in 1912 as a gift of friendship from the city of Tokyo (in 1952, cuttings were sent to Japan to replenish war-depleted groves). Annual Cherry Blossom Festival, usually about April 7–12, includes weekend pageant at the Jefferson Memorial. Tip on crowdless cherry blossoms: drive to suburban Kenwood, Maryland; Highland Street is best, an arch of blooms.

April 13, Jefferson Birthday services, Jefferson Memorial.

Mid-April, Baseball season opens. President tosses out first ball on one day a capacity crowd is assured at Griffith Stadium.

Late April, Washington Pilgrimage, a tour of religious shrines.

House and Garden, and Embassy Tours (late April or early May). Best chance to visit embassies and historic homes in Georgetown and Capitol Hill, while joining social leaders, Cabinet and Congressional wives at tea. Proceeds go to a worthy cause, such as Goodwill Industries and Washington Home for Incurables. For tickets, usually about $3, and exact dates, contract American Automobile Association, 1712 G Street, N.W. (ME 8-4000).

May, first or second Saturday, National School Safety Patrol parade; 25,000 to 30,000 youngsters take over Constitution Avenue with safety floats, banners, bands.

Third week, Armed Forces Day, open house at military and naval bases, plenty of jet planes, atomic cannons, latest weapons.

May 30, Memorial Day services, Arlington National Cemetery; Presidential wreath is placed at Tomb of the Unknowns.

S U M M E R—Can be hot, humid, sticky, though not as unbearable as it used to be before indoor air conditioning and motel swimming pools. Men wear tropical outfits (seersucker, Palm Beach, linen), women informal clothes, print dresses. When Congress, the big show, adjourns, hotel occupancy drops; hotels promote Summer Jubilee, June 15–Labor Day: family rates, children under 14 free, often free parking.

EVENTS

Early June to September 1, Carter Barron Amphitheatre, in the heart of Rock Creek Park, adjacent to 16th Street and Colorado Avenue. Programs under the stars feature big-name entertainers, ballet, symphony.

Early June–late August—Watergate Concerts, at open-air amphitheater just west of Lincoln Memorial. Marine Band, every Sunday evening; Army Band, Tuesday; Navy Band, Thursday; Air Force Symphony, Friday. (Free)

June–August—Sylvan Theatre Program, Washington Monument grounds. Friday evening. Half-hour concert or dance presentation, followed by illustrated hour lecture, usually on travel. For program call RE 7-1820, ext. 2557. (Free)

July 4—Fireworks display, Washington Monument grounds.

August—President's Cup Regatta, off Hains Point. Opens with rowing, followed by boating competitions in subsequent weeks.

A U T U M N—Best season except for spring; in some ways best of all. Crowds are thinner, less waiting in line, more personalized attention on government tours; wider selection of accommodations. Climate is dry, mild. If you are driving, color in the mountains is beautiful.

September, third weekend, President's Cup Power Boat Races, off Hains Point. A big-league show of champion drivers skimming the Potomac in hydroplanes.

*September–November–*Professional football; six Sundays at Griffith Stadium, George Preston Marshall and the Redskins tackle the rest of the National Football League.

*September–November–*College football, Saturdays. University of Maryland opposes the big-time at Byrd Stadium, College Park. George Washington University plays a fighting schedule at Griffith Stadium. Naval Academy is in its new stadium at Annapolis.

November 11, Veterans Day, Arlington National Cemetery.

*November–*Washington, D.C., International; join the celebrities at opening of the Fall Meet at Laurel Race Track, 18 miles from Washington on Route 1.

WINTER–Unpredictable, some years raw, cold, soggy; others, short and mild. You don't have to bring umbrella and galoshes, but come prepared to buy them.

EVENTS

*December 23–January 1–*Pageant of Peace, at the Ellipse, south of the White House; opens with lighting of national community Christmas tree by the President; concerts, reindeer, displays from many countries.

*January (first week)–*Congress opens; so does the social season.

*January 20–*Presidential Inauguration every four years at the Capitol, followed by parade on Pennsylvania Avenue. Inaugural ball (now held in two arenas to accommodate the exclusive battalion of ticket holders).

*February 12–*Lincoln's Birthday, services at Lincoln Memorial and Lincoln Museum.

*February 22–*Washington's Birthday, services at Mount Vernon. Pilgrimage to Washington Birthplace National Monument, 30 miles east of Fredericksburg, Virginia, on Route 3.

IV *Getting Around—and Where*

You have a day in Washington? A week? A year? You can see the high spots in almost any period of time and off-beat sidelights, too—providing you plot your program and learn the best ways to get around.

Don't try to kill yourself sightseeing. Keep your walking to a minimum and bring a good pair of comfortable shoes, preferably with rubber soles, to absorb the impact of marble and concrete floors. Learn which hours the places you plan to visit are open— some government buildings are closed weekends, some are open evenings. Find out where you'll have to pay admissions; they build up fast for a family group. Include activities for your youngsters; if they have fun, you will too. (See Chapter XIX.)

Get yourself a good map of the city and plan your schedule by areas—that is, on Capitol Hill, around the White House, the Mall. Best free map is issued by Esso Touring Service, 261 Constitution Avenue, N.W., where you can also get marked routings and travel guidance if you're driving onward from here. Another good map: the Gulf Tourgide, available at any Gulf station. For street details, including residential areas, the Shell map is very useful.

And another good one is issued by the Greater National Capital Committee, 1616 K Street, N.W., a travel promotion organization supported by local businessmen. If you have any questions, or need any guidance, visit this office or telephone ST 3-3535. Your Congressman's office also has guide pamphlets covering Washington points of interest.

Now let us say you have only one or two days in Washington. Here are the ten places you should visit, the approximate time involved, and a pointer or two:

1. LINCOLN MEMORIAL, the most nearly perfect structure in Washington. See it at night, when Lincoln will not only look you in the eye but speak to your inner self. Twenty-five minutes.

2. WASHINGTON MONUMENT, highest point in the city, excellent

for orientation of landmarks. Twenty minutes aloft, plus thirty minutes walking and waiting time below.

3. THE CAPITOL. Be sure to take the guided tour, which starts in the Rotunda; price (25¢) has remained the same since 1890. One hour. With more time, you can watch the legislative process in action. House and Senate usually convene at noon (sessions run from early January into summer) and you can obtain an admission card to the galleries at the office of your Congressman or Senator. Congressional hearings, usually held in morning hours, are open to the public, too.

4. THE WHITE HOUSE. Remember it's closed afternoons and all day on Sunday and Monday. Check with your Congressman on the early-morning guided tour. Thirty minutes.

5. SMITHSONIAN INSTITUTION. Don't get too absorbed or you may never get out. Concentrate on seeing the new exhibits. Two hours.

6. ARCHIVES (open evenings) to see the Declaration of Independence and Constitution, our charters of freedom. Forty-five minutes.

7. NATIONAL GALLERY OF ART. Take the one-hour tour at 11 A.M., then lunch at the cafeteria. Or else join the Sunday afternoon tour and stay for the evening chamber music concert.

8. LIBRARY OF CONGRESS (open evenings), headquarters of learning, its exhibit halls and reading rooms open to everyone—and that's part of freedom too. Check information and publications desk for pictures, prints, recordings for sale. Half hour for short guided tour, view of Main Reading Room.

9. CUSTIS LEE MANSION AND ARLINGTON NATIONAL CEMETERY. Be there on the hour to see guard changing at Tomb of the Unknowns. One hour, plus forty minutes round-trip driving. Avoid travel to and from Virginia during morning and afternoon rush hours.

10. MOUNT VERNON, George Washington's home on the Potomac, the nation's first shrine. It's loved and crowded by a million visitors a year. Come in the morning, avoid the weekend. One hour, plus an hour and a half round trip from Washington. While you're in the Mount Vernon area, visit Woodlawn Plantation.

Should you have additional time, add the following ten places and activities:

11. SUPREME COURT, temple of the rights of all men under law. Guided tour. Excellent cafeteria. Forty minutes.

12. WASHINGTON CATHEDRAL or the SHRINE OF THE IMMACULATE CONCEPTION, or both, regardless of your faith.

13. Go to church—where Washington worshiped, Abraham Lincoln, Teddy Roosevelt, Dwight Eisenhower, or to the church of your own denomination. Religion is part of the capital; there are sixty faiths here, including Moslem and Buddhist.

14. FBI Tour. Kids like it as much as grownups. One hour.

15. Drive through Rock Creek Park, woodland in the heart of the city, to the National Zoo. Make it at feeding time for Smoky Bear and the sea lions. Two hours.

16. Bring your rod and reel and throw a line in the Tidal Basin or the Potomac. Catch one a mile from the White House! (Time? Fisherman's patience.)

17. PHILLIPS GALLERY, the connoisseur's collection of modern art where everyone is welcome. Sunday afternoon or Monday evening for the concerts.

18. Walk through Georgetown and the eighteenth century. History may be everywhere in Washington, but antiquity is here only. Stop at Dumbarton Oaks. One hour and a half.

19. BUREAU OF ENGRAVING AND PRINTING, where $29,000,000 worth of paper money is printed every day. One hour.

20. ARENA STAGE, theatre-in-the-round and theatre at its finest —with orchestra seats for everybody at balcony prices.

How to get around in Washington? Besides walking, which you can't avoid but should reduce whenever possible, there are four other ways: car, streetcar or bus, taxicab, and sightseeing bus. Each has its proper time, place, and purpose.

Drive your car in Washington? Not downtown, if you can help it. L'Enfant designed a city of broad streets, which should carry a large volume of traffic smoothly but don't. Some streets are one-way downtown in the morning rush hour, then reverse in the evening. Others are posted NO TURNS or NO LEFT TURNS (7–9:30 A.M., 4–6:30 P.M.). If you make it okay on the straightaway, you're liable to get lost in the first circle.

Traffic safety is a serious problem. In 1958 there were 20,000 accidents, with 63 fatalities, 7000 injuries. The National Safety

Council rates Washington "low" in enforcement, public-safety traffic education, and public support. There are not enough police officers, not enough really trained men on the 2500-man force. We need additional manpower to cope with increasing traffic.

You will find parking handy and adequate at the Smithsonian, barely so at the Lincoln Memorial and none at all at many points of interest. Street parking meters cost 10¢ an hour—when you can find one open—but most are posted NO PARKING BEFORE 9:30 A.M. OR AFTER 4 P.M. Police can be tough about violations, too. You may figure it's safe to tear up a traffic ticket away from home, but during the work week (Monday–Friday) they may tow your car to the police garage and charge you $10 to get it back.

Very important: Whenever you park on the street, lock your car. If you're staying at a hotel or motel, unpack *all* your luggage and leave it in your room, not in your car trunk. An out-of-state license plate is an invitation to looters, in the neighborhood of places like the Capitol and Smithsonian, even on residential streets.

There is parking space in downtown garages, but it's expensive (except by New York standards). Rates are about 45¢ an hour, 25¢ each additional hour; for all-day parking you should be able to find a garage with a maximum charge of $1.50. Cheaper lots (75¢–$1 all day) are located around 23rd and C Streets, N.W., near George Washington University and the Department of State.

Tip: If you're staying at a Virginia motel, you can drive to the Columbia Island fringe parking lot (free) on Mount Vernon Boulevard near the Pentagon, leave your car locked and take a bus during morning rush hours into Washington, then pick it up in evening rush hours. There are two other fringe lots if you're coming in from Maryland: one at Carter Barron Amphitheatre, on 16th Street, on the Silver Spring route, the other at Soldiers' Home, Michigan Avenue and Irving Street, N.E., on the Prince Georges County route. Buses run past these locations all day.

Downtown parking tip: Drive your car into one of the 130 lots and garages displaying a circular PARK AND SHOP emblem. They will give you one hour free parking if you make a purchase at a participating downtown shop (though some have a minimum charge). You can park free all day if you get enough stickers by shopping at the right bank, beauty shop, restaurant, stores selling books, clothing, records, toys, liquor, furniture, furs, gifts. Check the list under "Park and Shop" in the Yellow Pages.

Streetcar and bus are the least expensive means of getting around—that is, when you're heading for a particular sightseeing objective rather than on a loop around the city. Fare is 20¢, with transfers issued by the driver if you're switching to another car going in the same general direction. Streetcars are now on their way out in Washington; a total changeover to buses is scheduled for completion by 1962. Fares may go up, too.

The best points of interest to visit by bus or streetcar:
Capitol Hill (Capitol, Library of Congress, Supreme Court), No. 30 or 54 from anywhere along Pennsylvania Avenue, or No. 40 from 14th and F Streets.

Bureau of Engraving and Printing, No. 50, from 14th and Pennsylvania; also puts you close to Washington Monument, Smithsonian Institution.

Federal Triangle buildings (Department of Commerce, Post Office, FBI, Archives, National Gallery), No. 54, 20, or 30.

White House, No. 30.

Union Station, No. 20 or 42.

Buses go to other attractions, too, but take time in waiting and walking. For example, you can reach the Lincoln Memorial (R-4), but first you've got to go to Farragut Square, 17th and K Streets, N.W. For route questions, call D. C. Transit, FE 7-1300.

Washington taxicabs are good and the drivers can be as interesting as those in New York if less garrulous. There are 8500 cabs, the highest number per capita in the country. Group riding is legal, so if the driver stops to pick up another passenger you have no recourse. Group riding became a necessity during the days of World War II and was either hectic or fun with all manner of people thrown together at close quarters. In those days our drivers were extremely courteous, in the Southern style. Now, many drive too fast and they're acquiring big city ways. However, the right driver will still tell you about his foolproof international peace

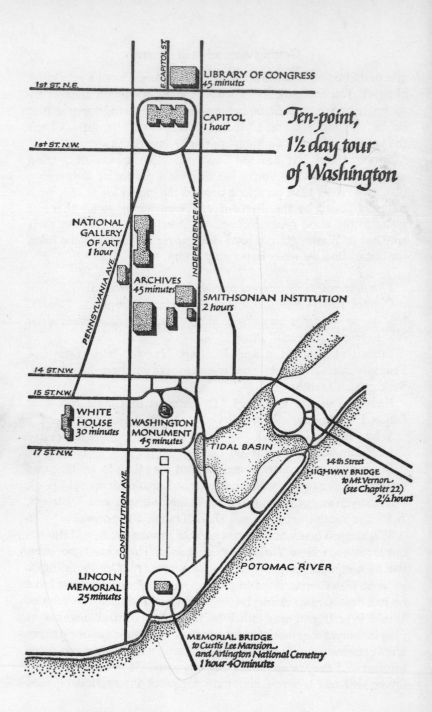

LIBRARY OF CONGRESS
45 minutes

E. CAPITOL ST.

1st ST. N.E.

CAPITOL
1 hour

1st ST. N.W.

*Ten-point,
1½ day tour
of Washington*

NATIONAL
GALLERY
OF ART
1 hour

PENNSYLVANIA AVE.

INDEPENDENCE AVE.

ARCHIVES
45 minutes

SMITHSONIAN INSTITUTION
2 hours

14 ST. N.W.

15 ST. N.W.

WHITE
HOUSE
30 minutes

WASHINGTON
MONUMENT
45 minutes

TIDAL BASIN

CONSTITUTION AVE.

17 ST. N.W.

14th Street
HIGHWAY BRIDGE
to Mt. Vernon
(see Chapter 22)
2½ hours

POTOMAC RIVER

LINCOLN
MEMORIAL
25 minutes

MEMORIAL BRIDGE
to Custis Lee Mansion
and Arlington National Cemetery
1 hour 40 minutes

plan, or his latest patent, or what he told Eisenhower before he became President, or what George Meany told him.

Cab rates used to be shamefully cheap. In the early 1930s five people could go anywhere in the city for 20¢—20¢ for all five, not per passenger. The single rate downtown is still a bargain and this is the only large city without metered cabs. The reason: Congress, which controls such things, prefers to maintain a low rate between the Capitol and hotels in the Northwest area. Consequently, you can travel from the Capitol or Union Station to the Sheraton-Carlton, Statler or Mayflower, all in the same zone, for only 50¢. This is a very good rate for one, but with two or more persons you get involved in group and party rates. For two persons in the first zone the group rate is 35¢ each (50¢ each into the second zone, 65¢ each into the third zone). For three or more persons riding together, the party rate applies—two group passenger fares, plus 20¢ for each additional passenger. This means a family of four will pay $1.10 within the first zone (downtown), $1.40 into the second zone (Zoo, Sheraton-Park Hotel), and $1.70 into the third zone (Washington Cathedral, National Shrine of Immaculate Conception).

Another complication: if you go from 22nd Street to the Capitol, a distance of two miles, you pay 50¢, but from 22nd Street to the Lincoln Memorial, only a few blocks, you pay 75¢ because you've crossed into another zone. It's hard to fathom and beat. On the long runs even the driver sometimes has trouble calculating the rates. He may overcharge, but he's just as likely to undercharge. Anyway, he can't take you the long way around to run up the meter and you can ask the cost before you start.

Tipping: No need on short ride. On a longer ride a tip is in order and drivers will accept it with appreciation, not as a matter of course.

If you want to go sight-seeing on your own, you can rent a cab for $3.60 an hour. The driver will take you to the principal shrines. He is not supposed to provide a lecture (unless he's paid his $10 sight-seeing guide fee), but no law forbids a passenger from asking questions.

Sight-seeing bus tours are very good, balanced to introduce you to the principal sights without strain. Then you can visit specific places that have most appeal on your own. Consider a guided tour if this is your first visit, if you have little time and want to make the most of it, or if you're traveling alone.

The four principal bus tour operators are:

D. C. Transit System, 1125 Pennsylvania Avenue, N.W. (FE 3-5200)

Diamond Sightseeing Tours, Union Station (RE 7-1716)

Gray Line of Washington, 1010 Eye Street, N.W. (DI 7-0600)

White House Sightseeing, 509 6th Street, N.W. (EX 3-3682)

They're all competent, though some buses are newer and more comfortable than others. If you have any feeling about air-conditioned buses in summer, ask before you book. Tours are generally the same and the guides are lively and knowledgeable (though some tend to rewrite history). Of the various tours, which they all offer, I like these three best:

"Beautiful Washington," the basic tour. You stop only at the Lincoln Memorial and Washington Monument, but drive past the White House, Capitol, Federal Buildings, and other points of interest. (Two hours; cost $4 to $4.50, half for children.)

"Washington-Georgetown-Arlington Cemetery" covers a lot of territory, too. You stop at the Jefferson and Lincoln Memorials and the Tomb of the Unknowns. (Three to 3½ hours; $4.50 to $5.)

"Washington at Night," a worth-while evening. You stop at the Lincoln Memorial and Archives, see the floodlit Capitol fountains and the skyline from the Virginia side of the Potomac. (Two and a half hours, $4 to $4.50.)

Other good tours: Alexandria and Mount Vernon (4 hours, $6), and the all-day combination of the city trip and Mount Vernon ($10 to $12). Ideal in summer: the tour-cruise to Mount Vernon, going there by bus and returning to the Washington waterfront aboard the SS *Mount Vernon* (for an additional $1.50). The Wilson Line operates the *Mount Vernon* spring and summer, leaving Pier 4 on Maine Avenue 10 A.M. and 2 P.M., and a moon-light dance cruise at 8:15 ($2 round trip). Latest addition to the flotilla, the yacht *Diplomat*, provides two-hour guided sightseeing cruises sailing 10:30 A.M. and 2:30 P.M. ($2, children $1, NA 8-2440).

Longer tours are operated, too—to Annapolis, Gettysburg, the Skyline Drive in Shenandoah National Park, and a three-day Virginia loop (Shenandoah Valley-Richmond-Williamsburg-Fredericksburg).

Besides the sightseeing lines, Trailways offers all-expense tours of one to three days to the Skyline Drive, Harpers Ferry, and Blackwater Falls State Park, West Virginia. From Trailways Terminal, 1201 New York Avenue N.W. (DI 7-4224).

Tip: if you're considering the public buildings tour on a weekend, remember the White House and Bureau of Engraving, two of the high points, are closed, and other buildings are substituted.

Sightseeing companies also rent limousines with driver-guide. If there are five or six in your group, the tariff is the same or only slightly more, depending on the trip. You'll cover more territory faster.

V *Lost in Circles, Found on Avenues*

Washington has such a simple, basic plan of geography that all you have to do is follow the rules and . . . and . . . and you may be lost before you know it. Don't despair: take your bearings from the Capitol dome or Washington Monument, if you can see them. If not, take heart in the long established fact that if you haven't been lost at least once, you really haven't been here.

The L'Enfant design of the city, so you'll know *why* you're lost, works as follows:

The Capitol is the center of the city. The city is divided into four quadrants, Northeast, Northwest, Southeast, and Southwest. Capitol Street divides the East and West; the Mall (extending from the Capitol to the Lincoln Memorial and ultimately, we hope, eastward to the Anacostia River) divides North and South. The streets are laid out at right angles, named alphabetically one way and numerically the other. This means the "first alphabet" extends from A to W Streets (there are no B or J Streets), followed by the second alphabet of two-syllable street names progressing from Belmont Street, and the third alphabet of three-syllable names from Allison Street. Streets on the Mall are named for the first four Presidents, Washington, Adams, Jefferson, Madison. House and building numbers follow the system; for example, the 700 block of H Street lies between 7th and 8th; the 700 block on 10th Street lies between G (seventh letter) and H.

Elementary so far? The L'Enfant plan has two focal points, the "House of Congress" and the "President's Palace" as he called them. From these two, broad avenues radiate outward like the spokes of a wheel, diagonally across the right angle grid patterns. These avenues, sometimes more like boulevards, intersect in landscaped circles, squares, triangles, and small parks, features which give Washington much of the atmosphere of space and vista—and which cause so much confusion. The diagonals are named for the states.

Most of the places you'll want to visit are in the Northwest
section. Become acquainted with these four principal avenues,
which lead to 75 per cent or more of the public buildings, monuments, churches, restaurants, and hotels—and to less-known points
worth noting:

Pennsylvania Avenue, the Main Street of the Nation, extending
a mile and a half from the Capitol to the White House, and
beyond to Georgetown. L'Enfant had great plans for the avenue
which never came off. It was in sorry shape until the south side,
a conglomeration of aged hotels, boardinghouses, saloons, and
Chinatown, was demolished in 1929 and replaced with the Federal
Triangle. Even today, the north side from 6th to 12th is pleading
for a face lifting. In the block east of 6th Street the bonus army
bivouacked in 1932 and was dispersed by Chief of Staff General
Douglas MacArthur. The intersection with 14th Street is the
busiest point on Pennsylvania Avenue, the crossroads of government, business, and visitors, probably our closest approach to
Times Square, without the bright lights. Halfway up to F Street is
the entrance to the National Press Building, the headquarters
of news bureaus and correspondents from every part of the
United States and points east and west, including Manila, Tokyo,
Moscow; other tenants are lawyers, publicists, and manufacturing
representatives, who like the address, and a school for secretaries,
which contributes charm if not news. In the city's process of
growing, newsmen have fanned out tremendously in their office
locations, but along about high noon the luncheon procession
begins to the National Press Club, a wonderfully unstuffy men's
club on the thirteenth floor, taken very seriously by the world
statesmen who have come to speak here; and also by the lady
journalists, who for years have been trying to crack the membership ranks. At 15th Street, Pennsylvania takes an unplanned bend
around the Treasury Building, then around past the White House.
At the northwest corner of 19th Street, a streamlined new office
building has pre-empted the very site occupied by the Department of State, when John Marshall was Secretary, and briefly as
the temporary White House of President James Madison after the
War of 1812. The Arts Club (2017), where James Monroe once
lived, is one of the few remainders of that era. The corner at

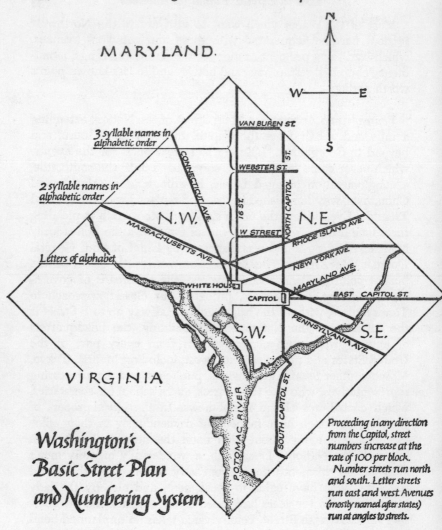

MARYLAND.

N

W   E

S

VAN BUREN ST.

3 syllable names in
alphabetic order

CONNECTICUT AVE.

WEBSTER ST.

NORTH CAPITOL ST.

2 syllable names in
alphabetic order

16 ST.

N.W.

W STREET

N.E.

MASSACHUSETTS AVE.

RHODE ISLAND AVE.

NEW YORK AVE.

Letters of alphabet

MARYLAND AVE.

WHITE HOUSE

CAPITOL

EAST CAPITOL ST.

S.W.

PENNSYLVANIA AVE.

S.E.

VIRGINIA

POTOMAC RIVER

SOUTH CAPITOL ST.

*Washington's
Basic Street Plan
and Numbering System*

*Proceeding in any direction
from the Capitol, street
numbers increase at the
rate of 100 per block.
Number streets run north
and south. Letter streets
run east and west. Avenues
(mostly named after states)
run at angles to streets.*

21st Street was site of the Franklin Hotel; the innkeeper's daughter Peggy O'Neale, the celebrated Gorgeous Hussy, defied Washington society when she married Senator John H. Eaton of Tennessee. The best people scorned her but President Jackson treated her as a favorite . . . Keep west, then around Washington Circle and you'll reach Georgetown.

Massachusetts Avenue, one of two "Embassy Rows" (16th Street is the other), cuts a wide swath across the heart of the city, forming major intersections at seven circles or squares. The most important is DuPont Circle, at the intersection with Connecticut and New Hampshire Avenues. The stone fountain and statue in the center are the work of Daniel Chester French, sculptor of the figure of the Great Emancipator in the Lincoln Memorial.

Around DuPont Circle are great mansions built in an earlier era. On the east side: the Elizabeth Patterson House (15 DuPont Circle), now the fashionable Washington Club; the Sulgrave Club (1801 Massachusetts), another rendezvous for nice ladies, and 1501 New Hampshire, designed by John Russell Pope, now occupied by the World Health Organization.

On the west side: James G. Blaine mansion (2000 Massachusetts Avenue); Indonesian Embassy (2020), built at the turn of the century by Tom Walsh, the Colorado mining king, whose daughter Evalyn owned the Hope diamond; The Phillips Gallery (1600 21st Street; the Larz Anderson House (2118), now headquarters of the Society of Cincinnati, formed by officers of the Revolutionary Army, used by the Secretary of State in official entertaining; and the Cosmos Club (2121), for men of letters, in the former town house of Sumner Welles.

Sheridan Circle is the most beautiful circle along Massachusetts Avenue and Phil Sheridan, in its center, the finest equestrian statue in Washington. Designed by Gutzon Borglum, fighting Phil is a figure of action. Embassies ring the circle: Greece (2221) Rumania (1607 23rd Street), Turkey (1606 23rd), Egypt (2301), Chile (2305), and Czechoslovakia (2349).

Prettiest street in Washington: S Street, to the right off Massachusetts. In spring, tulips spill across the lawn at 2347 (residence of the Dutch ambassador). Number 2340 was the home of Woodrow Wilson for three years after he left the White House. On Sunday morning, February 3, 1924, when it was announced that the ex-President was dying, crowds knelt and prayed in the street until the end came at 11:20 A.M. The house has been presented by Mrs. Wilson to the National Trust for Historic Preservation, although she still lives here and it will not be open to the public during her lifetime. The Textile Museum (2320, open 2–4, Monday, Wednesday, Friday, free) contains a collection of rugs, fabrics, tapestry and textiles from all over the world.

Farther out Massachusetts Avenue (3100), you'll come to the British Embassy, designed by the distinguished architect Sir Edwin Lutyens, largest and most imposing of the foreign delegations in Washington.

How to visit an embassy: A little girl once knocked on the door of the Russian Embassy (1119 16th Street) and asked to see the ambassador so she could report to her class on what he really thought of America. She didn't reach the ambassador, but half a dozen others spent an hour with her and served tea while they talked about communism and democracy.

It isn't that easy at all of the 80 embassies and legations in Washington, and very rarely at the Russian Embassy. These are essentially business offices, although most attractive ones, reflecting the art and décor of their countries. The best way to visit them is by joining the Embassy Tour in spring. If you're coming in some other season and are interested, you might arrange to visit one of these three by writing in advance to: Information Officer, Embassy of Japan, 2514 Massachusetts Avenue, N.W.; Embassy of Indonesia, 2020 Massachusetts Avenue, N.W.; or Embassy of Denmark, 2374 Massachusetts Avenue, N.W. For a complete list of all the embassies and legations in Washington, their addresses, telephone numbers, and the names of diplomatic officers, write the Superintendent of Documents, Government Printing Office, Washington 25, D.C., for a copy of "Diplomatic List of the Department of State" (price, 20¢).

Connecticut Avenue is the local version of New York's Fifth Avenue. It starts at the U. S. Chamber of Commerce Building, Lafayette Square. A block away, on the east side of Farragut Square, is the Army-Navy Club, favored for fifty years as a refuge in the city for military officers. All around K Street are signs of Washington's commercial building boom, new white, steel-trimmed office buildings.

From K Street to DuPont Circle are popular eating spots clustered around the Mayflower Hotel and shops of national reputation. Jefferson Place, in contrast to gleaming Connecticut and K, is an arty street of old homes done over into shops and offices. On upper Connecticut Avenue, above DuPont Circle, are more dining spots, hotels, the entrance to the Zoo, and the route to Chevy Chase, in case you're headed that way.

Sixteenth Street (a street in name but an avenue in fact) should be called Organization Row. Probably more headquarters of national associations are located along this street than any other in the country. Most have displays, if not museums. They welcome visitors and especially invite their own members.

Washington has boomed as an association town. No less than 300 national trade associations, plus 400 labor, farm, professional, and women's groups have their main offices here.

You may be a card-carrying member of one of these five 16th Street organizations. If so, stop in to see where your money goes. If not, you may be interested nonetheless in the:

HOUSE OF LABOR, headquarters of the 15-million-member AFL-CIO, two doors from the start of 16th Street at Lafayette Square. On the lobby wall a giant mosaic mural (17 by 51 feet) depicts progress of the American worker from the pick and ax days to the jet age. The Executive Council Chamber on the eighth floor would be worthy of any board of directors, but this is the only one with a balcony looking down at the White House.

NATIONAL HOUSING CENTER (1625 L Street, 10–6, Sunday 1–6), headquarters of the National Association of Home Builders, is a five-floor showcase of the latest architectural designs, techniques, and materials produced for the modern home. More than 150 industrial exhibitors keep it current without sparing expense. Guides available.

NATIONAL GEOGRAPHIC SOCIETY (corner of M, 9–4:30, Monday–Friday). Displays from its expeditions the world over and original illustrations from its magazine are on view in Explorers Hall.

NATIONAL EDUCATION ASSOCIATION (1201), headquarters of 750,000 teachers, a modern, blue-spandreled building opened in 1959. The library contains more than 30,000 books and magazines on education. NEA members are welcome to eat in the employees' dining room.

NATIONAL RIFLE ASSOCIATION (Scott Circle), opened in 1958, has unique appeal to sportsmen, including its 320,000 members. The fourth-floor museum (9–4:30, Monday–Friday) traces firearms development over 600 years and includes a specimen of every basic firearm in U.S. production. NRA members: don't miss shooting in the modern 12-point range in the basement (3–10 P.M.). Ammunition is 80¢ a box, plus 75¢ a half hour.

Beauty on 16th Street: Meridian Hill Park, part of National Capital Parks, is designed like a modern French-Italian garden, with cascades and fountains, a high terrace overlooking the city, long promenades and winding walks.

If you drive all the way out 16th Street, stop at Walter Reed General Hospital and Army Medical Center. Established in 1909, it comprises 113 landscaped acres with formal gardens and 148 buildings. Tulips presented by the Netherlands circle the main fountain in spring. The outdoor amphitheater is a beautiful natural setting for Easter sunrise services. Famous men have come here as patients (Dwight D. Eisenhower, George C. Marshall, John Foster Dulles) but the hospital prides itself on first-class treatment for privates as well as generals. General Pershing, who lived at Walter Reed seven years until his death in 1948, insisted on eating the same fare as the soldiers.

Walter Reed is a major research center as well as a hospital. Visitor volunteers from all parts of the country are wanted by the Whole Body Counting Facility to aid nuclear medical research. Step up and have your gamma rays (radioactivity) counted. It's painless and takes only 200 seconds in the detector tank. Call RA 3-1000, ext. 2212, for an appointment.

VI *The Capitol, Face and Inner Frame*

Approaching it by plane aloft, or from the opposite end of Pennsylvania Avenue, the Capitol of the United States appears perfectly proportioned, and thus a model representation of democratic government.

THE CAPITOL *is* a great structure, overpowering in form and concept. But looks from afar are misleading. The Capitol today results from disagreement and changing taste spread across 160 years. It is really not one building, but a series of additions, extensions and extended extensions to the tiny beginning.

As an office building designed to serve the two Houses of Congress, the Capitol has been outmoded and inadequate for years. Capitol architect George Stewart says: "Since the turn of the century, the population of the country has doubled. The responsibilities of Congress have increased at least that much. But there has been no basic expansion of facilities or improvement in this building (except for renovation of the two chambers ten years ago) since before the turn of the century."

Now the Capitol is in the midst of its newest face lifting, extending from the figure of Freedom atop the dome (cleaning, repairing and reinforcing) to new footings and piers 60 feet underground. During your visit you may be inconvenienced and have to pick your way around the building. Parts of it may be closed, but don't miss the chance to witness the inner frame of the old Capitol laid bare and construction underway.

In a sense, the Capitol is almost a complete, self-sustained community, with barbershops, post office, underground railroad, restaurants, a place of worship, its own 158-man police force. Five million visitors annually enter the Capitol doors (9–4:30, later if Congress remains in session), averaging 15,750 a day, except for Thanksgiving, Christmas, and New Year's days when it is closed. By act of Congress the flag flies over the Capitol day and night.

Consider Capitol Hill as more than the Capitol alone but as the entire hilltop, encompassing the cluster of office buildings where Congress does most of its work, the Supreme Court, and the Library of Congress. The Hill is easily worth a full day of any visitor's time.

Start at the office of your Congressman or Senator. Better yet, write him first of your plans; his staff will help with arrangements where possible. If you're from one of the distant, less-populated states, say Arizona, Nevada, or Alaska, your Congressman will probably greet you himself. But if you're from a nearby state (like Maryland, New Jersey, New York, Pennsylvania, Ohio), don't expect a royal welcome, though any constituent will receive a cordial, helpful reception from a staff member. If you have a bright, eager boy (14 to 17) in tow, you may want to inquire about vacancies on the page-boy list. Fifty of these fortunate youngsters run errands for the House, twenty-eight for the Senate. They earn $306 monthly, while Congress is in session, attend school from 6:30 to 9:30 at the Library of Congress. Be sure to ask for an admission card to the Congressional gallery. When the session gets rolling these offices are the busiest places in Washington; it's not unusual for everyone, including the boss, to work six and seven days, and often evenings.

From your Senator's office, ride the underground subway to the Capitol Building—a must for youngsters. New cars, installed in 1959, travel at 20 miles per hour (41 seconds from the old Senate Office Building, 55 seconds from the new one). A new subway to link the Capitol with the House side (which now has only an underground tunnel) is due for completion in 1962.

The only real way to see the Capitol for the first time is on a guided tour (25¢), which you join in the Rotunda. It introduces you to the highlights in 40 minutes; when you're through you can probe further on your own, but without it you might be hopelessly lost in the long corridors, engulfed in the tide of lobbyists, correspondents, pages, Capitol employees, and Congressmen. But this great building is a world of pleasantly human surprises, too. One day, my little boy, unlooking, walked smack into the House Republican leader, then Joe Martin of Massachusetts, who shook his hand as if he were a long lost constituent and kindly talked to him about Congress. One evening, a friend who works here was

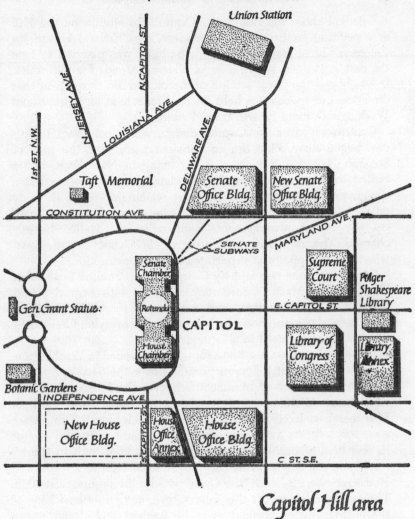

Capitol Hill area

driving two foreign students around the Capitol grounds when he found his boss, Senator Clifford Case of New Jersey, waiting for a streetcar. The Senator declined the offer of a lift home, but countered by spending an hour showing the visitors around. Were they surprised at politics in America!

L'Enfant chose the site of the Capitol. He envisioned the Hill as a pedestal waiting for a monument, the "Federal House for Congress." Most historians say the building was planned to face the east as it does, where a level plateau extends for two miles. It was hoped the finest section of the city would develop in that direction, but speculators held the land for sale at high prices and Washington's main growth turned westward.

Controversy over the Capitol design, which continues to this day, began early. First the commissioners accepted the plan of Stephen Hallet, a French architect living in New York. But a skilled amateur draftsman, Dr. William Thornton, presented a design to Washington and Jefferson which impressed them so much the President asked the commissioners to adopt it and cancel the Hallet arrangement—"with delicacy." Hallet bitterly charged Thornton with architectural theft, but cooled down when he was appointed superintendent of construction.

The cornerstone was laid by George Washington on September 18, 1793, in a Masonic ceremony complete with martial music, flying colors, fine oration, and a barbecue feast. Within three years federal construction funds gave out but Maryland helped by donating money raised in a lottery.

In November 1800, the Sixth Congress convened in Washington, with Vice-President Jefferson presiding over the Senate, Speaker Theodore Sedgwick of Massachusetts over the House. Only one wing (now adjoining the Rotunda on the north) was finished. Few members liked this "palace in the wilderness." The House was crowded into an outer room in the Senate wing and almost its first item of business was to order a chamber built in the incompleted south wing. But this proved uncomfortably warm and House members called it "the Oven" without the slightest affection. The small bridge across the Tiber Creek, at the western base of the hill, was often washed away by freshets and Congressmen riding to the Capitol were compelled to tie their horses to the farther side and pick their way across the swollen stream on fallen trees.

Benjamin Latrobe, first of the major Greek revival architects in America, gave shape and form to the Capitol when he was appointed in 1803 to construct the south wing, remodel the cupolas and design the interior. The walls were made of sandstone from nearby Aquia Creek in Virginia, the bricks in kilns on the Capitol grounds. By the time the British arrived in 1814, the new Capitol looked quite imposing on its hillsite.

But what a target! The invaders had disembarked, nearly 500 strong, at the Patuxent River (facing Benedict, Maryland, now on Route 231). General Ross and his troops advanced unchallenged until a sniper shot the horse from under him as he entered Washington. This enraged them; they marched to the Capitol and filled the House chamber. "Shall this harbor of Yankee democracy be burned?" shouted Admiral Cockburn from the Speaker's chair. The response was uproarious: "Fire the building!"

The beautifully sculptured House chamber was filled with pine-pitch boards from the passageway between the two buildings; books from the new Library of Congress, then in the Capitol, and paintings from the walls were scattered over the floor. The torch was applied. The soldiers fired through the roofs while they waited until the bonfire really glowed. Then they headed up Pennsylvania Avenue to spread their celebration to the White House.

The interior was well ruined, but the walls were saved by a night-long rainstorm. After the war Latrobe resumed his work but he lamented that the damage to Thornton's plan should have been more complete.

In 1818, the eminent New England architect Charles Bulfinch succeeded Latrobe and directed construction of the Rotunda (as Thornton had planned it) covered with a low wooden dome. Four huge historical paintings (Signing of the Declaration of Independence, Surrender of Burgoyne at Saratoga, Surrender of Cornwallis at Yorktown, Washington Resigning His Commission) by John Trumbull, who had been aide-de-camp to Washington in the Revolution, were hung on the Rotunda walls. Congress admired the new handiwork, yet neither house exercised jurisdiction over the Rotunda; as a twilight zone it became a market place for hucksters selling everything from ribbons and mousetraps to stoves and pianos.

In 1850, first steps were taken to enlarge the Capitol anew, extending the wings with greater wings. In the process, it became evident the marble extensions would dwarf the central dome, "that small wooden thing," and the new dome, nine million pounds of cast and wrought iron, was begun. During this period architect

Thomas Ustick Walter was constantly harassed by Captain Montgomery C. Meigs of the Corps of Engineers, the construction supervisor. Walter protested to Secretary of War Jefferson Davis, "If Captain Meigs is to have charge of the architecture, I shall take pleasure in retiring!" But Captain Meigs replied simply, "I have labored faithfully and diligently to construct this building in such a manner that it would last forever as a creditable monument of the state of the arts at this time in this country."

Regardless of its quality as art (which *is* subject to question), the great dome, 135 feet, 5 inches in diameter, has an impressive dignity visible for miles. And one hundred years later it is still a remarkable engineering phenomenon. It took nine years to build, during which time the Capitol walls were girded, trussed, and bolted. The dome is composed of two shells, a series of 36 ribs supporting large outer plates. It follows the path of the sun like a flower, oscillating three to four inches from east to west, then returning when the sun sets. The 19-foot statue of Freedom was raised in 1863, after the Civil War began, but the Confederacy really had the last word; Jefferson Davis, while still Secretary of War, had the headdress changed from a liberty cap to eagle's feathers to avoid it becoming a symbol of liberation from slavery.

Now in a five-year period (1958–63) the greatest changes are being made in the Capitol since the addition of the dome. The east central front is being extended, by 32 feet, 6 inches, with the present architectural details of sandstone—pedestals, columns, cornices, and pediments—reproduced in marble. And a third House Office Building is being erected at a cost of $66,000,000. Another vast program under serious consideration provides for extension of the west front, a four-level underground parking garage, tunnels to the Supreme Court and Library of Congress, as well as subways to House office buildings.

Sound and fury surrounded the proposal to extend the east front. Many architects and historic preservationists argued that the sandstone was too closely linked with tradition to be destroyed. At one point Capitol architect Stewart introduced to a Senate group an aerial photo taken almost directly overhead showing the building was anything but symmetrical, that the dome, while it is 60 feet from the west front, actually overhangs at the east front. "Yes," countered Senator Theodore Green, the remarkably astute Rhode Island nonogenarian, "but how many people see it from that angle?" The east front extension will not eliminate the asymmetry, but lessen it by about half. Whether it was proper to sacrifice the cherished, symbolic east front, history will judge; if the verdict of time is affirmative, the marble facing will, in a sense, be a memorial to Speaker Sam Rayburn, who championed the proposed change through Congress.

While the forces of historic preservation lost the battle, the Capitol architects pledged to preserve "the architectural dignity and majesty of the Capitol, while carrying out their commission to accomplish authorized changes and improvements in a manner to serve effectively the needs of Congress, now and in the future." This has involved incredible diligence and difficulty. For example, each of the 24 east front columns (24 feet high, 3 feet in diameter) had to be carved from a single block of Georgia marble weighing as much as 20 tons. The sandstone statues in the central portico had first to be reproduced in plaster, then in marble by the best of the vanishing breed of artistic stonecarvers, working under supervision of the noted sculptor, Paul Manship. Georgia marble, incidentally, was chosen for its imperviousness to wind, rain, frost. The newness you see should endure a thousand years or longer.

The west front is rather neglected and overlooked in all the controversy, but it should not be. The terraces were long closed because of unsafe macadam surfacing, but now they are rebuilt, paved, and bordered with flowers abloom in spring and summer. From the west front, the view of the Mall and the city around is superb.

The Capitol grounds, 131 acres, trenched and torn during the construction period, will be relandscaped, although many of the historic trees are being saved. The newest addition to the grounds, the Robert A. Taft Memorial, is on the northwestern slope, a 100 foot-high tower built of Tennessee marble with a 10 foot statue of the late Ohio Senator, "Mr. Republican," at the base. Twenty-seven bells, the largest seven tons, hang in the upper part of the tower; they toll the quarter hours and the hour.

The Capitol is not only the seat of legislation, but a mammoth museum of history and art. The exterior pediments are decorated with marble sculpture, the doorways with ornamented bronze.

The interior is copiously ornamented with tiled and mosaic floors, murals, frescoes, and paintings. Some of the décor does not stand up too well under the test of time. The classic example: the marble statue of George Washington, which Congress more than a century ago ordered from Horatio Greenough for the huge sum of $45,000. He worked on it for ten years. "It is the birth of my thought, and I have sacrificed to it the flower of my days and the freshness of my strength," he wrote. "I would not barter away its association with my name for the proudest fortune avarice ever dreamed of." Today you will see this statue (Washington in a toga), in an obscure corner of the Smithsonian. Perhaps the most curious item presently on view is the white marble block with busts of Susan B. Anthony, Elizabeth Cady Stanton, and Lucretia Mott, best known as "Three Old Ladies in a Bathtub."

The Rotunda, the center of the Capitol, contains a variety of art. Its finest works: the marble head of Lincoln, by Gutzon Borglum, a gift of the late Eugene Meyer, publisher of the Washington *Post;* the bronze bust of Washington, by David d'Angers, a gift of France in 1905, and the full-length bronze of Washington, by Edward Valentine, presented by the State of Virginia originally for Statuary Hall. Looking straight up into the "eye" of the dome, you can see light streaming through the 36 long windows and the decorative coffers surrounding the monumental fresco, "Apotheosis of Washington." Some of the figures are 15 feet tall, painted by the artist Constantino Brumidi while he was flat on his back on a scaffold 180 feet in the air.

Once it was possible to ascend a winding staircase to a gallery directly under the dome and look down at the Rotunda and out across the Mall. "Well," as Mark Twain rationalized, "you ought not go up in the dome anyhow, because it would be utterly impossible to go up there without seeing the frescoes in it—and why should you be interested in the delirium tremens of art?"

Tip: If you're really interested and have plenty of energy, check with the office of the Architect of the Capitol, who will assign a Capitol police guide to lead you the 365 steps up to the gallery.

Constantino Brumidi, if not a great artist, was a dedicated craftsman, who labored more than a quarter of a century decorating the Capitol. When he died in 1880, he was in the midst of painting the circular frieze 75 feet above the Rotunda, depicting important events in American history; Filippo Costaggini, a fresco artist, completed most of the painting, but the last three scenes (Spanish-American War, Civil War, and the Wright Brothers in Flight) were done by Allyn Cox in 1953.

Below the frieze are eight gigantic historic murals depicting the Landing of Columbus at San Salvador, Embarkation of the Pilgrims, Baptism of Pocahontas, De Soto's Discovery of the Mississippi, and the four of the Revolution by Trumbull.

The Rotunda has been the scene of solemn, sorrowful hours. Americans honored have lain in state here to receive the tribute of the nation. The first was Abraham Lincoln in 1865, the most recent were the Unknowns of World War II and Korea in 1958. Pierre L'Enfant, scorned in his lifetime, was honored here too before his reburial in Arlington.

Adjoining the Rotunda on the north is the Small Rotunda, in the oldest part of the Capitol, and the old Senate Chamber, used by the Senate until 1859, then as Chamber of the United States Supreme Court until 1935.

Adjoining the Rotunda on the south is marble-columned Statuary Hall, chamber of the House of Representatives from 1807 to 1857. John Quincy Adams returned here as a member of the House after he was President; you can see the spot where his desk stood and where he was fatally stricken while delivering a speech.

When the House moved to its new, larger wing, the states were invited to send marble or bronze statues of two deceased leading citizens. In 1933 the weight had become so heavy that the number in Statuary Hall was reduced to one per state and the remainder have spilled into the corridors. Some of the statues are deeply impressive. Look especially for Will Rogers of Oklahoma by Jo Davidson, Samuel Adams of Massachusetts by Anne Whitney, and Zebulon Vance of North Carolina by Gutzon Borglum. By all means, look for those chosen by your own state.

For that matter, the Congressional art gallery does include a number of fine works: portraits by Stuart, Peale, Sully; two landscapes by Albert Bierstadt; 17 paintings of Indian scenes and army forts by Seth Eastman; sculpture by Daniel Chester French, Saint-Gaudens, Jo Davidson, and that massive marble Lincoln head in the Rotunda. And the President's Room in the Senate wing, reserved for the chief executive when he visits the Capitol (very rarely now), is pre-eminent in its furnishings and decorations.

Near the Rotunda on the west is a beautiful small room set apart for prayer and meditation by members of the House and Senate. It is nondenominational in design, with prayer benches and ten chairs. The central figure in the stained-glass window is the kneeling figure of Washington, with the etched words, "Preserve me O God, for in thee do I put my trust."

Beneath the Rotunda are a crypt and empty tomb, once intended to hold the body of Washington; the plan was to have a galleried opening in the center of the floor through which the sarcophagus could be seen. Martha Washington consented, but after her death the heirs decided that, by the terms of his will, Washington must remain at Mount Vernon. But in the tomb itself is a catafalque, a simple funeral bier draped in black broadcloth, used only for those who lie in state in the Rotunda.

The basic function at the Capitol is the enactment of legislation. During the course of a guided tour you will briefly visit the galleries of both House and Senate; you can return with a pass from your Senator or Congressman.

The two houses of Congress have their traditions, differences—and jealousies. The Senate for a time sat with closed doors and still occasionally conducts executive sessions, while the House has always transacted its business openly. Once it was customary for Representatives to sit in the House wearing hats; in the Senate, to this day, there is a box containing choice snuff (though supposedly no longer any snuff users).

Representation in the House is based on population; members serve two-year terms, so are always running for office and are, theoretically, more responsive to the people. Senators, two from each state, serve for six years. The Vice-President acts as president of the Senate, but has no vote except to break a tie. The House elects a speaker.

Congressmen in the early years received six dollars a day. When they tried to raise their pay to $1500 a year such a furor was raised they settled for eight dollars a day. Now they receive $22,500 plus allowances for secretaries and administrative staff (based on population), expenses for one trip home yearly, plus telephone and telegraph.

Before a bill becomes law it must have approval of both houses. To follow its course, the bill first is referred to the appropriate committee, which may hold hearings before it passes (rejects or modifies) the measure and submits it to the full House or Senate. When it wins approval in one house, it is forwarded to the other, referred again to committee before it comes to the floor. On passing both houses, the bill goes to the President for his signature; if he chooses to veto the bill it takes a two-thirds vote to override.

In the Senate, the presiding officer, the Vice-President (or a Senator who may be sitting in) occupies a carved chair on the rostrum facing the 100 Senators seated at mahogany desks in a semicircle, Republicans on the left, Democrats on the right. The House Chamber, much larger, provides space for its 437 members; here joint sessions are held when the President or a foreign leader addresses Congress. House members sit on leather-covered chairs arranged in benches; unlike the Senate, where seats are assigned by seniority, House members may sit anywhere. When the House is in session, look to the right of the Speaker for the Mace (13 ebony rods fastened with silver bands, surmounted with silver globe and eagle), the symbol of authority and order adopted in 1789.

House members are allocated speaking time on the floor, usually five or ten minutes, by their party leaders, although on a normal day two thirds of the House seem to be out for a short coffee, or reading the morning paper. Actually, it is difficult to judge diligence by attendance, since much business is done off the floor and in committee rooms. Senators can speak more freely. Sometimes, particularly late in the session, there may be night meetings and, if a good filibuster is going, queues waiting to enter the steeply rising public galleries as late as 10 P.M. The two champion senatorial filibusters have been the late Huey Long and Wayne Morse (the record holder with 22 hours, 26 minutes).

Each side has its legendary heroes and personalities. In 1811 Henry Clay entered the House (he had earlier been a Senator) and was elected Speaker the first day, a position of power he held for eleven years. Davy Crockett was a House member from Tennessee. James G. Blaine and Joseph Cannon were prominent in the line of Speakers, although probably none in history has had the extensive influence of Sam Rayburn. The Senate, "the world's most exclusive club," has been known for its individualists and personalities: John C. Calhoun, Thomas Hart Benton who served twenty-nine years, Daniel Webster, William E. Borah, Robert M. La Follette, Robert A. Taft, and Alben Barkley, the "Veep."

Congress at times can be a curious institution. The Reverend Edward Everett Hale, when he was Senate chaplain, was asked, "Do you look at the country and pray for the Senate?" "No," he replied, "I look at the Senate and pray for the country."

Sessions open at noon with prayer, followed by the "morning hour," when members are allowed to insert "extended remarks" in the Congressional Record, the most unusual document published in Washington.

"The Congressional Record is an important publication," explained Representative Charles Teague of California recently in *Roll Call*, the sprightly unofficial newspaper of Capitol Hill. "It is printed each night, when Congress has been in session during the day. It sets forth word for word the debates and speeches made on the floor of the House and Senate. This is information to which the people are entitled, even though the cost is $81 a page and the daily volume runs to hundreds of pages."

But Representative Teague said he was not completely satisfied with the procedure. "I object," he continued, "to the long-standing custom which permits Senators and House members to insert huge numbers of items such as recipes, obituaries, poems, jokes, and all manners of material in the Appendix of the *Record*. I have discovered that some members have made as many as two hundred insertions in a single session of Congress—some of them several pages in length. In a few days there were such items as: Old World Quality Retained in Famed St. Vincent Bread; National Association of Plumbing Contractors Will Hold 77th Convention in Florida; Asbury Park, N.J., Observed Loyalty Day, Sunday, May 2; Subsidies for Farm Drainage in the Prairie Pothole Area." Representative Teague felt this was really too much and suggested his colleagues limit themselves to ten insertions a year.

Sessions normally continue until 5 or 6 P.M. Generally, there is not too much excitement on the floor or major bills called up until March or April; activity intensifies from then until adjournment sometime in the summer.

Be sure to visit the new Senate Office Building, a modest $25,000,000 structure. In speaking of it on the floor one day, Senator William Fulbright called it a "marble palace" and an "unfortunate edifice." He reminded his colleagues that after spending $100,000 for rubber tile floors, they had voted another $150,000 for carpeting, which meant that 600 doors had to be trimmed a half inch.

The new building has an auditorium seating 500 for hearings and other large rooms for the 15 Senate committees, much improved over facilities in the Capitol. Attend committee meetings to get to the core of lawmaking. They normally are held January to August, starting at 10 or 10:30 A.M. Plan to arrive ten or fifteen minutes early, though most spectators don't stay long and you shouldn't have trouble getting a seat. A list of hearings appears daily in the Washington *Post* (page opposite editorial); they're open to the public unless specified as executive sessions. They will be listed in the *Post* in such manner as: SENATE—Select Committee on Improper Activities in the Labor-Management Field, to begin hearings on activities in the coin-operated machine industry, 10:30 A.M., 318 Senate Office Building. Or HOUSE—Committee on Agriculture, to hear Secretary of Agriculture with respect to the administration's farm program proposals, 10 A.M., 1310 New House Office Building.

In the spectacular hearings you see the McCarthys, McClellans, Hoffas, Kefauvers—the TV personalities. The less-publicized hearings, sober, serious, sometimes dashed with humor, are essentially factual explorations designed to build laws and not headlines.

When you're on the House side, visit the U. S. Botanic Garden, at the western foot of the Hill (Monday–Friday 9–4, Saturday 9–12). In the midyears of the last century it rivaled the conservatory in London's Royal Kew Gardens. It was also called the "bouquet garden of Congress," supplying flowers free for members to send their wives and friends and at session's end one large box of choice plants for each member to carry home. Today it produces an unusual variety. Look for the Justice rose that resembles a bursting skyrocket, the Eucher plant with a blossom as large as a watermelon, fragrant South American lilies, several hundred types of orchids.

Places to eat at the Capitol? Probably the best is the 750-seat cafeteria in the new Senate Office Building. If you want beer with your lunch, go to the cafeteria in the House Office Building. There are restaurants in the Capitol itself, but these are small, crowded; nice places if you're a guest of a Senator or Congressman. Both House and Senate claim credit for inventing the delectable Capitol bean soup, a staple since the turn of the century. Another specialty is Senate rum pie, served Wednesday.

Good private eating spots on the Hill are scarce. If you're taking out a Congressman, or his secretary, suggest the Congressional Hotel or Carroll Arms.

Off-beat curio: Congressional Cemetery, 18th and E Streets, S.E., burial place of Congressmen, diplomats, architects, and Washington native John Philip Sousa. The government erected memorial cenotaphs over Congressional graves until Senator George Hoar of Massachusetts protested in 1877 that the prospect of burial beneath one of these atrocities added a new terror of death.

Before you leave the Hill, cross Capitol Plaza to visit the United States Supreme Court, the white marble temple on the north, and the Library of Congress, which behind its sprawling Renaissance front contains far more than books on shelves.

The massive, Corinthian-columned Supreme Court Building reflects the power of the High Court, as one of three separate branches of the federal government, and respect for the rights of man under law. This temple was completed in 1935; before that the Court was a stepchild of the Capitol, meeting in one room or another, with a 75-year stretch in the old Senate chamber.

Try to come when the Court is in session. "The Constitution is what the Supreme Court says it is," a Chief Justice once declared. And this is where you hear lower court decisions appealed, laws defined, and historic decisions handed down. The Court meets Monday through Thursday from noon to 4:30 P.M., with a half hour out for lunch. The term normally opens in October and extends until June. The best days are three Mondays a month when the justices deliver their opinions; these are known among lawyers as "judgment days." If there's a major case or constitutional interpretation involved, the Court Room is crowded with government and private attorneys, the side aisles crowded with standees.

The Court Room is like a great theater. Heavy red velvet draperies form the backdrop. Columns of light Italian marble line the wall, and bronze grilled screens extend along the side aisles. There are three hundred seats altogether, about half for attorneys, whether practicing or visiting, and half for the public.

The opening of the daily session is announced formally in the long tradition of the Court by the crier: "Oyez! Oyez! All persons having business before the Honorable, the Supreme Court of the United States, are admonished to draw near and give their attention, for the Court is now sitting . . ." Before the nine justices on their bench, the first order of business is presentation of attorneys for admission to the bar, which takes $50, a law degree and endorsement by an attorney already admitted. Then oral arguments in pending cases are heard, with each side normally permitted one hour.

The justices once were law professors, politicians, judges of lower courts. They line up as the liberal bloc (smiling Chief Justice Warren, Black, Douglas, Brennan); the generally conservative side (Clark, Frankfurter, Whittaker, Stewart), and the independent, Harlan. They are characters in the unending drama begun when John Jay sat as first Chief Justice and continued through the careers of John Marshall, who won incontestable power for the Court by establishing its right to declare an act of Congress unconstitutional; Roger B. Taney, who handed down the Dred Scott decision; Charles Evans Hughes, who almost became President; William Howard Taft, the only ex-President who sat on the Court; Louis D. Brandeis and Oliver Wendell Holmes, known as the great liberals, whose dissents are more quoted than most majority decisions.

"The Constitution is an experiment," Holmes, the champion of free speech and the free mind observed, "as all life is an experiment. I think we should be eternally vigilant against attempts to check the expression of opinions that we loathe and believe to be fraught with death, unless they so imminently threaten immediate interference with the lawful and pressing purposes of the law that an immediate check is required to save the country."

Should you come when the Court is not sitting, join a conducted 20-minute tour (Monday–Friday 9–4:30, Saturday 9–12), starting from the marshal's office, Room 111. Besides the Court Room, you will be shown conference rooms, the oak-paneled reading room and offices of Court officials. Note the marble and bronze stairways seemingly without support but actually overlapped and partly extended into the walls.

The cafeteria is excellent (the Justices eat the same food, on trays sent to their chambers). It is open for breakfast, 8–9:15 and lunch 11–2.

THE LIBRARY OF CONGRESS has so many facets that rarely does a visitor appreciate them fully, or realize how to use them to his advantage.

Most people come to see the publicized display material: the Gutenberg Bible, one of the earliest books printed with movable metal type; the so-called "rough draft" of the Declaration of Independence in the handwriting of Thomas Jefferson with changes in the handwritings of Benjamin Franklin and John Adams, and Abraham Lincoln's first and second drafts of the Gettysburg Address.

Let these exhibits be your starting point. The Library's two buildings, the ornate Renaissance structure and the white marble annex behind it, house 11,500,000 books and pamphlets, plus millions of newspapers, manuscripts, maps, photographic prints, negatives, volumes and pieces of music, sound recordings, motion pictures. These are accessible to you—and you can obtain photo copies of source material that is in public domain at a reasonable fee.

Or enjoy the Library as a center of culture and the arts. In beautiful 525-seat Coolidge Auditorium, you can hear chamber music at its finest one or two evenings a week from late September through April. The famed Budapest String Quartet performs in fall and spring with instruments made by the master Antonio Stradivari and bows by François Tourte. (The instruments are encased in carefully regulated temperature and humidity and you may see them when the Pavilion is not in use by asking permission of the Music Division.)

Major poets and writers, like Robert Frost, Carl Sandburg, and Eudora Welty, are also presented in Coolidge Auditorium, usually Monday evenings, October through May. A unique experience for the audience, to hear a creative artist read his own work.

The admission price: postage and a letter. For concerts, write the Music Division, Library of Congress, Washington 25, D.C., to learn whether there will be a program during the period you are in town and whether tickets will be available. For literary readings, write the Poetry Office. When in Washington, tickets are also available at the Hayes Concert Bureau, 1108 G Street, N.W., starting the Monday morning before the program. Service charge is 25¢.

Aside to critics of cultural "extravagance": gift and trust funds, not the federal government, underwrite music and poetry programs.

Another excellent event is the National Exhibition of Prints, held May through August, when the Library presents about 100 lithographs, itaglios, woodcuts, and perigraphs by distinguished modern artists. If you're decorating or Christmas shopping and want quality art, these original works are printed in small "editions" and you can purchase one from the artist, for about $15 to $50. An exhibit catalogue lists their names and addresses.

Many fine items are available for sale at the Library: copies of rare prints, engravings, and old photos, including Mathew Brady's Civil War scenes; long-play poetry readings (like T. S. Eliot reading *The Waste Land*, $4.50); a facsimile of Lincoln's own scrapbook on his debates with Douglas; folk songs and tales collected by the Library's experts, including Alan Lomax, Ben Botkin, Duncan Emrich.

Even to the casual visitor, there's a right way to see the Library of Congress. Join a guided tour (30 minutes) starting at the office of the captain of the guard, Monday through Friday (9:15, 10, 11 A.M., 1, 2, 3, and 4 P.M.). The building is also open evenings, including Saturday, until 10, and Sunday 11:30 A.M. to 10 P.M.

The interior of the Library reminds one of the foyer of the famous Paris Opéra, with marble floors and columns, statues, and balustraded stairways. It crawls with murals, mosaics, ceiling panels, and paintings, all reflecting the taste for Old World grandeur in the 1890s. Marble stairs (also an elevator) lead to the gallery overlooking the massive main reading room, with 30,000 books around its shelves and reading desks for about 300 persons. The rotunda, 100 feet in diameter, is thoroughly ornamented: carvings, statuary (sixteen "Men of Mark") and, of course, a painting in the eye of the dome. It's the kind of place that delights American visitors when in Europe.

The Library opened in two rooms in the Capitol with 964 books and nine maps. Many were used as kindling in the British bonfire of 1814; subsequently, Thomas Jefferson, a bibliophile, made his 50-year collection available so the Library could start anew. Since 1870 the Library has been the official copyright agency, receiving two copies of every book registered for copyright in America, including the one you're reading now. It also administers the national program of "talking books" and braille to the blind.

Though the Library has grown in scope, it still serves Congress. One department, the Legislative Reference Service, is the research arm of Congress. Another, the Law Library, which probably contains the largest law collection in the world, has a branch in the Capitol to provide Congress with books; it also conducts Congressional research in the legal field.

Just north of the Library of Congress stands the Folger Shakespeare Library (11–4:30, Monday–Saturday). It probably belongs in Stratford, England, or Stratford, Connecticut, but a wealthy oilman, Henry Clay Folger, felt that *his* Shakespeare collection should be in the national capital. You can tell the building by the white marble statue of Puck out front. The interior suggests the Elizabethan age and the oak-paneled walls bear 200 paintings, prints, and playbills associated with Shakespeare and his plays. Collections in the vaults are a prime source of Shakespeare research. At the end of the building, the reproduction of a seventeenth-century inn courtyard represents a typical theater of the Elizabethan period.

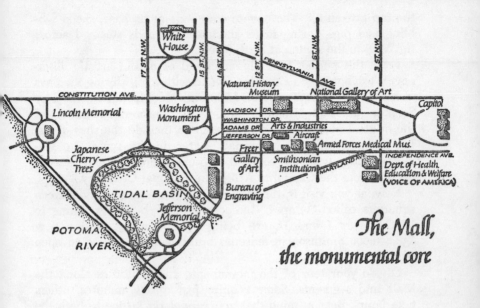

The Mall, the monumental core

VII *Of Monuments and Museums*

Let us explore the Mall (pronounced mawl, not mell), which sweeps across the monumental core of Washington from the foot of Capitol Hill two miles westward to the Lincoln Memorial.

This expansive greensward is the handsome central axis of our national capital. Yet the Mall has had its share of trying, incredibly dismal days, which are too easily and too soon forgotten.

L'Enfant planned the Mall, though not by that name, to extend between the White House and Capitol, bordered by mansions, gardens, and sloping lawns. But in the nineteenth century, when L'Enfant went out of fashion, so did the plan.

At one period an unsavory settlement called "Murderers' Bay" grew up at the edge of Tiber Creek on the Mall's south side. The Washington Monument was begun but it took 40 years to complete and for a time it looked like a factory chimney with

the top broken off. There were cowsheds at its base, sheep nib-
bling and pigs dozing in its shadow. Railroads steamed across
the Mall to the station at Sixth Street.

From this period, later characterized as one of artistic illiter-
acy, Washington and Congress awoke with a jolt during the days
of McKinley and rediscovered L'Enfant. A commission headed by
Senator James McMillan of Michigan sponsored restoration of
the original plan and its enlargement to include the sites of the
Lincoln and Jefferson Memorials. Later, in the 1930s, the Memorial Bridge was built across the Potomac, creating a monumental line from the Capitol to Arlington National Cemetery.

Now, as you visit it, the Mall is acquiring new beauty. Fifteen
squatters called "tempos," temporary office buildings dating to
World Wars I and II, are being cleared away. And a new
$36,000,000 Smithsonian museum building is scheduled to open
in 1962.

Divide your tour of the monuments and buildings along the
Mall into segments. Some require just a few minutes, others
take hours. Bear in mind that you cannot do justice to both the
north and south sides in a single afternoon—or in a day. However,
starting from the Capitol, plan to see these principal points of
interest:

GRANT MEMORIAL, 1st Street, the largest statue here until the
Marine Corps Memorial was built. This bronze shows General
Grant as a cloaked, somber commander overlooking massed groups
of cavalry and artillery at each end of a granite base. The sculptor,
Henry M. Shrady, worked twenty-two years on the statuary, then
died just before its completion in 1922.

THE NATIONAL GALLERY OF ART, Constitution Avenue between
4th and 6th Streets (10–5 weekdays; 2–10 Sunday), a young
institution as art galleries go (opened in 1941), yet it displays
many fine works produced since 1200 A.D., with choice examples
of Italian, Flemish, Dutch, Spanish, and French schools of painting.

The National Gallery succeeds in rendering art palatable and
understandable. The pictures are beautifully hung and lighted
(largely natural light, filtered through skylights). Flowering plants

in the two Garden Courts soften the setting of the paintings and bring color and fragrance. In fact, the horticultural displays alone will make your visit worth while. There is a restful public lounge, free check room, wheel chairs, and baby strollers at no charge.

The National Gallery, built of rose-white Tennessee marble at a cost of $15,000,000, was presented to the government by Andrew W. Mellon, financier, Secretary of the Treasury, and art collector. His collection is largest among the 27,000 works of art, but there are other distinguished collections (Kress, Widener, Dale, Rosenwald). The sum total may be, as an occasional critic suggests, newly bought art in contrast to centuries-old European galleries, but none denies the art was bought with taste as well as determination. In the early '30s, for example, when Mellon learned the Russians were willing to sell paintings from the Hermitage in Leningrad in order to raise money, he didn't hesitate to pay $7,000,000 for 21 of their finest, including $1,000,000 for Raphael's Alba Madonna.

The Gallery offers many activities. An introductory tour (45 to 60 minutes) starts 11 A.M. and 3 P.M. Tuesday–Saturday; 3 P.M. Monday, and 5 P.M. Sunday. There also are a Tour of the Week (1 P.M. Tuesday–Saturday, 2:30 Sunday), concentrating on a type or school of painting, and a Painting of the Week (12 noon, 2 P.M., Tuesday–Saturday; 3:30 and 6:30, Sunday).

Visitors are welcome at the excellent, moderately priced cafeteria (Monday through Saturday 11–4 P.M., hot foods until 2; Sunday 4 to 7 P.M.). It has one shortcoming—popularity, and you're liable to have a long wait in line. Try to eat early. Take the 11 A.M. tour, then lunch around noon.

If you miss the guided tour, take advantage of the unique Lectour (rental 25¢), a radio device with small receiving set covering 19 exhibition galleries; pleasant, easy to listen to.

Sunday evenings (except mid-July through mid-September) a free concert is presented by the National Gallery Symphony Orchestra, conducted by Richard Bales (sometimes by chamber music groups) in the East Garden Court. These are popular, too, so arrive early to be sure of a seat. Suggestion: arrive at 4 for the Lecture of the Week and motion picture, have dinner at the Gallery, then attend the concert at 8. A full course of art and music at the cost of $1.25 or $1.50 for dinner! If you have any money left, you can buy reproductions ranging from a 5¢ postal card to a large framed one for $20.

(Paintings are arranged so you can start with the earliest period and trace the development of art through the centuries.) As you walk through the galleries, be sure to note these treasures: Madonna and Child, by Giotto, founder of the Florentine school, one of a handful outside Italy, Gallery 1; Adoration of the Magi, begun by Fra Angelico, completed by Fra Filippo Lippi, Gallery 4; Raphael's four paintings, including that million-dollar Alba Madonna and Cowper Madonna, Gallery 8; the Venetians: Feast of the Gods, by Bellini, Venus with a Mirror, by Titian, and Adoration of the Shepherds, by Giorgione, Galleries 21 and 22; Laocoön, by El Greco (cleaned in 1958, it revealed a fragment of one new figure; stripped loin cloths from other figures showing they first were done nude; and brought out the brilliant El Greco colors), Gallery 30; Annunication, by Jan Van Eyck, founder of the Flemish school, Gallery 39; the Dutch: Woman Weighing Gold, by Vermeer, nine masterpieces by Rembrandt, especially his two Self-Portraits and The Mill, and An Elderly Lady, by Hals, Galleries 44–48.

Three canvases by Velázquez, among the few outside Spain, Gallery 51; Wivenhoe Park, by Constable, Gallery 58, among the British; Marquesa de Pontejos, by Goya, a Mellon favorite, Gallery 61; Mrs. Yates, by Gilbert Stuart and the historically important Washington Family, by Savage, Gallery 67; Chester Dale's modern French collection of Picasso, Matisse, Derain, Braque and others, Galleries 60, 62, 64; the popular French Impressionists and Post-Impressionists including Degas, Renoir, Manet (note especially Gare St.-Lazare), Corot, Gauguin, Cézanne, Van Gogh, and Toulouse-Lautrec, Galleries 72–90.

Most prominent among the sculpture is the polished bronze Mercury by Giovanni da Bologna on the Rotunda fountain. But look also for the life-size David by Donatello, Gallery 11, and two works of Sansovino, which Napoleon once carried as loot from Italy, in the West Hall.

THE SMITHSONIAN INSTITUTION, on both sides of the Mall between 9th and 12th Streets (9–4:30 daily), contains at least 51,000,000 catalogued items and someone estimated that if you were to spend thirty seconds at each object for eight hours a day, five days a week, you would see them all in 44 years. I mention this so you will know precisely where to begin and how long to stay.

The Institution (note: not Institute) was founded in 1846 with a bequest from James Smithson, a British scientist. In pique with his own country, he left $550,000 to create at Washington, a city he had never seen, "an establishment for the increase and diffusion of knowledge among men." The Institution started by conducting research in natural history, which led to collection of reports, specimens, and expansion into other fields. The National Zoological Park, for instance, began in the '80s when a buffalo herd was sent for study and tethered on the Mall.

Most people think of the Smithsonian as a museum. This it is, on a grand, monstrously cluttered scale, covering nearly every conceivable phase of human experience and achievement. But as you view the displays, let yourself meet the Institution as a center of scientific research in many fields and many places of the world. Joseph Henry, its first secretary, or director, invented the electromagnet, the basis for all subsequent developments in electricity. A later Secretary, Samuel Langley, pioneered in aviation. Today the Smithsonian is pre-eminent for identifying and naming living things—birds, plants, mammals, insects, fishes. Among its ten divisions: The Astrophysical Observatory, Cambridge, Mass., which together with 200 observation stations around the world tracks space satellites with telescopic cameras; Canal Zone Biological Area, and the International Exchange Service, which conducts interchange of scientific findings with other nations. It also is the administrative agency of three art galleries (Freer, National Gallery, National Collection of Fine Arts) and the National Zoo.

Yet only now is the Smithsonian coming of age as a museum, shedding its cobwebs as the "nation's attic." The greatest part of its modernization program, begun in 1952, revolves around the new building between 12th and 14th Streets, which will open in 1962 as the Museum of History and Technology. Primarily it will trace the development of science and the growth of the United States.

In the meantime, do not try to cover everything in the present Smithsonian buildings, unless you have 40-odd years to spare.

Pick the high spots, particularly the dozen new exhibit halls which have opened in the past five years; they provide a co-ordinated, tangible picture. Allow an hour bare minimum on each side of the Mall.

The Natural History Building, on the Constitution Avenue side, contains, among its twenty million-or-so specimens, stuffed birds, mummies, whales, big game bagged by Theodore Roosevelt in Africa; pianos, woodwinds and violins; mammals of North America, lifelike and complete with terrain.

Five highlights you will especially enjoy:

1. Fenykovi Elephant, in the Rotunda, the newest (1959) major addition. This is the biggest land animal ever bagged, 13 feet high at the shoulders, weighing twelve tons when it was shot by a Spanish sportsman in Angola, Africa; it took him 19 bullets and a full day to fell it. Mounting it proved the crowning achievement in the 51-year Smithsonian career of William L. Brown, the famed, recently retired taxidermist, who used 10,500 pounds of clay, wire screening, and wooden ribs within the elephant's skin.

2. Hall of Evolution, directly behind the Rotunda, featuring the 70-foot-long skeleton of a Diplodocus, better known as Gertie the Dinosaur, dug out from rock in the Rocky Mountains. Another prize item is the Stegosaurus, the plated, spike-tailed dinosaur, bully of the fields 150 million years ago.

3. Hall of Gems and Minerals, where the fabled, beautiful blue Hope diamond has come to rest after belonging to French royalty (whom it supposedly afflicted with a "curse") and more recently to Evalyn Walsh McLean. Here also are the world's largest flawless crystal ball, weighing 106¾ pounds, cut from a block mined in Burma; a 316-carat star sapphire, star rubies, diamonds, opals and the Cave of the Swords, reproduction of a Mexican mine paved with swordlike crystals.

4. Hall of American Indians, recounting civilization in America as far back as 10,000 years. Among the lifelike scenes are the Indians who met Columbus; a Hopi pueblo, a prehistoric apartment house; Navaho and Zuni silversmiths.

5. Hall of Latin American Archaeology, a collection of Aztec, Toltec, and Inca gods, goddesses, relics of ancient art in metal

and stone. The greatest piece, a colossal stone head from southern Mexico, stands nine feet high, weighs 20 tons.

The Natural History Building also houses the National Collection of Fine Arts, originally called the National Gallery until it was overshadowed by the Mellon bequest. Paintings here, given by American collectors, include works by European masters Rembrandt, Titian, Rubens, Gainsborough, as well as sculptures in marble, bronze, and silver. The collection is unique as an Albert Ryder shrine, with 17 paintings by the American genius of the nineteenth century, including his Storm at Sea and Flying Dutchman. Other American paintings include seascapes by Winslow Homer and watercolors by Childe Hassam.

The National Collection will move into its own home, in one of Washington's oldest, most interesting buildings, at 10th and F Streets, N.W., when the Civil Service Commission moves out. Built in 1837–40, with its great stone pillars it looks much like the Madeleine in Paris seen from the Rue Royale. It was the setting of Lincoln's second inaugural ball in 1865.

Across the Mall, the red-brick Arts and Industries Building houses tremendous exhibits covering history, engineering, and industry, including thousands of clocks, watches, telephones, typewriters, ceramics, sewing machines, ships from dugout canoes to models of ocean liners, live bees flying in and out a wall opening to collect nectar. The following are among the highlights and new displays:

1. THE WRIGHT BROTHERS' PLANE, suspended from the ceiling as you enter, the world's first heavier-than-air craft in which man made free, controlled, and sustained flight—for 12 glorious seconds on December 17, 1903. The Smithsonian once credited Langley with the first successful flight; this angered the Wright Brothers, who allowed their plane to be shown in England for many years.

2. THE SPIRIT OF ST. LOUIS, directly behind the Wright Brothers' plane, the remarkable little Ryan monoplane in which Charles A. Lindbergh flew nonstop from New York to Paris in 33½ hours in May 1927.

3. FIRST LADIES HALL, displaying the inaugural gowns worn by the Presidents' wives starting from Martha Washington. The

collection is divided into eight period settings, with each case spanning twenty-five years and First Ladies grouped around White House furnishings of the period. The first case, covering 1789–1817 shows Abigail Adams, Martha Jefferson Randolph (the widower Jefferson's daughter), and Dolly Madison gathered around Martha Washington at her tea table. The room is almost completely furnished with Washington family original items. Martha Washington's gown, though earliest, is one of the loveliest: hand-painted with 50 different tiny insects set in wreaths or garlands. The last case, the modern one, shows Bess Truman (in a simple gray gown), Eleanor Roosevelt (white satin, long train, worn at the third inaugural) and Mamie Eisenhower, wearing the most glamorous gown in the collection, a Nettie Rosenstein pink taffeta with 4000 sparkling pink and rose stones. The case includes wall paneling, cut down to fit dimensions here, the Siena marble mantel, and Steinway gold piano, all brought from the East Room of the White House after its renovation during the Truman administration.

4. HALL OF POWER, left of the entrance, working models of steam, gas and oil engines, water turbines, and electric generators. Children love this place because they can press buttons and watch the engine models work.

5. HALL OF MILITARY HISTORY, six dioramas showing dramatic moments in military history, tracing weapons and uniforms from the time of the colonial militia to modern missilery.

6. THE ROTUNDA, a cluttered crossroads, where you can see the plaster cast from which the bronze statue of Freedom surmounting the Capitol dome was cast, and a duplicate of the Navy Vanguard rocket which launched the first successful U.S. satellite.

7. AUTO HALL, a tight little corner with two dozen choice motorcars, starting with the tiller-steered 1893 Duryea, America's first practical gas-driven vehicle. Others include the Winton Bullet in which Barney Oldfield blazed across the Daytona sands at 83.7 miles per hour in 1904, steamers, electrics and a 1912 chain-driven red Simplex raceabout, *the* sports car of its day.

8. HALL OF HEALTH, where you can listen to your own heartbeat on an electronic stethoscope. Here's one place you can sit, while watching film strips and the new "transparent woman," an electronic creature explaining how the body functions.

The original Smithsonian Building, the adjacent red one resembling a Norman castle, contains displays and a directory of all the Smithsonian's activities. Printers and publishers who visit the Graphic Arts Exhibit in the west end will be greeted by Horatio Greenough's toga-clad statue of Washington, surrounded by Benjamin Franklin's printing press, rotogravure, and halftone equipment.

The Aircraft building, west of Arts and Industries, is really an old, inadequate steel hangar built in World War I for experiments with plane engines. Historic planes are on display: Billy Mitchell's World War I Spad; Navy NC-4, first to fly the Atlantic (1919); the Polar Star, which carried Lincoln Ellsworth across the Antarctic (1935); Bell X-1, first to break the sound barrier (1947), and others. Propellers, balloons, engines, parachutes, and models illustrate the age of flight. Plans call for a National Air Museum on the Mall, and *that* will be another great day in the history of the Institution.

FREER GALLERY OF ART, 12th and Independence Avenue (9–4 daily except Monday), a kind of independent appendage of the Smithsonian, is one of Washington's oft overlooked wonders, a treasure house of Near Eastern and Asiatic fine arts, with a spicy dash of Whistler.

Charles Freer of Detroit built and sold so many freight cars in his youth he was able to retire in his 40s and take up collecting oriental arts, pioneering in this exotic realm. In 1923, he presented the building and his collection to the government.

In the Asiatic wing are Chinese bronze, wood and stone sculptures dating to the fifteenth century B.C. There are stone buddhas, gilded bronze, carved jade, paintings of the great Tang and Sung dynasties. Japanese rooms include examples of lacquer and pottery, decorated folding screens, a distinctive mural form. The Near East is represented by Greek biblical manuscripts, examples of calligraphy, glasswork, and painting.

On the south corridor is the "Peacock Room," a lavish nook decorated by Whistler. Originally he had painted a picture, "The Princess from the Land of Porcelain," for F. R. Leyland, a London shipbuilder—but he subsequently disliked the arrangement of the room around it and offered to do it over, while his patron was away. He splashed the gilded Spanish leather walls and shutters with gold peacocks and lavish turquoise. Two facing peacocks: one with elegant dignity represented Art and himself, the other, disorderly, stamped with coins, Wealth and his client. It disturbed Mr. Leyland, but Mr. Freer was intrigued enough to buy it for $63,000.

ARMED FORCES MEDICAL MUSEUM, 9th and Independence Avenue (9–5 daily), though not part of the Smithsonian, is convenient to visit at the same time. It was founded during the Civil War to collect information about war-caused wounds and diseases but now includes thousands of microscopes, stethoscopes, and other medical equipment dating to Roman and Chinese days. The anatomy section contains some lively looking skeletons; and human embryos pickled in alcohol. Best time: 2 P.M. weekdays, for the guided tour.

THE WASHINGTON MONUMENT (9–5 daily, 10¢) is not quite as simple to visit as it used to be, before it became the target of a million or more visitors a year and parking was eliminated at the base. Now you park at a new lot at Constitution Avenue and 16th Street (allow ten minutes for the walk uphill and return). You will get no closer by cab, sightseeing bus, or streetcar from the east side. And in the popular periods, which are almost any time, you're likely to be at the end of a 30 or 40 minute waiting line, which winds and rewinds around the base.

It *is* worth the time and effort to ascend the elevator to the observation room 500 feet aloft. Be philosophical. Rest on the benches while you wait and contemplate the Monument, which you've already seen as a landmark visible for miles in daylight or in floodlit night. It weighs 81,000 tons and its foundation extends 37 feet into the earth. The walls are 15 feet thick at the base next to you, but taper to only 15 inches at the aluminum capstone 555 feet up.

Like the Mall, the Washington Monument had to endure a horrible time before its eventual day of glory. A monument to George Washington, envisioned as an equestrian statue, was agreed on by Congress during his lifetime. But it was only an idea until 1833, when the Washington National Memorial Society was founded. Fifteen years later, funds in hand and oratory in the wind, the cornerstone was laid and construction begun on this obelisk. Memorial stones were sent to honor Washington from all parts of the country and the world. However, the arrival of a block of marble from the Temple of Concord in Rome, a gift of Pope Pius IX, provoked the anti-foreign, anti-Catholic Know-Nothing party to dispatch a band of night raiders and make off with it.

Harassment by the Know-Nothings, who at one point stole the records of the Memorial Society, brought construction to a halt and for twenty years the Monument was an unsightly stump in the midst of a marsh. Finally, Congress appropriated funds and it was completed in 1888. If you look about one-third up you can see a change in the color of the stone, where work had stopped.

There is no waiting, and you can save ten cents, should you care to walk up the Monument. The long climb, of 15 or 20 minutes, is fine for athletes in training and those enviably tireless high-schoolers. Otherwise, wait for the elevator; the new steel cab, installed in 1959, takes less than a minute—in contrast to the 12 minute "precarious ascent" aboard the first elevator before the turn of the century.

The observation-room windows provide the best vantage point anywhere from which to view the Washington panorama. Looking down one side the Federal Triangle is plainly defined. On another you get an unusual perspective of the Reflection Pool, extending 2000 feet between the Monument and the Lincoln Memorial. On a clear day, visibility extends for 20 miles and you can easily identify the Washington Cathedral on Mount St. Alban and the Washington Masonic Temple in Alexandria.

If you're in good health, you needn't hesitate to walk down the 898 steps. There are 50 landings along the way and you'll see the carved tribute blocks within the shaft presented by states, cities, territories, colleges, churches, and foreign nations.

THE JEFFERSON MEMORIAL (open 9 to 9) is a pretty, photogenic sight reflected in the Tidal Basin, especially when framed by cherry blossoms in spring. But it is not a major point of interest in itself and as a memorial to Thomas Jefferson is disappointing.

Within the circular, low-domed memorial stands a bronze Jefferson 19 feet high. To sense the spirit of the man, take note of the inscription, *I have sworn on the altar of God eternal hostility against every form of tyranny over the mind of man,* and the passages from his writings on the wall panels.

Parking space is ample, but the traffic pattern is complicated. Visit the Jefferson Memorial if you're heading over the 14th Street Bridge to Virginia, or north along Ohio Drive to the Lincoln Memorial.

LINCOLN MEMORIAL (open 9 to 9) appears to belong perfectly on its site, bordered by boxwood and lawn. Though little known today, this is reclaimed land dredged from the Potomac River fifty years ago as part of the McMillan Plan. In those days the location of the Memorial was opposed by "Uncle Joe" Cannon, Speaker of the House, who warned, "If you put it in that marsh, it will shake itself to pieces in no time with loneliness and ague."

Since it was dedicated on Decoration Day 1922, however, the Lincoln Memorial, like the man whose memory it enshrines, has grown in appeal with the years. Thirty-six columns, one for each state in the Union at the time of Lincoln's death, form an exterior colonnade around the white marble Memorial. Fifty-six steps, one for each year of his life, lead to the chamber and the 21-foot statue of the seated Emancipator. It was designed by Daniel Chester French, then carved over a four-year period in twenty blocks of interlocked marble by the Piccirilli brothers of New York. Take the time to read the timeless words of Lincoln's second inaugural address ("With malice toward none, with charity toward all. . . .") on the north wall, the Gettysburg Address on the south wall.

You can park around the side of the Memorial. There aren't too many spaces, but they change frequently. Return at night when floodlights create an entirely different effect around the homely, tender, piercing-eyed Lincoln.

Westward, low-arched Memorial Bridge extends the monumental line of the city across the Potomac River to Arlington National Cemetery. The two statues at the Bridge entrance, representing the "Arts of War," (as well as the two others at the Rock Creek Parkway entrance, symbolizing the "Arts of Peace"),

were surfaced, in Italy, with pure gold by fire-gilding, an ancient
process.

THE MARINE CORPS WAR MEMORIAL, a tribute to all Marines
who died in action since 1775, when the Corps was founded,
borders Arlington Cemetery on the north. The huge figures (32
feet high, bearing carbines 12 feet long), cast in bronze by Felix
de Weldon, re-create the flag raising on Iwo Jima, first recorded
in the dramatic photograph taken by Joe Rosenthal in 1945.

Inscribed at the base is the tribute paid by Admiral Chester
Nimitz to the 5500 Marines who perished at Iwo Jima: *Un-
common Valor was a Common Virtue.* A Marine Corps color
guard raises the flag at 8 A.M., lowers it at sunset, but the best
time to visit is 4:30 P.M. Tuesday when Marine units and band
parade.

Note: At the Marine Barracks, 8th and I Streets, Southeast,
the oldest post (1801) of the Corps, Sunset Parades are held
Friday at 5 P.M. during spring and fall, 9 P.M. during the summer,
with drum and bugle corps, drill team, barracks troops, and band.
Plenty of seats for spectators.

NETHERLANDS BELL TOWER, newly installed neighbor of the
Marine Memorial, a carillon 131 feet high with 49 bells, presented
by Queen Juliana in 1952. The largest bell weighs 6½ tons.

ARLINGTON NATIONAL CEMETERY (9:30–4:30, October–March;
9:30–6, April–September) comprises hallowed ground where military men—famous generals and admirals and unknown but equally
honored enlisted men—have been buried for a century.

Before the Civil War these wooded hills overlooking the Capital
made up a great Virginia estate owned by George Washington
Parke Custis, Martha Washington's grandson, whom George Washington adopted as his son. Custis built Arlington House, a classic
of Greek Revival architecture. In 1831, a young lieutenant named
Robert E. Lee appeared on the scene and married his daughter;
later Lee lived at Arlington House and left from here for Richmond to command the Confederate Army.

At the outbreak of the Civil War the Arlington estate was
fortified as part of the defense line around Washington, then

became a field hospital after the battle of Manassas. First burials were made in 1864 and have not stopped since. By 1883, when the government officially purchased the estate from the Lee family, there were 15,000 interments, including many unknowns and Confederates who had died in Washington hospitals. By 1935 the total burials was 35,000, but today it has passed 100,000 and is rising at the rate of 18 a day, five days a weeks. Interment in these 408 acres of sloping greens, shaded by 18,000 trees and shrubs, is open to all servicemen and servicewomen. Their wives, husbands, and minor children may be buried alongside.

The best way to tour Arlington: from the semicircular stone Memorial Gateway, on a direct line from Memorial Bridge, drive through iron gates to the right (Schley Avenue). Soon you will pass the grave of William Howard Taft, the only President buried in Arlington. Notice the fields of uniform headstones: flat markers, with grave numbers only, mark the unknown; markers with rounded top bear the name, state, and dates of birth and death. Principal sections along the way will be the "Field of the Dead," containing thousands of Civil War gravesites; the Spanish-American War Section; the field of Confederate dead around Jackson Circle, and Pershing Hill, where General John J. Pershing is buried in the area of 5000 World War I dead.

Follow Schley into Sherman Avenue and the parking space at the cemetery headquarters west of Lee Mansion, otherwise known as Arlington House and officially as Robert E. Lee National Memorial (admission 25¢). The restored mansion reflects the period when Lee lived here. The long central hallway divides family dining room and parlor. Notice the Duncan Phyfe table in the dining room; the portrait of Light Horse Harry Lee in the drawing room; the playroom and bedroom of the three Lee girls. In the yard around the house are slave quarters, smokehouse and icehouse, typical of Virginia mansion outbuildings. On the portico steps of the Mansion, overlooking the Potomac River and Washington, the first Decoration Day services were held May 30, 1868.

Close by are beautiful and important memorials which most visitors unfortunately overlook completely: the old wisteria-covered amphitheater, used for Memorial services from 1873 to 1922; Temple of Fame, a domed arbor dedicated to twelve Civil

War heroes; Tomb of the Unknown Dead, a granite sarcophagus over a common vault containing 2100 unidentified Civil War dead; the statue of fighting, one-armed General Phil Kearny, who fought in twelve battles before his death in 1862; the tomb of General Phil Sheridan, the fearless cavalryman, and, beneath a granite slab engraved with the plan of Washington, Pierre Charles L'Enfant.

From Lee Mansion, follow Wilson Drive past the Maine Memorial, mast of the U.S.S. *Maine* with its conning tower still in place, raised from Havana harbor after the Spanish-American War. Stop and park at the National Memorial Amphitheatre. This elliptical white marble amphitheater, built in 1920, seats approximately 5000 persons at Memorial Services every May 30. The marble chair in the center of the platform is for use of the President. Above the platform, the Trophy Room displays decorations bestowed on the Unknown Soldier of World War I by every allied nation.

Directly in front of the Amphitheatre on the east are the Tombs of the Unknowns, honored dead symbolic of all who gave their lives in war. In the center is the tomb of the Unknown Soldier of World War I, a 50-ton rectangular marble block, inscribed, *Here rests in honored glory an American soldier known but to God;* it is flanked by the flat stones of the Unknowns of World War II and Korea. Over 100 wreath-laying services are held at this sacred spot during the course of a year. A Presidential wreath is placed each Armistice Day; foreign dignitaries, presidents, kings, queens pay similar respect when they visit Washington.

Selection of the first Unknown was made by Sergeant Edward S. Younger, the most decorated enlisted man of World War I, at Chalon, France, from among caskets bearing four unknowns. He walked among them, placed a spray of roses on one, indicating his choice. This casket was returned to the United States to lie in state in the Rotunda of the Capitol. The Unknown Soldier was honored by all the states, awarded the Medal of Honor, and decorated by allied nations. On November 11, 1921, he was buried in Arlington.

In May 1958, aboard the cruiser *Canberra,* Hospitalman First Class William R. Charette, the Navy's only active enlisted holder of the Medal of Honor, selected the Unknown of World War II, from two caskets, one representing the European Theatre of Operations, the other representing the Pacific. At the same time, Master Sergeant Ned Lyle, U. S. Army, chose the Korean War Unknown, from among four flag-draped caskets at the National Cemetery in Hawaii. Both were brought to Norfolk, Virginia, transferred to the destroyer *Blandy* for the final voyage up the Potomac River to Washington. They rested in state at the Capitol Rotunda from May 28 until May 30, then were moved to the Memorial Amphitheatre; before a distinguished assembly, the President awarded each the Medal of Honor and then they were buried to a 21-gun salute.

The Unknowns are guarded by a sentry both day and night. Soldiers who perform this assignment consider it an honor. They are chosen men of the "Old Guard," the 3rd Infantry Regiment stationed at Fort Myer, which also serves as guard of the Presidents at inaugurals and ceremonial functions. Watch the sentry as he begins his march at one end of a long, narrow rubber mat. His pace is regulated at 128 steps per minute; at the opposite end he does a right face, stands motionless for a count of 30, shifts his rifle to the other shoulder (always away from the Tombs) and marches back. Sentries are on duty 24 hours, standing guard for one hour at a time, with the next two hours off. Be sure you're here on the hour for the impressive changing of the guard, when a noncommissioned officer relieves one sentry after a rifle salute to the Unknowns and posts his replacement.

VIII *A Call on Lafayette Square*

You don't exactly get to rub shoulders or shake hands with the President, as visitors once could when there were fewer of them, but the White House during certain hours (10 A.M.–12 Tuesday through Saturday) is open to all callers.

If you ask your Congressman, he will arrange for you to join the early-morning tour (8:50), when you're conducted by a guide.

Everyone enjoys the White House, for reasons of his own. I like it, among other reasons, because it retains the essentials of its beginning, along with the riches and echoes acquired through the years. The White House proves the wisdom and practicality of saving the finest in America, even when the plaster starts to crack and floors give way.

I like it also because the home and offices of the President are so much a part of the human scene in Washington—like living in a goldfish bowl, as Harry Truman said—and you can watch our First Citizen take off in a helicopter, or, as in Mr. Truman's case, meet him walking down the street at 7 A.M. Best of all is the realization, any time you go past on Pennsylvania Avenue, that somebody, who was neither born to the job nor claimed it by force, is on duty inside running the government. And, if we don't like the way he does it, we can always say so on Election Day.

The White House began as the first public building in the capital-to-be. It was Saturday, October 13, 1792, when the cornerstone-laying procession, led by the Masons, set forth from Fountain Inn, Georgetown. Everyone felt the "President's Palace" was endowed with an excellent design by the Irishman James Hoban. His plan had won $500 in a competition which included an entry—the second-place winner—anonymously submitted by Thomas Jefferson. The site was still a marshland but this only stimulated the peroration led by Brother Casanova, master of the Georgetown Lodge. After the ceremony, the entire assemblage repaired quickly to Mr. Suter's Fountain Inn for an elegant dinner accompanied

by sixteen toasts, to everyone from the Marquis de Lafayette
and the French Nation, to Thomas Paine, author of *Common
Sense;* the fair daughters of America, and General Anthony Wayne
and the Western Army.

History is not quite clear as to whether George Washington was
present at the ceremony; that day he appears to have been in
Philadelphia, where the capital was still located. President Washington was never to occupy the White House, but he loved to
watch it a-building with light gray sandstone quarried at Aquia,
near his home at Mount Vernon. The President and Mrs. Washington walked through the house in 1799, a few weeks before his
death.

When President John Adams and his wife Abigail arrived along
with the government the following year, this was the only completed public building in the city—and it was not too complete
either. The President elected to stay at Union Tavern the first
six months, but even when he and Mrs. Adams did move in conditions were on the primitive side. Water had to be hand-carried
from a spring five blocks off. There were no bathroom, fence,
yard, or lamps, and since there was no staircase the Adamses had
to enter and leave via temporary wooden stairs and a platform.

But in time the building improved. President Thomas Jefferson,
who originally had criticized it as being big enough for "two
emperors, one pope and the grand lama," collaborated with
architect Benjamin Latrobe to add porticoes and landscaped terraces (as well as stables, icehouse, and hen house). Across Pennsylvania Avenue, incidentally, on the site of Lafayette Park, a
race course attracted upward of 200 carriages and 4000 spectators during this period.

Then came the Madisons, the President, a man of good taste
who brought quality furnishings from France, and his wife Dolly,
the first queen of capital society. She presided at dancing parties
and social events with the glitter of Old World courts. Dolly had
a dinner planned the night the British arrived in 1814, but
before leaving she gathered up a trunkful of valuables, including
the famous Stuart portrait of Washington from the East Room
wall.

The invaders were about as thorough here as they had been at
the Capitol. In their wake the light sandstone walls were left

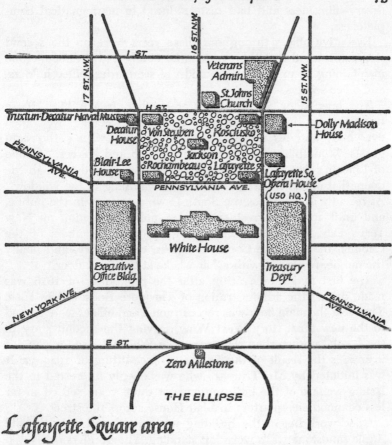

Lafayette Square area

blackened with smoke and the interior almost completely gutted.

When the building was reconstructed, James Monroe, the next President, brought furniture, linen, dishes, and silver which he had acquired in France. From then until the end of the nineteenth century interior changes and remodelings were made with almost each succeeding administration, from which the White House did not exactly benefit. At one point the East Room, today the epitome of stateliness, was said to resemble a saloon and the State Dining Room to have the décor of a fashionable bar. After the Civil War, on the other hand, the interior was dreary—flimsiness and bad taste reduced to mathematical completeness.

Executive offices throughout these years were on the second story, so located that the Presidential family had a difficult time maintaining its privacy in the midst of secretaries, office holders, and office seekers.

The open door, in one form or another, is a White House tradition. Andrew Jackson, the "People's President," welcomed everybody and his receptions were thronged with a thousand guests, "a jumbling together of honest men and knaves." At one of Lincoln's first receptions so many people poured through the doors that others found an easier route climbing in the windows. As recently as the 1880s the South Lawn was open to the public, and until 1932 the President held a public reception on New Year's Day, when he would greet, in order, members of the Cabinet, the Supreme Court, Congress, the military, and finally the public, rewarded with a handshake at the front door.

The first major renovation after the rebuilding of 1816 was made during the administration of Theodore Roosevelt in 1902. That year the main floor was reconstructed and offices were moved to the new three-story West Wing, leaving the second story to the family, undisturbed. However, the White House, as you see it now, is the result of the $5,500,000 face-lifting of 1949–52. It was initiated by Mr. Truman, who was deeply interested in the lasting welfare of the building and for three years settled in far less commodious quarters in Blair House across the street.

Once work began the building was gutted and only the old Aquia sandstone walls were left standing. The builders excavated to add basement and mezzanine, so now there are 132 rooms and 20 baths, almost double the previous number. New steel supports were set in place, the building was air conditioned and a bomb shelter, equipped with protection against radioactivity and poison gas, installed for the President's safety.

Today the White House stands as a new classic in architecture and decoration, preserving and highlighting the best of its original furnishings and design. You enter at East Executive Avenue, the same entrance used by guests at evening social functions. Five rooms on the first floor are open to view, predominantly eighteenth-century Georgian but retaining in harmony other elements of historic interest. The rooms and corridors are decorated with portraits of Presidents. These vary in quality: in 1944 the grandson of James A. Garfield, in a letter to Franklin D. Roosevelt, raised the question of changing the portrait of his grandfather. F.D.R. was all for it, conceding the picture in question was one of "three or four horrors of former Presidents" hanging on the walls. In contrast is the bronze bust of Abraham Lincoln, cast from the marble original in the Capitol Rotunda; this was a favorite of Theodore Roosevelt.

The East Room, the first one you see, is a great hall (87½ feet long, 45 feet wide) used for large receptions and affairs of state. It has been the scene of weddings (President Grant's daughter Nellie who married Captain Algernon Sartoris in 1874; Alice Roosevelt who married Nicholas Longworth in 1906; and Jessie Wilson who married Francis B. Sayre in 1913), and funeral services. The last service for a President was in 1945, on the death of Franklin D. Roosevelt. Others close to the White House have been buried from here, too, most recently including G. Hall Roosevelt, the President's brother-in-law (1941); August A. Gennerich of the Secret Service, bodyguard, friend, and great helper physically to the invalid Roosevelt (1936), and Louis McHenry Howe, his long-time political ally (1936). Looking back a little further, there is a seldom-told but poignant story about the funeral service in the East Room of Calvin Coolidge, Jr., in July 1924. The sixteen-year-old youth suffered a blistered heel playing tennis at the White House court, contracted blood poisoning and died at Walter Reed Hospital. Seemingly emotionless at the service for young Calvin, five years later his father said, "With the boy's death went all the glory of the Presidency."

On one wall of the East Room is the full-length portrait of George Washington which Dolly Madison rescued from the British and a companion portrait of Martha Washington painted later. Around the room are busts of Washington, Jefferson, Franklin, and Lincoln. Three immense gold-plated chandeliers hang from the ceiling and huge gold mirrors are over two marble mantels. Hundreds of events in this room have been recounted in history. Once Lincoln was receiving a long line of handshakers. "Mr. President," someone called out from down the line, "in my state they say the welfare of the nation depends on God and

Abraham Lincoln." To which Lincoln replied, "My friend, you are half-right!"

The adjoining Green Room, used for informal receptions, could be called the Monroe-Hoban Room. The cornice was an original Hoban design and the marble mantel imported from Italy by the architect in the rebuilding of 1816. The hand-tufted green rug, bearing the Presidential seal, is a reproduction of the original Aubusson rug brought from France by President Monroe; the Hannibal clock and gilt vase also were purchased in France during his administration.

The oval-shaped Blue Room was the scene of the only Presidential wedding in the White House, when Grover Cleveland married Frances Folsom in 1886. This room, directly behind the Entrance Hall from the North Portico, is where the President receives foreign diplomats and other official guests. The Louis XV white and gold mantel was purchased for the White House during the 1902 renovation.

The Red Room, decorated in rich silk damask, is the First Lady's reception room. The portrait of a thoughtful, seated Lincoln, by G. P. A. Healy, was moved here during the Eisenhower administration from the State Dining Room. The cornice of the room is an original Hoban design with added Greek fretwork; the gilt bronze clock and candlesticks, gifts of the French government in 1952.

In the State Dining Room, at the west end, there is a great horseshoe table; for large evening functions, often attended by 100 guests, it yields to a complete rearrangement of smaller, E-shaped tables. The landscape painting above the marble fireplace, Sundown, by George Inness (on loan from the National Gallery) replaced the Healy Lincoln. At the north wall, the gilt-framed mirror and candelabra were presented by Queen Elizabeth, when she was a princess, in behalf of her father, the late King George VI.

The rest of the house is private domain. The smaller dining room, adjoining the State Dining Room, contains a true chandelier—lighted by candles, without electric wiring. Living quarters for the Presidential family are on the second and third floors, in rooms as attractively furnished as the five you have seen. The most interesting are the Victorian Lincoln Room, with the nine-foot-long rosewood bed used by the Civil War President; the Oval study, above the Blue Room; and the Monroe Room, decorated by an eighteenth-century fruit-and-flower print in the draperies and slip covers. On the third floor are a new air-conditioned sun parlor with blue-green glass walls and bamboo furnishings; six bedrooms done in Williamsburg style, and eight servants' rooms.

Below the first floor, on what is called the ground floor, the principal rooms are the oval Diplomatic Reception Room; the Library, paneled with old White House timbers; the Broadcasting Room, China Room, and the new stainless-steel kitchen.

The President's office and Cabinet Room are in the West Wing. More news flashes have probably been telephoned from the press room in the northwest corner of this building than from all the rest of the world put together, with probably a similar record for hands of poker in between.

The whole White House operation, like the responsibility of the President, has mushroomed over the years. Two dozen people are required to open the President's mail, an average of 4000 pieces daily. No longer are weekly press conferences held in the President's office, but in a 200-seat conference room in the Old State Building across the street. The executive staff of the White House has grown in size to such an extent that a $35,300,000 building is now planned in the block diagonally across Pennsylvania Avenue.

After your visit within, have a look at the White House grounds. You can feed the squirrels through the fencing or take pictures of the north portico framed behind flower beds and circular fountain sprays. The English boxwood banked in front of the main entrance are as old as the house itself, and the trees have been planted by Presidents since Madison. Elsewhere in Washington, elms and other wonderful trees are falling under the ax, but these, at least, are safe. Most of the 18 acres of lawn are on the south side.

Cross Pennsylvania Avenue to Lafayette Park and pull up a bench at Bernard Baruch's old spot, where you can feed the pigeons and watch the world go by. This section around the White House known in its day as President's Square, is a unit of interest in the same sense as Capitol Hill. There's a lot worth seeing and learning about here.

Notice the White House is flanked by two massive buildings. On the east side, the Greek revival Treasury Building is the subject of a favorite Washington legend (which may be *pure* legend). Andrew Jackson reportedly is responsible for placing the building where it breaks the straight line of Pennsylvania Avenue with a bend around 15th Street. He became irked, the story goes, with delay in building a new Treasury (the previous one had burned several years earlier); one morning he stalked out of the White House, examined this site and drove his cane into the ground. "Right here," he ordered, "is where I want the cornerstone!"

The lobby exhibit room (9:30–3:45 weekdays) illustrates the activities of the Treasury Department with such items as the $7,200,000 draft paid to Russia in the purchase of Alaska; counterfeit currency, which looks almost but not quite as good as the real thing, narcotics and other contraband seized by T men, the Treasury agents. From the gallery, you can observe the cash room, where warrants for millions of dollars are cashed daily. This currency, as well as part of the country's gold and silver reserve, are stored in steel-cased, concrete vaults below.

West of the White House, the dirty gray Old State Building, now used for White House offices, stands as a relic of the "gingerbread age" of the 1880s, a curio of endless cascading columns, granite porches, mansard roofs, and pediments. The practical modern eye sees it as a monstrosity, or as President Herbert Hoover once said, an architectural orgy foisted on Washington despite the splendid taste of Congress. Yet eminent architects rank it as a classic. And if anyone were to ask my judgment, which is unlikely, I would say let's try a good scrubbing to save a sentimental landmark. At least we could point to *the* building that once housed the entire State, War, and Navy Departments under one roof!

There is not too much remaining of the old Lafayette Square, and that's a pity. The park is pleasantly landscaped around the galloping statue of Andrew Jackson and the four corner figures of foreign revolutionary heroes—Lafayette, Rochambeau, Kosciusko, Von Steuben. But in its day the Square was lined with the city's finest mansions, the homes of wealthy statesmen, literary figures (John Hay, Henry Adams), and diplomats. It was a highly social, zestful, and sometimes impolitely violent corner of town.

Several of the old buildings still stand, and each is important in its own right. The first one built, for instance, St. John's Church, facing the White House from H Street, has been the house of worship for thirteen Presidents, from James Madison to Franklin D. Roosevelt.

St. John's was designed by Benjamin Latrobe in 1816. Three years later the same architect prepared plans for the mansion of Commodore Stephen Decatur, the young but wealthy hero of the Barbary wars, at the corner of Jackson Place and H Street. Decatur enjoyed fame, fortune, a lovely new home and bride. His only lack was a good dueling pistol, or at least a better one than Navy Captain James Barron used when he won in their match at the Bladensburg dueling ground in March 1820. The house, however, continued as a residence of distinction, with three Secretaries of State, Henry Clay, Martin Van Buren, and Edward Livingston, among its occupants.

Soon the palatial three-story Decatur House will be the only antique on Jackson Place. The others are being razed to make way for the new White House office building, and Decatur House was saved only through the efforts of the National Trust for Historic Preservation. Mrs. Truxtun Beale, its last owner—and the last socialite on Lafayette Square—bequeathed the house as a property of the Trust on her death, in 1956. It is now open Wednesday and Saturday, 12–5 P.M. (admission, 50¢).

The former carriage house of the Decatur residence, 1610 H Street, is now the Truxtun-Decatur Naval Museum (12–5 Tuesday–Friday; 10:30–5 Saturday; 12–5 Sundays and holidays), a compact collection maintained by the Naval Historic Foundation. Principal exhibits change three times yearly, but the permanent display includes busts of John Paul Jones and Matthew Maury, models of the frigates *Raleigh* and *Constitution* (*Old Ironsides*).

But back to the trail of violence on Lafayette Square.

Next door to Decatur House on Jackson Place lived Congressman Daniel E. Sickles of New York (later a Union general at Gettysburg), with his pretty wife. She was, according to reports, enjoying an occasional rendezvous with District Attorney Philip Barton Key, son of the author of "The Star-Spangled Banner." On February 27, 1859, in the middle of Lafayette Park, Sickles denounced Key as a scoundrel of the deepest die and filled him full of lead. The Congressman was tried and acquitted under the unwritten law—then returned home to his young wife.

A few years later, across the Square on Madison Place, where the Belasco Theatre stands (it opened as the Lafayette Square Opera House in 1895 with Lillian Russell, presently is USO headquarters), Secretary of State Seward was asleep in bed at his home the night of Lincoln's assassination. He was a target, too; Lewis Payne, one of John Wilkes Booth's psychotic troop, stabbed him in the throat and very nearly killed him.

The house on the corner of H and Madison Place, incidentally, was the home of Dolly Madison until her death in 1849. Toward the end she was almost destitute, until Congress purchased her husband's papers.

The last act of violence hereabout was in November 1950 at the Blair-Lee House, 1651 Pennsylvania Avenue, two historic houses joined together as the "guest house of the Nation" to accommodate visiting heads of state. It was in the Blair House at the start of the Civil War that Robert E. Lee was sounded out by Postmaster General Montgomery Blair on taking command of the Union Army and declined. In 1948 President Truman moved in with his family while the White House underwent reconstruction; the streetcar stop at the corner was eliminated, but anyone was free to walk past the President's front door. Thus arrived the two Puerto Rican nationalists, who tried to assassinate the President, but succeeded only in killing a brave White House guard, Pvt. Leslie Coffelt, and in getting themselves disposed of. The street that day was spattered with bullets and blood.

The scene has been peaceful since. The official title of the Blair-Lee House is the President's Guest House, where you can be treated like a king—if you are one, or a president, or boss of the Soviet Union. President Manuel Prado of Peru asked for and was served breakfast at 5 A.M. of boiled turkey, potatoes, and spinach. King Ibn Saud of Arabia was welcome to have his three bodyguards sleep on the rug outside his door, because that's the way he wanted it.

Comfort is the word. We have come a long way from those crowded days at the White House, as when poor President Buchanan yielded his bedroom to the Prince of Wales (the future King Edward VII) and slept on a couch in his study.

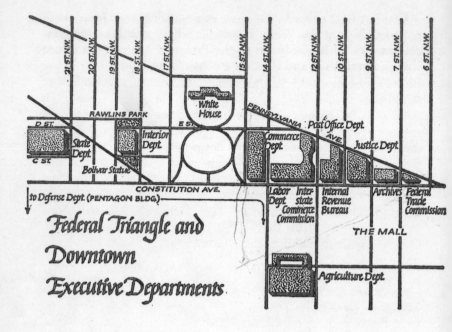

Federal Triangle and Downtown Executive Departments

IX *The Executive Branch*

The government is like a growing boy already the size of a basketball player. Today the Civil Service payroll in metropolitan Washington covers 230,000 men and women. There are more alphabetical agencies than during the New Deal, and every one of them, it seems, has subagencies willing to become basketballers, too.

The executive branch of government, of course, has changed over the years. The Federal system has greater impact on everyone: more influence on our lives, more responsibility and demands, more difficulty in interpreting mandates from Congress. About the only quality it could not have more of is complexity.

Yet you will find government immensely fascinating and you're welcome to visit almost all its buildings. Many have museums, displays, guided tours. Few visitors realize it, but you are welcome to eat at most government cafeterias, which serve wholly adequate meals at reasonable cost.

Start with the Federal Triangle, which extends from the Apex Building, housing the Federal Trade Commission at 6th Street and Pennsylvania Avenue, N.W., to the base, the three-block wide Department of Commerce at 14th Street and Pennsylvania Avenue, N.W. The Federal Triangle was developed between 1930 and 1937, when the government purchased 70 acres, leveled them and built nine new buildings at a cost of $78,000,000. The individual most responsible was Secretary of the Treasury Andrew W. Mellon. Modern architects criticize the neoclassic design of Triangle buildings, but with few exceptions have they done as well since to express the timeless spirit of the national capital.

The principal buildings of interest, starting from the Apex, are:

NATIONAL ARCHIVES, Constitution Avenue between 7th and 9th Streets (9 A.M.–10 P.M. weekdays, 1–10 Sunday) which "holds in trust the records of our national life and symbolizes faith in the permanency of our national institutions." You can enter from Pennsylvania Avenue, but come around to the Constitution Avenue side, the classic entrance, guarded by two bronze doors 38 feet high. It opens into the Exhibit Hall and the three documents which contain America's charter of freedom—the Declaration of Independence, Constitution of the United States, the Bill of Rights.

This beautiful semicircular hall, 75 feet high, was designed for the purpose it fills. The three parchments, especially the Declaration of Independence, were much traveled and handled before coming here in 1952. Now they are sealed in helium-filled glass cases, screened by filters from harmful light rays. They can be lowered at a second's notice into a steel and concrete vault under the floor.

You'll find this one of Washington's most interesting rooms. One large mural represents Thomas Jefferson and his committee presenting the Declaration of Independence. Another mural depicts James Madison submitting the Constitution. While you wait in line—and you will—for a closeup of the principal documents, you will pass fifty others of importance relating to the founding of the Union. These include the rebellious Articles of Association of 1774, which decried the "ruinous system of colony administration adopted by the British ministry"; Washington's acceptance of the post of commander in chief of the Continental Armies, and the Articles of Confederation of 1777, which preceded the Constitution.

Don't miss the semicircular corridor behind the Exhibition Hall. It's lined with Federal documents relating to all the states of the Union, including yours. This is a wonderful spot to let children loose on a treasure hunt to locate their own state displays. Among them: Colorado—map of the Pikes Peak region from the journal kept by Zebulon Pike; West Virginia—Colonel Robert E. Lee's report to the War Department on quelling John Brown's band at Harpers Ferry; New York—deed of gift of the Statue of Liberty from the French people.

Behind the scenes: National Archives holds the selected permanent records of the Federal government, military, diplomatic, and domestic, dating from 1774. These include still pictures, sound recordings, motion picture film, all of increasing value with the passing years.

Documents for sale: "Charters of Freedom," beautiful facsimile of the Constitution, Declaration of Independence, and Bill of Rights, with historical notes, 25¢. Photographs of Abraham Lincoln, Robert E. Lee (both by Mathew Brady), Sitting Bull, John J. Pershing, Dwight D. Eisenhower, Wilbur and Orville Wright, 20¢ each.

DEPARTMENT OF JUSTICE, 9th and Pennsylvania Avenue, N.W., for the guided tour of the Federal Bureau of Investigation (one hour, 9:30–4, Monday–Friday). The tour is far better than watching a TV thriller and the G men are hard to beat as courteous hosts—tours start every 15 minutes, every three minutes during peak periods.

During the tour you see FBI laboratory experts examining evidence in current cases. These may be microscopic examinations of minute hairs, soil fragments, or bullet shells. Exhibit rooms portray different phases of the FBI in action. One, on the gangster era of the '30s, contains John Dillinger's guns, hat, and death mask, pictures of desperadoes like Pretty Boy Floyd, Baby Face Nelson, and Machine Gun Kelly. Another room traces the G men's successful efforts in coping with foreign agents and espionage. And another is devoted to the million-dollar Brink's holdup, complete with the scale model of the Boston crime. A loud, emphatic high point: a visit to the firearms range, where a special agent demonstrates marksmanship with revolver and submachine gun.

POST OFFICE DEPARTMENT, 12th Street and Pennsylvania Avenue, N.W., a philatelist's must. Not the old "shudder in stone" but the new building across the street. Visit the Philatelic Agency and Exhibit Room, Room 1315, (9–5 Monday–Friday, to 4:30 Saturday). Here you can buy any U.S. stamp still in stock, from a half-cent to $5 issue. More than 100,000 stamps are on exhibition, dating from the first U.S. issue in 1847; there also are 1100 major foreign varieties furnished by the International Postal Union.

DEPARTMENT OF COMMERCE, 14th and Pennsylvania Avenue, N.W., the mammoth base of the Federal Triangle (8:30–5, Monday–Friday; 8:30–12:30, Saturday). This building cost $17,000,000 to build in the 1930s. In the lobby you come face to face with the nation's dramatic, slightly terrifying "Census Clock," an electric timing scoreboard which records population and its changes. It flashes the average intervals between every birth (7½ seconds), death (20 seconds), immigrant arrival (1½ minutes) and emigrant departure (20 minutes)—a net increase of one every eleven seconds. At this rate, the U.S. population will pass 200,000,000 in 1967.

There is always another display in the Commerce lobby, either prepared by the Department or by industrial corporations, ranging from electronic distance measuring equipment, foreign trade services available through the Department, to models of industrial parks and inventions under the U. S. Patent System. To find out which display is current, call the Department of Commerce, ST 3-9200, or Greater National Capital Committee, ST 3-3535. Another permanent display is the Coast and Geodetic Survey's seismograph, recording earth vibrations underneath the building and photographs of recent earthquakes in the western United States and Japan.

The Aquarium in the basement contains a variety of American game fish, muskellunge, catfish, trout; terrapins, and tropical fish, including the flesh-eating piranha. Feeding time: 2 P.M., Monday and Thursday.

Across the Mall: *Voice of America,* in the Health, Education, and Welfare (HEW) Building, 3rd Street and Independence Avenue, S.W., offers guided tours of its studios at 11 A.M. and 3 P.M., Monday through Friday. This is probably the world's major radio network; broadcasts originating here are beamed through 83 overseas transmitters. The Voice, a major instrument of U.S. foreign policy, largely avoids propaganda but sticks to the news and reports on cultural life in America.

BUREAU OF ENGRAVING AND PRINTING, 14th and C Streets, S.W., (8–11 and 12:30–2, Monday through Friday), is one of the most popular government buildings. Mark the hours carefully; the Bureau is not open too long. There's really no place to park so take the streetcar (No. 50), cab, or sightseeing bus. The 30-minute tour shows a part of the plant that prints $29,000,000 in paper currency a day, five days a week. Of this amount, two-thirds are one-dollar bills, the highest denomination $10,000. In the examining room only one per cent of all bills printed are found with imperfections. The Museum of Currency displays government bonds, stamps, engravings, currency back to 1861 and a $100,000 bill, last printed in 1935.

DEPARTMENT OF THE INTERIOR, 18th Street between C and E Streets, N.W., holds strong appeal if you're interested in conservation of resources or the American West. The Interior Museum on the first floor (8–4:15, Monday through Friday), includes models, charts, and maps of geological surveys; a model of gigantic Hoover Dam; paintings of explorers and fur traders, dioramas of an old Indian trading post, oil fields, and a rescue at a mine disaster. The Interior Department Craft Shop has a fine display of authentic Indian and Eskimo arts and handicraft—and the items are for sale.

THE DEPARTMENT OF STATE, between 21st and 23rd and C Streets, N.W., (8:30–5, Monday through Friday), exemplifies the growing government. With its brand-new $57,400,000 enlarged headquarters, it now occupies the second largest building here, topped only by the Pentagon.

The eight-story contemporary-style State Building, covering four blocks, is an expansion around the previous smaller building. It contains special rooms for international conferences, an 800-seat auditorium and dining rooms for diplomatic functions. Use the Diplomatic Entrance on C Street, where glass panels rise three-stories high. Among points of interest in the building is the Seal of the United States, which you can watch being affixed to official documents with the President's signature.

The Department of State, the oldest executive department, was established in 1789 with Thomas Jefferson as the first Secretary. He had five clerks, one interpreter, two messengers, three diplomatic missions abroad (Paris, London, The Hague). Today the Department has 25,000 employees in this building and at 279 posts overseas.

THE PENTAGON, headquarters of the Department of Defense (7 A.M. to 6 P.M., Monday through Friday), is only 15 minutes from downtown over Arlington Memorial Bridge or 14th Street Bridge, and is well worth the trip just for the chance to see it from the inside.

Five Capitol buildings would fit within its walls, with room to spare. It has three times the office space of New York's Empire State Building. More than 30,000 military and civilian personnel come to work here daily, including 600 to keep it clean.

The Pentagon has direct approach by helicopter, rail, highway, and water (service morning and afternoon for high offices). Buses operate 900 trips daily. Parking areas can accommodate 8300 cars. You are welcome to use Visitor Lanes 12 and 13 in South Parking, and 54 B in North Parking.

Stop at the information desks for a Visitor's Guide and Tour Route. A map will make all the difference when you start cruising around the "Puzzle Palace." With one, you'll find that, while it's a distance of about a mile around the outer ring, no two offices are more than six minutes apart—by following escalators and ramps. Without one, you may be lost for days.

On the third floor, walk past the impressive office of the Secretary of Defense, then take the escalator up to the fourth floor to see the models, pictures, and planes in the Air Force area; the ships, planes, and paintings in the Navy area; and the trophies, pictures, and models in the Army area.

Then take the escalator down to have lunch and see the shopping facilities on the concourse. Nearly 30,000 meals are served daily in six cafeterias, two restaurants, nine beverage bars and a tenth in the center court open during warm weather.

The shops: tailor, barber, jeweler, Brentano's bookstore, drugs, department store, dry cleaner and laundry, florist, pastry shop, airline and rail ticket offices, post office.

X *The Outdoor Scene*

Parks, trees, and the spacious outdoors are as basic to Washington as government, although some people now think such a concept of land use is outmoded.

Two thousand varieties of trees and shrubs, representing 200 distinct species, grow in Washington. No other city and few arboretums have such a wide range. You can find thirty types of oak, six of maple, ash, elm, dogwood, magnolia, holly (it blooms along the Mall at Christmas), black birch, beech, poplar, tulip, pines, cedars, firs, and flowering fruit trees—apple, quince, plum, and cherry.

George Washington loved trees and nurtured them with a forester's know-how. The most famous tree ever to grow in Washington was the great elm he planted on the Capitol lawn. It lived 150 years, until 1948.

Dating from L'Enfant, parks and open spaces have been part of the architecture of the city, providing settings of dignity for public buildings. Thomas Jefferson, for his part, planted four rows of poplars along Pennsylvania Avenue from 1st to 15th Streets and contributed the concept of height limitation—which is under criticism today, although it sets Washington apart from all other cities.

Every President has enjoyed and contributed to the outdoor scene. Theodore Roosevelt, hiker and horseman, was an enthusiast of Rock Creek Park. Herbert Hoover was a fisherman on the Rapidan River, in what is now Shenandoah National Park. Franklin D. Roosevelt, though physical infirmity restricted his active participation, loved boating on the Potomac and Chesapeake Bay. Harry Truman, the walking enthusiast, bounded from the White House to the Capitol and back for his morning constitutional. Dwight D. Eisenhower turned for his recreation and renewed vigor to golfing.

Parks comprise 7000 acres or about one-tenth of the national capital land area. Ours is a different type of city park system. It belongs to the nation. It shows the world, and our own future generations, that we believe government is enhanced by an environment of growing, living things.

These are parks for everyone. You can fish, ride, camp, swim, skate, play golf or tennis, follow wilderness trails, or watch football and baseball played at the Ellipse, back of the White House.

My favorite is the one and only Rock Creek Park, nearly 2000 acres which Congress purchased for the nation in 1890 for its "pleasant valleys and deep ravines, its primeval forests and open fields, its running waters, its rocks clothed with rich ferns and mosses, its repose and tranquillity, its light and shade, its ever-varying shrubbery, its beautiful and extensive views."

One day follow part of the ten-mile drive through the Park (but avoid morning, afternoon rush hours when traffic is routed one way). From the Lincoln Memorial drive out Rock Creek Parkway, past the new Watersports Center on the Potomac, then "Ickes Beach," the banked lawn where hundreds of Washingtonians sun themselves in summer. On Beach Drive, principal road in the Park, you will see the waters of Rock Creek splashing over rocks and boulders and colonies of ducks swimming and fluttering about; you'll also drive through four fords, so slow down and test brakes after each crossing. Two good stops are at Pierce Mill, an early waterpowered grist mill, and the old log cabin of Joaquin Miller, built and lived in by the "Poet of the Sierras" (moved here many years ago from Meridian Hill near 16th Street.

Choice activities in the Park:

Riding—from the new stables near Military Road and Oregon Avenue. Leave car fumes behind and ride the Black Horse and White Horse trails through the woods and along the creek, without once crossing the highway. Riding is a great Rock Creek tradition, enjoyed by many Congressmen, diplomats, Westerners. Rate $3 an hour, with an escort accompanying each party. Phone Pete Hendrick, EM 2-0117. Open all year, best in mornings. Another new stable, under Taft Bridge, is convenient to Sheraton-Park and Shoreham Hotels. Phone AD 4-9664.

Picnicking—in 48 scenic groves. Reserve a choice table by telephoning AD 4-2050.

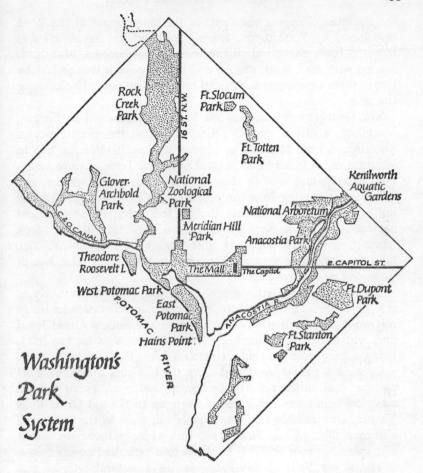

Rock
Creek
Park

16 ST. N.W.

Ft. Slocum
Park

Ft. Totten
Park

Glover-
Archbold
Park

C & O CANAL

National
Zoological
Park

Kenilworth
Aquatic
Gardens

National Arboretum

Meridian Hill
Park

Anacostia Park

Theodore
Roosevelt I.

The Mall   The Capitol

E. CAPITOL ST.

West Potomac Park

POTOMAC

East
Potomac
Park

ANACOSTIA R.

Ft. Dupont
Park

Hains Point

RIVER

Ft. Stanton
Park

*Washington's
Park
System*

Golf—good, hilly public course, 16th and Underwood Streets;
90¢ for 18 holes, $1.50 on weekends.

Guided nature walks—conducted by National Capital Parks.
Also twilight campfire programs twice weekly in summer, near
16th Street and Colorado Avenue. Call RE 7-1820, ext. 2557.

Especially for children—National Zoo and the Nature Center.

For an unusual park experience, take the mule-drawn canal
clipper barge on the historic Chesapeake & Ohio Canal, parallel to

the Potomac. This was once part of the water route to the West envisioned by Washington. During its heyday (the 1870s) five hundred boats navigated all the way to Cumberland, Maryland, loaded with coal, flour, grains, and lumber. Each was pulled by two or three mules, and raised and lowered through 75 locks along the way.

The Georgetown Division has been reconstructed to Seneca, Maryland, a distance of 22 miles, of which the clipper covers 4.6 miles. A park historian or naturalist accompanies the trip to interpret canal history and natural features. Trips operate Saturday, Sunday, and holiday afternoons May through October, and Wednesday evening June through August. Tickets (75¢, children under 12, 50¢) are on sale during the week at Government Services, Inc. (NA 8-7363), or before departure at the barge landing, one block south of 30th and M Streets, N.W. *Tip:* take the barge one way, then return on the Cabin John bus or by hiking on the towpath.

The canal is lush with water vegetation. And you're likely to see wood duck, black vulture, and many species of warbler in migration season. If you're driving your car, follow Canal Road and rent a canoe at Fletcher's (look for the sign on the left). Bring fishing gear—you might catch a bluegill, bass, or crappie.

Or pack a picnic lunch and drive up to Great Falls, the most popular area on the restored section of the canal. There you see a typical trim stone lockhouse, a museum in the old Great Falls Tavern, and trailside exhibits. Best of all, walk to the top of the cliff overlooking Great Falls, a 200-foot-wide, 50-foot-deep waterfall, splashing over upthrust boulders into turbulent rapids below.

The Great Falls of the Potomac are a natural wonder you would scarcely expect at Washington's back door. If it weren't for all the attractions of the city, this would be considered one of America's finest scenic areas of the East—and is probably the most overlooked.

You can also reach Great Falls on the Virginia side via the beautiful new 5½-mile extension of the George Washington Memorial Parkway, from Spout Run just above Key Bridge, and Route 193. Great Falls Park (admission 50¢ per car), owned by Fairfax County, has fine facilities: picnic tables, refreshment stand, self-guided nature trail, and carousel for children.

Theodore Roosevelt Memorial Island, a complex of plants and animals in a wild state, is a living memorial to Theodore Roosevelt, who, while he was in the White House (1901–09), did more than any other President to preserve the nation's natural resources through establishment of the national forests and wildlife refuges. Even in Washington he loved to probe the outdoors. On long walks in Rock Creek Park, as William Allen White recollected, Roosevelt would invite "fat military officers with him, who panted along a step or two behind."

Roosevelt Island, one mile long and a half mile wide, lies south of Key Bridge in the Potomac. The only approach, till now, is by ferry from the foot of Wisconsin Avenue in Georgetown, Saturday and Sunday 1 to 4:30 P.M. (no charge). *Best Time:* 2 P.M. for the guided nature walk. The woods are full of raccoon, muskrat, and other small animals, while along the shore you may see an egret in shallow water, or a red-winged blackbird, possibly even a great blue heron in summer.

The island has a long history. It was called Analostan by early explorers, later was owned by George Mason. The next chapter will open with the new Constitution Avenue Bridge crossing its southern tip, something which Theodore Roosevelt's admirers opposed but couldn't halt.

In the Northeast section—

Kenilworth Aquatic Gardens, in Anacostia Park, reached via Kenilworth Avenue, N.E., was started by a government employee as a hobby eighty years ago. Now it contains more than 100,000 water plants, including rare exotic species like the Nelumbium, the famous lotus of history; the deep rose Egyptian lotus, and the South American Victoria cruziana with immense leaves up to six feet in diameter. Best time is mid-June, when thousands of plants are in bloom. Late July and August are good, too, to see the tropical water lilies open. Many flowers close in the heat of day, so visit in mornings. *Parents:* children will love the frogs, turtles toads, birds.

National Arboretum, Bladensburg Road and Montana Avenue, N.E., is a living laboratory of trees, shrubs and plants grown in this area, maintained by the Department of Agriculture (open Saturday and Sunday, mid-April to mid-May; rest of the year by appointment—phone LI 3-9373). Roads and foot trails through the 400-acre Arboretum enable visitors to observe thousands of plants and flowers arranged in patterns. The azalea display includes some 65,000 plants covering the slopes of Mount Hamilton. Prettiest time is April–May, but there is color and fragrance from early spring to late autumn.

Parks and monuments are administered by National Capital Parks, a unit of the National Park Service, thus a federal agency yet very much a part of local life. A week does not pass without a program of activities—nature walks, evening lectures, color movies, historical tours on the Mall, photo tours, motorboat trips. To learn the full opportunities, order the booklet "National Capital Park System," from the Superintendent of Documents, U. S. Government Printing Office, Washington 25, D.C. (price 15¢), and the booklet "Outdoor Program" from the Superintendent, National Capital Parks, Department of Interior, Washington 25, D.C. (free).

For the Sports-minded—

Fishing: "It aboundeth in fish," exulted Captain Henry Fleet, one of the earliest explorers of the Potomac. And in 1832, almost 300,000 herring were reported taken from the waters off Washington. Today fishing is still fun, but pollution—a constantly worsening problem—claims a heavy toll.

Spring, when salt-water fish come upstream to spawn, is a very good season for the fisherman. First come great schools of herring, followed by white perch and crappie, then the delectable white shad and rockfish after mid-April. The rocks near Chain Bridge are popular, sometimes dangerous. Between Cabin John and Great Falls, you can catch walleyed pike, bass, catfish. In summer, try the Tidal Basin for carp; a good fighter on light tackle. In autumn, small-mouth and large-mouth bass are caught on both shores of the Potomac.

The National Capital Casting Club gives instructions in casting at the Reflection Pool every weekend (Noon Saturday, 10 A.M. Sunday). Call KI 0-6554. Recommended reading: *Washington Area Fishing Guide,* by Charles Covell, Outdoors Editor, the *Evening Star* (50¢). A free Fishing Map and Time Table is published by the Washington *Daily News,* available at the newspaper office, 1013 13th Street, N.W., and at sporting goods stores.

Boating: Rent sailboats at Sailing Marina, Mount Vernon Memorial Highway, south of National Airport, OT 4-7783. Rent powerboats at Columbia Island Marina, near the Pentagon, DI 7-0173. Rent canoes at the beautiful new $350,000 Watersports Center. Park your car at Virginia Avenue, where Rock Creek empties into the Potomac. The Center is also used for housing and launching racing shells. Even if you're not boating, stop for refreshments and the Potomac view. Canoes and rowboats may also be rented at the Tidal Basin, and at Dempsey's in Georgetown (via K Street), Jack's and Fletcher's, on the Potomac off the Chesapeake & Ohio Canal ($2 for rowboats, $4 for canoes, all day).

Tennis: Excellent Har-Tru courts at Sheraton-Park Hotel, $2 an hour single, $3 double. One hundred and twenty free courts are operated by the D. C. Recreation Department, AD 4-2050. Pay courts at Hains Point and Rock Creek Park (clay courts 75¢ an hour, hardtop 20¢).

Cycling: Rock Creek Park, Hains Point, Chesapeake & Ohio Canal towpath. Near Rock Creek Park rent bikes at 1458 Park Road, open every day (50¢ an hour, $2 a day, slightly more for English bikes).

Golf: Public courses are Hains Point, Rock Creek, and Fort DuPont near Minnesota and Massachusetts Avenues, S.E., and Langston Golf Course, at Benning Road, N.E., and the Anacostia River (18 holes for 90¢ weekdays, $1.50 weekends).

Baseball: American League baseball, featuring the Washington Senators, cellar dwellers often, but favorites still, from April through September at Griffith Stadium, DU 7-6333.

Football: Professional variety—Washington's team is the Redskins—from September to November, also at Griffith Stadium. Call the Wigwam at DI 7-6140. College football: George Washington University at Griffith Stadium; University of Maryland at College Park; U. S. Naval Academy at Annapolis.

Racing: Great horse country surrounds Washington and twelve tracks are within reach. One mile tracks: Bowie (20 miles), Laurel (18 miles), Pimlico (40 miles), Charles Town (60 miles). Half-mile tracks: Bel Air (50 miles), Timonium (55 miles), Hagerstown (75 miles), Marlboro (25 miles), Shenandoah Downs (60 miles, night racing). Harness Racing: Rosecroft (10 miles), Laurel, Baltimore (40 miles), Ocean Downs (104 miles). All tracks in Maryland, except Charles Town and Shenandoah Downs which are in West Virginia.

Bowie season opens early February and Pimlico's closes mid-December, so the ponies are usually running somewhere in the area. Consult sports pages of the newspapers for schedules.

Ice Skating: Outdoor rink at the Marriott Motor Hotel, Virginia side of 14th Street Bridge, mid-October–March, $1 an hour for children, $1.25 for adults. Plus new rinks at the Sheraton-Park Hotel and C. P. Skating Club, Route 1, College Park, Maryland. Indoors at Uline Arena, 3rd Street and Maryland Avenue, N.E. When it freezes, which is rarely, bring your skates to the Reflection Pool, Kenilworth Gardens, or Chesapeake & Ohio Canal (above Brookmont).

Camping: Potomac Park Motor Court, Hains Point. Space for about 50 tents, 50¢ per night per person, no charge for youngsters under 6; showers, washroom, laundry facilities. Trailer space, too, for about 56 trailers, equipped with electric and water connections, $2. This area, east of Jefferson Memorial, is operated by Government Services, Inc., in co-operation with National Capital Parks. Also available are rooms ranging from dormitory-type without baths, $1.50 per person, to more modern type with bath, $8 double. Write to Potomac Park Motor Court, Washington 4, D.C., or call NA 8-0037.

XI *Culture in the Capital*

Does Washington wallow in the cultural backwoods or is it finally "arriving"? That's an interesting question to be argued out one day in the back of a bookstore. But here's another, better subject for the present: the matter of really using the cultural facilities we do have.

"There is nothing esoteric or beyond the comprehension of the average man in that incessant spiritual activity we call art," comments Duncan Phillips, director of the Phillips Memorial Gallery. "The sense of well-being and enriched capacity which art can give is a privilege of the many as well as of the technically trained few."

This is sound philosophy for expression in Washington. Properly, art, like the outdoors, the city itself and the whole scheme of democracy, offers a share of enrichment to everyone. As an example, Mr. Phillips' own gallery is not only inviting, but symbolizes the freer spirit we are acquiring; his collection, *sans* conformity, displays the innovators in art as well as the accepted and understood.

The Phillips Gallery, 1600 21st Street, N.W. (11–6 weekdays, Monday to 10; Sunday 2–7; gallery tour 3 P.M. Saturday), was opened in 1918, probably the earliest museum of modern art in the United States. It is housed in the converted four-story brick mansion of the Phillips family and the best part of it, after the paintings, is the atmosphere: uncrowded, non-institutional, totally unlike a public place. In one of the softly lighted rooms on the first floor you can sit at ease in an overstuffed chair or sofa alone, or nearly so, to appreciate and admire the paintings. In such a setting art was meant to be hung.

As a museum of "modern art and its sources," it includes a painting by sixteenth-century Giorgione and other early works. The large, though still intimate Main Gallery displays familiar paintings and artists, including Renoir's Le Déjeuner des Canotiers

(Luncheon of the Boating Party), Daumier's The Uprising, and versions of The Repentant Peter painted by El Greco and Goya.

The Gallery accents Bonnard (and was perhaps first to display him in this country), Matisse, Derain, Roualt, Picasso. Entire rooms are devoted to Braque and Klee. The Phillips is the only public place in Washington where you can see the works of Jackson Pollock, Arthur Dove, de Kooning, de Stael and Rothko—and an entire room in its new wing displays contemporary abstractions.

Concerts: chamber music is performed in the Main Gallery Sunday afternoon and Monday evening, October to June (free). Performers are largely young people who deserve to be heard or older artists who play because they love the Phillips Gallery.

The Corcoran Gallery of Art, 17th Street and New York Avenue, N.W. (10–4:30 Tuesday through Friday; 9–4:30 Saturday; 2–5 Sunday), is Washington's oldest gallery, founded by W. W. Corcoran in 1859. Its original building, the reddish Victorian memento at the corner of Pennsylvania Avenue and 17th Street (now occupied by the U. S. Court of Claims), was designed by the great American architect James Renwick, who is perhaps best known as the architect of St. Patrick's Cathedral in New York and the Smithsonian Institution in the capital. The Corcoran has always emphasized and encouraged American art and includes 550 works in its American collection. Among the European paintings, most of them given by the late Senator William Clark of Montana, are a room full of paintings by Corot, early master of the impressionists, and another room of paintings by Monticelli, who strongly influenced Van Gogh.

Several historically important American paintings include Samuel F. B. Morse's huge portrait of The Old House of Representatives; Albert Bierstadt's Last of the Buffalo; Seth Eastman's Lacrosse Playing among the Sioux, and George P. A. Healy's portrait of beardless Abraham Lincoln, painted in 1860 when he was President-elect.

Other outstanding American works include portraits by Copley, Washington Allston, George Inness, Gilbert Stuart and Rembrandt Peale; Battersea Reach by Whistler; A Light on the Sea by

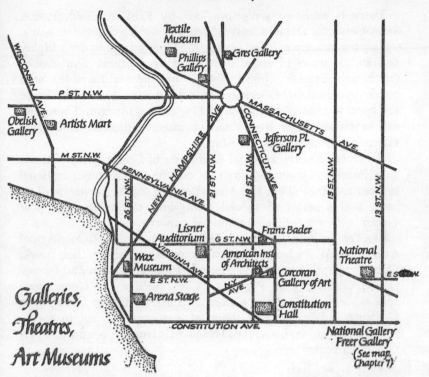

Galleries, Theatres, Art Museums

Winslow Homer, purchased by the Corcoran at its first Biennial Exhibition in 1907; The Pathetic Song by Eakins; Woman with a Dog by Mary Casatt, and the Oyster Gatherers by Sargent. More recent paintings are Two Kids by George Bellows, representing the "Ashcan School," and Sunny Side of the Street by Philip Evergood. Among the latest acquisitions: watercolors by Alexander Calder and John Marin, and lithographs by George Biddle.

In the European section be sure to note these masterpieces: Judgment of Midas by Rubens; An Elderly Man in an Armchair by Rembrandt; Lake of Terni, among the thirty paintings by Corot; The Advocate by Daumier; Drama of Woods and Sunlight, among the several by Monticelli; the Seine at Paris by Pisarro; five by Degas of the ballet and theater; Willows of Vetheuil by Monet, and Esterel Mountains by Renoir.

There is excellent sculpture, too: by Paul Manship, Rodin, Saint-Gaudens, Daniel Chester French.

As a community cultural center, the Corcoran presents a highly worthwhile series of about 25 concerts, receptions, film classics (such as *Potemkin, Grand Hotel, Les Enfants Terrible*) with coffee by candlelight, lectures on art, theater, literature. These are open to members at a fee of $10, or $15 for two. There also are seven or eight free chamber music concerts on Sunday afternoons from October to May.

Recurring Events: Biennial Exhibition of Contemporary American Painting, January–March in odd years, a major national competitive exhibition; the Annual Area Exhibit, November–January, and a series of special exhibitions throughout the year (consult the art columns in Sunday papers).

Smaller galleries of merit: Jefferson Place, 1216 Connecticut Avenue, N.W., where avant-garde members show their work; Gres, 1729 20th Street, N.W., largely Latin American and foreign talent; Obelisk, 3241 P Street, N.W., fashionable Georgetown spot where you can buy a Miro or Picasso; Franz Bader, 1705 G Street, N.W., changing shows of contemporary art in a convenient downtown bookshop; Howard University, Negro and pre-Columbian art.

THEATERS

Arena Stage is a first rate new cultural institution—the largest one of four, theatres-in-the-round outside New York (the others: Margo Jones Theatre, Dallas; Alley Theatre, Houston; Fred Miller Theatre, Milwaukee).

As a repertory theater, *Arena* presents more than 90 plays, encompassing Shakespeare, Shaw, O'Casey, Turgenev, O'Neill, Arthur Miller, Tennessee Williams, Jean Anouilh, Christopher Fry. Under Zelda Fichlander, its producing director, Arena, since it opened in 1950, has earned professional honors and distinction as a training ground for playwrights, actors, directors.

At last glance, Arena was bidding adieu to its home, a converted brewery in Foggy Bottom standing in the way of the projected Theodore Roosevelt Memorial Bridge, and preparing to move. By early 1961, Arena should be relocated in its own $350,000 building, designed for theatre-in-the-round and three-quarter

staging (ideal for Shakespeare), in southwest Washington. This
modern, 700-seat theater results from a $50,000 grant (from the
Eugene and Agnes E. Meyer Foundation), plus $300,000 in loans,
grants, bequests raised by Arena enthusiasts. In its first nine
years attendance rose 33 per cent yearly until it reached nearly
100,000, which is no small group of theatergoers. Check newspaper
theater pages for current productions.

The National Theatre, 1321 E Street, N.W., (NA 8-3393), is
Broadway's only outlet for the legitimate stage in the capital,
popular for both try-outs and road companies. The original
National opened in 1835 with a play entitled *The Man of the
World*. The present National—built in 1917—is the sixth structure
to be erected on the same original site. All the great names of the
theater from the days of Junius Brutus Booth, Edwin Forrest, and
Jenny Lind to Katharine Cornell, Helen Hayes, and the Lunts
in our time have trod the boards of the National. Of all
the Presidents who have attended—and they all have since
the days of Martin Van Buren—Franklin D. Roosevelt was the
most ardent theatergoer. A ramp was built for the fire escape so
he could enter directly into the Presidential box in his wheel chair.
The box is the last on the left facing the stage.

Keith's Theatre, on 15th Street at G, is a Washington landmark,
now a motion picture house of nostalgic and sentimental interest
because of its important place during the halcyon days of big-time
vaudeville. It was President Woodrow Wilson's favorite theater
and, during his years in the White House, he was a regular patron
of Keith's to see Nora Bayes, Eddie Foy, Irene Franklin, Bert
Williams and all the great headliners of the golden era of Keith
Vaudeville.

Catholic University Theatre, 4th and Michigan Avenue, N.W.,
top-flight college group, stages five plays, each in a two-week
run, from October to May. These include Shakespeare, Moliére
and original works. Tickets are $2; subscription seats are sold.
Call AD 2-6000, ext. 358.

Players, Inc., a high quality Catholic University graduate group,
performs at the area's most durable summer theater, the Olney,
in Montgomery County, Maryland, WH 6-8100; downtown
ticket office at Jordan's, 13th and G Streets, N.W.

MUSIC

The National Symphony Orchestra under conductor Howard Mitchell has advanced to rank with the country's major symphonies. The orchestra plays a thirty-three week series, October to April, at Constitution Hall, 18th and C Streets, N.W., part of the headquarters of the Daughters of the American Revolution. (Box office, 1108 G Street, N.W., NA 8-7332.)

Dr. Mitchell, who was first cellist under the late Hans Kindler, the orchestra's founder, is a constant campaigner for new music enthusiasts. The orchestra plays 44 concerts for area youngsters (including an elementary school subscription series for as little as 50¢ a concert and another series in the schools without admission charge). For visiting teen-agers in school groups the five-week Music for Young America series in April and May offers free nightly concerts at the Pan American Union, 17th Street and Constitution Avenue, N.W. These provide many youngsters their first opportunity to hear live orchestral music. For tickets, write manager, National Symphony Orchestra, Hotel Roosevelt, 16th and V Streets, N.W., Washington 9, D.C.

The military bands—Army, Navy, Air Force, Marine—perform free concerts during winter months at the Department of Commerce Auditorium, 14th and Pennsylvania Avenue, N.W., and at the Departmental Auditorium, 12th Street and Constitution Avenue, N.W. Consult the newspapers or call ST 3-3535, Greater National Capital Committee, for the schedule.

The Opera Society of Washington, since it started in 1956, has earned a national reputation by quality performances of difficult operas, such as Mozart's *Cosi Fan Tutte*, Stravinsky's *The Rake's Progress* and Debussy's *Pelléas et Mélisande*. Under direction of Paul Callaway, choirmaster at Washington Cathedral, three or four operatic productions are staged during the year at Lisner Auditorium, 21st and H Streets, N.W. They are given in performance "runs" from Thursday through Sunday. The "twilight matinee" at 5:30 P.M. Sunday is a choice time to introduce youngsters to the world of opera. The auditorium at George Washington University is not quite an opera house, but performances are fully staged and the roles are sung by able, youthful singers. The audience is studded with Washington personalities, if that counts. Tickets are sold at the Opera Society office, 1745

K Street, N.W., RE 7-0700, or the Talbert Ticket Office in the Willard Hotel, NA 8-5575.

Speaking of art forms, Washington is truly the architects' city. The work of some of America's best, from Dr. William Thornton and his archfoe Benjamin Latrobe (who once sued him for libel) down to Stanford White, John Russell Pope, Paul Cret, and Horace Peaslee, is manifest in private homes, headquarters, embassies and bridges, as well as the monumental public structures. The American Institute of Architects (AIA) has a classic in its own national headquarters, the Octagon House, 18th Street and New York Avenue, N.W., (Tuesday–Saturday, 9–5; Sunday, 2–5, free). It was designed by Dr. Thornton, Washington's favorite, as a town house for wealthy Colonel John Tayloe, and completed in 1800. Among its architectural features are the six-sided floor plan (Octagon is a misnomer), combination of oval and rectangular rooms, curved front wall, unique secret doors and a hidden staircase. In its early days, the Octagon was the scene of receptions and balls, possibly the most elegant in the city; it achieved historic importance in 1814 as the residence of President and Mrs. Madison for the greater part of a year, after the burning of the White House.

The AIA has spent a half million dollars in restoration since it acquired the Octagon, in a sorrowful, run-down condition, at the turn of the century. Now you can see the circular entrance hall, dining room and drawing room restored with many original furnishings, and the round inlaid table on which the Treaty of Ghent, ending the war with Britain, was signed in this temporary White House. From time to time, exhibits on architecture and allied arts are held on the second floor. A few years ago the AIA, which has its headquarters in the annex beyond the walled garden, found itself in a quandary: whether to tear down the stable in order to expand the office space, or to prohibit any move that would mar the authentic 1800 town house. The decision was an architectural compromise, and now the stable is the AIA library.

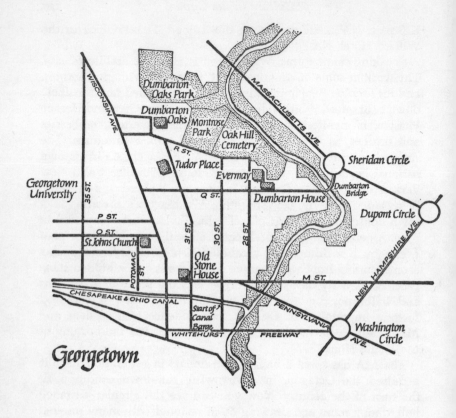

Georgetown

XII *A Stroll in Georgetown*

Fountain Inn, otherwise known as Suter's Tavern, was the proper place in Georgetown for men of distinction to drop in for a short one, or for a night's lodging. It was convenient, but not too close, to the wharves and the ferry to Virginia. And Mr. Suter believed in providing parking at the premises so that a guest could always find a space in the stables for his horse or coach.

Suter's was a favorite spot of George Washington's. He had stopped off as early as 1774, when he was riding with Patrick Henry and Edmund Pendleton to the first Continental Congress in Philadelphia. One morning seventeen years later, in 1791, he met there with leading Georgetowners to study the L'Enfant-Ellicott surveys for the new capital. In the afternoon he conferred with the three commissioners, dined and spent the night. Next day he inspected the site of the new city and met with the Georgetowners again. They were embroiled in contention with Carrollburg on location of public buildings. Patiently, Washington warned they were serving neither the public interest nor their own, that if they didn't co-operate and compromise the federal city might go elsewhere.

By this time not only was Suter's Tavern (now long gone from its site near Wisconsin and M) well recognized, but so was Georgetown. It sniggered at Carrollburg. Georgetown was then settled almost a century, from the time the first land grant for the "Rock of Dumbarton" tract had been issued to Colonel Ninian Beall; since 1751 it was officially a "towne" under charter from the Maryland Assembly. The water at its wharves was deep enough for large sailing ships and the Georgetown port carried on a lively commerce with the West Indies and England.

Today Georgetown is the one corner of Washington with full-flavored antiquity. Lafayette Square and other sections have been plowed under, Capitol Hill is finally coming back, but Georgetown stands unique as the residential area where you can stroll for block after block and sense the charm and fruitfulness of the past.

In composite terms, Georgetown would be one part New Orleans' Vieux Carrée, one part Charleston or Savannah, a small part Greenwich Village, and the closest thing in the East, temperamentally, to San Francisco. Here are soft and mellow tones, an appreciation for living, and for the decorative arts, without and within. In recent years, many old homes, almost lost in misuse and decay, have been restored with new paint, new flowers, new doorways complete with burnished knockers and door lamps. A large number are furnished with eighteenth-century pieces and are complete with garden, however small.

Georgetown is something of a state of mind, too. As a community it retains an insular identity, though it yielded its sovereign rights as a separate city on merging with Washington in 1871. Characterizing the typical Georgetowner, however, is another question. Here live government officials and Congressmen, intellectuals, a sprinkling of wealthy, a smattering of snobs and oddballs, and many average citizens. Not too long ago the atmosphere was more casual than fashionable, and places like the drugstore at Wisconsin and O or Martin's corner restaurant were as convivial as a country store. Not that there's anything wrong with them now, but there are so many other places: a multitude of shops, restaurants, a coffee house.

The best time to visit is late April or May, when you can join the Georgetown House Tour or the Georgetown Garden Tour and experience the heart of it from better than street level. Whenever you come, plan at least some strolling (for one thing, you won't be entangled in one-way streets). Driving or walking, here is an itinerary to follow:

Start from the Georgetown side of Dumbarton Bridge, the "Bridge of Buffaloes," across Rock Creek Parkway from Massachusetts Avenue and Sheridan Circle. Stop first at Dumbarton House, 2715 Q Street, headquarters of the National Society of Colonial Dames and the only authentically furnished house and garden open to the public all year (10–5, Monday through Saturday, free). The brick mansion, built around 1800 on the original tract belonging to Ninian Beall, once blocked the way from Q Street to Rock Creek and was moved in 1915 to its present site. Furnishings include pieces associated with famous names; on the second floor are items of clothing that belonged to General and Mrs. Washington, George Mason, Dolly Madison. Be sure you visit the restful terraced garden, which reveals the circular bays of the house unseen from the front.

Turn right at the corner and up 28th Street. Notice Evermay (number 1623), built about 1792, one of Georgetown's great houses, preserved in eighteenth-century lines with dormers and towering chimneys. It was built by an eccentric bachelor who preferred privacy to people and advertised a warning in the daily press against intrusion, especially directed to those "amorous bucks with their dorfies, and all sporting bucks with their dogs and guns."

Atop the hill on R Street, Oak Hill Cemetery (7–5 daily;

8-5 Sundays) contains several notable monuments in its 25 wooded acres. The Gothic chapel, which you can see from the road, was designed by James Renwick, who has been mentioned previously. Look for the Carrara marble and bronze bust over the tomb of John Howard Payne (who in 1823 wrote "Home Sweet Home") and the circular white marble temple, the tomb of W. W. Corcoran, banker, founder of the Corcoran Art Gallery and Washington's leading civic figure of the nineteenth century. The most distinguished monument, on the easternmost heights, is the columned mausoleum of General and Mrs. John Peter Van Ness, designed by George Hadfield after the Temple of Vesta. Among others buried here: Peggy O'Neale Eaton, the innkeeper's glamorous daughter, and her husband; Joseph Henry, first secretary of the Smithsonian; James G. Blaine, and Edwin M. Stanton.

Beyond Montrose Park, visit Dumbarton Oaks, 1703 31st Street (Tuesday-Sunday, 2-5, closed Monday, free), the area's most important single point of interest, even though it is not true Georgetown. The original mansion was built in 1800, once was occupied by John C. Calhoun of South Carolina, and most recently by Mr. and Mrs. Robert Woods Bliss. Mr. Bliss is a former Ambassador to Argentina and a distinguished art collector. In the course of extensive alteration years ago, an entire ceiling was brought from a French château and the main room built to fit. In this Renaissance setting the Big Four Dumbarton Oaks conference was held in 1944, a step in organization of the United Nations; now it is used for lectures and chamber music concerts (invitation only).

In 1940 the Blisses presented their estate to Harvard University as a center for scholarly work in the Early Christian and Byzantine periods; officially it is the Dumbarton Oaks Research Library and Collection.

The collection, rare objects of art, spans Grecian and Roman eras through the Byzantine into the Middle Ages. There are small, delicate pieces—rings, bracelets, gold and silver jewelry—and larger tapestries, stone, wood, and bronze sculpture.

The estate covers 15 acres but, surrounded by parkland, seems far more extensive. Lovely gardens, designed by Beatrice Farrand, include azalea, tulips, forsythia which blaze yellow in spring, one area entirely of white flowers. (Gardens open 10-4 weekdays,

1–4 Sunday). The tennis courts and swimming pool are for use of
the scholars in residence. From the loggia above the pool you can
see one of Washington's most unusual sights: the slender minaret
of the Islamic Mosque beyond the treetops of Rock Creek Park.

On leaving Dumbarton Oaks, continue west on R Street. The
house at 3238 was used as a summer White House by President
Ulysses S. Grant, who found this higher elevation cooler than the
lowlands in town. At Wisconsin Avenue, turn left but first observe
the town houses on the southwest corner; they once were part
of "Friendship," the last residence of party-giver Evalyn Walsh
McLean.

Shops along Wisconsin Avenue, the main shopping street, and
those elsewhere in Georgetown, display attractive restored fronts.
They offer art, antiques, books, interior decoration, clothing, dining. Arpad and Henry (1400 Wisconsin), for example, does quality silverwork for the Smithsonian and other museums as well
as the public. The Early American Shop (1323 Wisconsin) is
very good for antique furniture (mostly Virginian) in rough
condition suitable for refinishing by amateurs and hobbyists. The
Attic (1531 Wisconsin) has fine prints, and a collection of carved,
early decoys, as well as furniture. Madame Santina (1408 Wisconsin) is the only woman I ever heard of who is a man's tailor. She
started by working for Schiaparelli to pay her way as an opera
singer. And around the corner, the Savile Book Shop (3236 P)
handles rare books, art, poetry, belles lettres. The Francis Scott
Key, 28th and O, is another excellent bookshop.

Turn right on N Street (watch the one-way arrows carefully
throughout Georgetown), lined with typical nineteenth-century
Federal houses. The five in a row on the north side just east of
34th Street were built around 1805 by Mayor John Cox of Georgetown, who lived in the ivy-covered corner house (3339). Notice
that each house has its garden in the rear. Visible straight ahead is
the Gothic tower of Healy Hall, on the campus of Georgetown
University. Turn right on 35th Street, then right on O. Note
especially the cream-colored Bodisco House, 3322 O, with graceful
twin stairs and wrought-iron railing, named for Baron de Bodisco,
who came here as a bachelor Russian minister and threw lavish
parties attended by up to 800 guests. St. John's Church, O and
Potomac, was built from plans drawn by Dr. William Thornton,

architect of the Capitol, and completed in 1806. In those years, when Georgetown was the "court end" of town, Dolly Madison, the British minister (followed by two liveried servants with drawn swords), and other leading figures attended church here.

On the east side of Wisconsin Avenue, drive (or walk) to Q Street to see Tudor Place, the gem of all Georgetown's old houses, a great yellow stucco mansion also designed by Dr. Thornton. Built for Thomas Peter and his wife Martha Parke Custis, granddaughter of Martha Washington, it has been the home of the Peter family ever since. Thornton was a family favorite; Woodlawn, in Virginia, the home of the younger Martha's sister, Nellie Custis, was designed by him, too.

On M Street, near 31st, the "Old Stone House," built about 1765, was long thought to have been Washington's headquarters, or at least L'Enfant's. Though now known to have been neither, it is an historically important representative of colonial Georgetown, a landmark rescued and newly restored after much embattlement locally and in Congress.

Preservation does pay, commercially as in other ways. At 30th and M, Historic Georgetown, Inc., has done over three houses into pleasant shops (gifts, yarns, florist) and a restaurant, France's. M Street, as a composition of old shops and houses, once attractive, is slowly following this lead.

Eating in Georgetown:

Martin's Tavern, 1264 Wisconsin, the old Georgetowners' last stand. Plain but popular. Good spot for bean soup and beer. Eat well for $1.50.

Billy Martin's Carriage House, 1238 Wisconsin. Martin's down the street and gone modern, complete to carriage lamps out front. Open to 2 A.M.; Sunday brunch (10:30–3). Count on spending $5 per person for dinner.

France's, 1204 30th Street, a pleasant terrace bar and restaurant, intimate atmosphere. Try the beef Burgundy dinner with artichoke hearts vinaigrette, brandied peach flambé for dessert. Closed Sunday. About $6 per person.

Chez Odette, 3063 M Street, a pleasant bistro, the big brother of the little unpretentious Parisian transplant at 3027 M Street.

Make a meal of pâté de foie gras, lentils with Italian sausage, and home-made pastry for $1.75.

Rive Gauche, Wisconsin and M, an excellent French restaurant. To midnight, closed Sunday. About $8.

Cordon Bleu, 3125 M Street, fine French food, aussi. To one A.M., closed Sunday. About $8.

Town House, Wisconsin and O, should appeal to most gourmets, for it is run by one, John Prince. He might suggest, if you asked him, gazpacho followed by shrimp Norfolk à la Française with sherry and rice pilaff, or tournedos Henry IV. About $5. You can drop in for a late bite or drink; Town House is open till 2 A.M., with pleasant piano music.

Gallery Coffee House, 3213 O Street, an arty little corner serving European coffee and pastries. To midnight.

XIII *A City of Churches*

Most of the time Perle Mesta or the Washington Senators draw bigger headlines than religion. But never a bigger crowd. Washington rarely may be considered an especially spiritual kind of a place, but it is and on a very large scale.

Today there are almost 500 churches of 60 different faiths. The President attends regularly. Cabinet officers and Congressmen teach Sunday school. Congress opens it daily sessions with prayer and the Capitol's Prayer Room provides a quiet corner where its members can discuss their problems privately with God.

God has always been influential in high places around Washington. George Washington was a praying man who spent his rightful time and more in a church pew. Three Episcopal churches in Virginia (Pohick, Christ Church, Alexandria, and Falls Church) claim him as a vestryman. At his first inaugural he said it would be "peculiarly improper to omit in this first official act my fervent supplications to that Almighty Being who rules the Universe." John Adams, his successor, on moving into the White House, wrote: "I pray Heaven to bestow the best of Blessings on this House and All that shall hereafter inhabit it." Abraham Lincoln read a chapter of the Bible each day in his favorite chair in the White House study, while the family assembled for breakfast. Harry Truman was not only a Bible reader but collector, and has a case full of Bibles in Independence, Missouri.

The city, without planning it, has become a world religious center. Two of the largest churches anywhere, comparable to the cathedrals of Europe except in antiquity, are open and . . . a-building to completion. The most unusual church, to Americans, is probably the new Mosque, the only Moslem house of worship on our continent.

Half a dozen national churches of individual denominations are in Washington. So are headquarters of religious organizations and seminaries.

And some of Washington's most beautiful, interesting buildings are small, older churches associated with figures and events in history.

You should plan to visit a church in Washington. Attend a service, if that is your normal practice—the religious page of the Saturday newspapers will provide details. Even if you're not normally a goer, you are welcome. Remember that religion is part of the fabric of Washington; but a free kind of religion which allows everyone to worship in his own way. Many churches are open during the uncrowded weekdays; feel free to walk in and sit in the pews or on benches once occupied by Presidents and others who have influenced the course of history.

Following are the most interesting and representative churches:

Washington Cathedral, properly the Cathedral Church of St. Peter and St. Paul, Massachusetts and Wisconsin Avenues, N.W., is roughly three-fifths complete, or about $12,000,000 worth. The building process, underway since 1908, depends on funds available and hand labor for carving stone blocks into Gothic towers, spires, buttresses, and vaulted arches. It may not be finished for fifty years but this Episcopal cathedral should last for 3000.

Already, magnitude is its first unmistakable characteristic. The four central pillars, for instance, are each 37 feet in diameter at the base; the main church can accommodate 3000 persons at one sitting.

In the tradition of the Middle Ages, the cathedral is richly detailed with wood and stone carvings and with no less than 80 stained-glass windows. The great circular Rose Window, a representation of the Last Judgment, set high in the north wall, is composed of 9000 individual pieces of glass. Look at it carefully; under the right conditions it creates a seeming purple-violet twilight.

Cathedral tours are conducted by volunteer aides 9 to 4:30 weekdays and after the 11 A.M. and 4 P.M. Sunday services. The guide will show you the cross-shaped outlines of the building, the north-south transepts forming the arms and incomplete nave forming the longitudinal shaft. At one corner of the Crossing, the Canterbury Pulpit, made of stone from Canterbury Cathedral, depicts in bas-relief the history of the English Bible.

Despite its Gothic form and religious roots in the Church of England, the cathedral is an American expression. You will see ornamental grilles by Samuel Yellin, the artist-in-iron; and panels, in the Chapel of the Holy Spirit, painted by the famous illustrator, N. C. Wyeth.

A number of distinguished Americans are buried within the cathedral, including President Woodrow Wilson, Secretaries of State Cordell Hull and Frank B. Kellogg, and Admiral George Dewey. Funeral services have also been held here for other national leaders—Secretary of State John Foster Dulles, Chief Justice Fred M. Vinson, Admiral William F. Halsey, and others.

If you appreciate religious music, note that the finest is performed here; try to attend one of the four major concerts given yearly, including Easter and Christmas, by the Washington and Cathedral Choral Societies. They present such works as Brahms' Requiem and Haydn's Creation, with nationally known soloists and members of the National Symphony.

Walk through the surrounding grounds as well as the cathedral. In the Bishop's Garden (9–5:30, to 6 in summer), paved walks lead to English boxwood, holly, an ivy-banked pool and a multitude of flowers. Souvenir note: at the Herb Garden you can purchase gift jars of thyme, savory, marjoram, vinegars, mustards and jellies, all raised in these vineyards. Best day of the year is the first Friday in May, when the Flower Mart, an outstanding garden show, is held as a money-raiser for further landscaping.

Before leaving, stop at the west entrance (Wisconsin Avenue), where rows of limestone blocks, cut and numbered, are ready to be hoisted aloft to the stone carvers. You may see Philip Hubert Frohman, the architect for thirty years, who is still in daily supervision. Think for an instant of how long these newly carved gargoyles, buttresses, and arches will remain in place, God willing.

National Shrine of the Immaculate Conception, on the grounds of Catholic University, Michigan Avenue and 4th Street, N.E., (7–6 daily), now the largest Catholic church in America. Its completion, or rather its opening in partial completion (late 1959), is the realization of a century-old Catholic hope to build in Washington a great church comparable to Europe's finest.

The architectural style, a combination of Byzantine and Roman, harmonizes with the classic Washington skyline. Its dominant feature from a distance, the Great Dome, rises 237 feet and the slender bell tower, or campanile, 102 feet higher.

The Shrine was proposed in 1912 by the late Bishop Thomas J. Shahan, Rector of Catholic University, as a dedication to the Blessed Virgin Mary, and was accepted as a responsibility of all the bishops in the United States. By 1926, the crypt church, below the main level, was complete, but five years later building halted with the depression. The pace since 1954, when it resumed, has been tremendous—$15,000,000 in delicate construction within six years. Although modern techniques are used, materials are the cathedral traditionals—masonry, brick, tile, and stone.

The exterior is ornamented with symbolic sculpture, mosaics, and inscriptions. Flanking the center door are eight stone panels representing the women of the Old and New Testaments, carved by Lee Lawrie; above the door, the tympanum (recessed half-moon) represents the Annunciation, the central moment in the life of Mary when she heard God's message, carved in high-relief figures by John Angel.

The interior is vast, 399 feet long, 306 feet across the sacristies and 159 feet from floor to crossing dome. It has a capacity of 6000 persons. The floor, covered with patterned marble, leads to the main altar, beneath a canopy and figure of Mary Immaculate. In the arched apse behind the altar, a colossal mosiac figure of "Christ in Majesty" by John de Rosen overlooks all. The interior, however, is far from finished. Walls will be covered with marble, the seven domes with mosaics; eleven chapels will be installed as funds become available. Total cost will exceed $30,000,000.

Don't overlook the crypt church, which has been in use twenty-five years. Onyx, granite, and marble from fifty countries compose the columns supporting the low-vaulted ceilings. The central altar, a huge onyx block, is open on all sides, facing the circular bays. An air-conditioned cafeteria at the Shrine is open to the public from 7:30 A.M. to 7:30 P.M.

A nearby church gem: *Chapel of Notre Dame* at Trinity College (for girls), Michigan Avenue and Franklin Street, N.E. For this artistic chapel, the architects Maginnis, Walsh, and Kennedy, who are also responsible for the National Shrine, were awarded the American Institute of Architects' gold medal for ecclesiastic design.

The Franciscan Monastery and gardens, 14th and Quincy Streets, N.E. (8–5 daily), about a half mile from Catholic University, contains striking reproductions of principal Holy Land shrines, including the Holy Sepulchre and the Grottos of Nazareth—and the same Indulgences are accorded here as at the sacred places in Jerusalem. Another feature is an underground facsimile of the catacombs, the hiding place of early Roman Christians.

The 40-acre grounds surrounding the Monastery church comprise one of Washington's most beautiful outdoor corners. Among the flowers, shrubs, and trees are reproductions of the Garden of Gethsemane and the Grotto of Lourdes. Thousands of flowers burst into bloom starting with daffodils in early spring, followed by lilies at Easter (250 pots are brought inside to decorate shrines), then by roses—some of the prettiest you'll ever see—running red across the hillsides in June.

The Washington Mosque, 2551 Massachusetts Avenue, N.W., (9–5 Monday through Friday, 9–12 Saturday and Sunday), is a symbol of Islam in America. For anything comparable you would have to travel 4000 miles; even there this Mosque would be exceptional, for it combines the best efforts and materials of fifteen Moslem nations.

The Mosque, built of carved white limestone surmounted by the traditional minaret and crescent, was completed in 1956. As part of the Islamic Center, its dual purpose is to care for the religious needs of Moslems in Washington and to promote understanding of the Moslem world. Curiously, it is off the city building lines in order to face most directly the holy city of Mecca, in Saudi Arabia. Five times daily the religious chant called the Athan is sounded (on tape recorder, in lieu of a muezzin, or caller), summoning the faithful with the opening verse of the

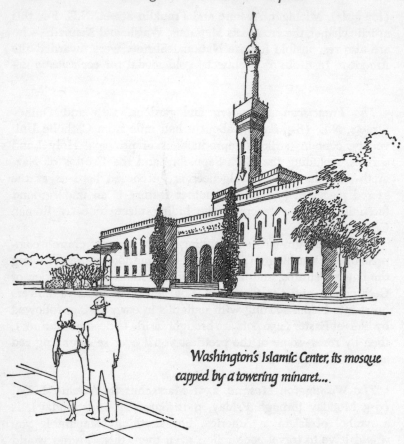

Washington's Islamic Center, its mosque capped by a towering minaret...

Koran: *La Illahah illa Allah, Muhammedum rasulu Allah—There is no God but Allah, Mohammed is his prophet.*

Highlights of the interior: tiles from Turkey; huge two-ton chandelier of bronze inlaid with nickel, from Egypt; large Persian rugs, woven for this setting by order of the Shah of Iran; and the pulpit, or Minbar, composed of 10,000 hand-carved sections inlaid with ebony and ivory.

The best day to visit is Friday for the noon services. Non-Moslems are welcome to sit in the rear and observe the Moslems kneel on their prayer rugs and worship God in their way.

St. John's Episcopal Church, Lafayette Square (7 to 7 daily), was built in 1816 in the fast growing center of city life lying between Georgetown and Capitol Hill. Designed by Latrobe in the form of a Greek cross, the "Church of Presidents" is a pleasing example of Federal architecture, with white pillars, pale yellow walls, bell tower, and cupola. Pleasing and restful within, too; have a seat in pew 54, the Presidential pew, and observe the graceful chandeliers, arches under the dome and stained-glass windows.

Madison was the first President to come across the Square from the White House to pray here, and so did the next six occupants of the White House—James Monroe, John Quincy Adams (although he came to afternoon service, reserving the morning for the Unitarian Church), Andrew Jackson, Martin Van Buren, William Henry Harrison, and John Tyler. Chester A. Arthur was not only a member, but presented a window in memory of his wife Ellen, who died in 1880, the year before he became President. Franklin D. Roosevelt was the last Presidential member of St. John's.

Services are conducted in French Sunday afternoons at 4 P.M.

Foundry Methodist Church, 16th and P Streets, N.W., was born during the War of 1812, when Henry Foxall, wealthy Georgetowner, gratefully gave ground and funds to build a chapel (at 14th and G) because prayers to save his foundry from destruction had been answered. The present church was built in 1904.

Several Presidents have worshiped here (Rutherford B. Hayes with most regularity), but it is most associated with two who were not members. One was Abraham Lincoln, who came to hear its anti-slavery preacher. A stained-glass window memorializes the Great Emancipator and his words, "Thanks be to God who in our great trial giveth us the churches." The other was Franklin D. Roosevelt who, with Winston Churchill (and a cortege of secret service men and armed troops), attended the Christmas service here in fateful 1941. Their presence is recalled in the chapel windows of the Four Freedoms.

Church of Jesus Christ of Latter-day Saints, the Mormon chapel, 2810 16th Street, N.W. (tours on Sunday at 12 noon and 8 P.M., weekdays by phoning AD 4-7275), is built of 16,000 pieces of stone cut in the Utah mountains and shipped to Washington on 32 railroad cars. The 176-foot tower follows the design of the great Tabernacle of Salt Lake City, even to the figure on top, the horn-blowing Angel Moroni. The organ in the amphitheater-like chapel has 5000 pipes; recitals are given frequently.

All Souls Unitarian Church, 16th and Harvard Streets, N.W., built in 1924, follows the design of famed St. Martin's in the Fields, London, complete with portico, Corinthian columns, clock tower, and belfry. The bell, however, was cast in 1822 for the original church building by Paul Revere's son Joseph. It has lasted a little longer than the one year covered in Revere's warranty! All Souls has had distinguished members, including John Quincy Adams, Millard Fillmore, William Howard Taft (who taught a young people's Sunday school group when he was Chief Justice), John C. Calhoun, and distinguished ministers, most recently the late Ulysses Pierce and A. Powell Davies.

First Baptist Church, 16th and O Streets, N.W., is in a new $2,000,000 Gothic building, although it was founded in 1802. Stained-glass windows portray the lives of great Christians of all denominations, such as George Fox the Quaker, and John Wesley the Methodist. President Truman, who was a member, arrived unannounced one day for the early service. The minister, embarrassed because a Sunday school promotion was scheduled rather than regular worship, met the President at the front door and explained. When the President replied that he was fond of children, the minister asked if he would say a few words. The President delivered the Sunday school commencement address, speaking simply about the benefits of growing up in a religious democracy.

Friends Meeting House, 21st and Florida Avenue, N.W., the simple Quakers' house of worship, without pulpit, pastor, or music. Services are held in silence since the Quakers believe that God speaks if you are still and listen; the only interruption of this quiet time occurs when members are moved to rise and express themselves. The colonial Pennsylvania-style meeting house, of quarry stone and slate roof, was built when President Herbert Hoover attended regularly, sitting on a plain bench midway down the center aisle. He is still a member.

National Presbyterian Church, Connecticut Avenue and N Street, N.W., has maintained a President's pew since the 1830s. The most recent Presidential member, Dwight D. Eisenhower, came to worship (in pew number 41) his first Sunday in the White House and later joined the church (his wife was already a Presbyterian). Normally, the Eisenhowers would arrive before the services and be escorted to their pew by the minister; like any other parishioners they would follow the order of service and sing hymns from the songbook. Afterwards, the congregation remained standing until their departure.

New York Avenue Presbyterian Church, 1313 New York Avenue, N.W., the "Lincoln Church," and also the Church of the late Reverend Peter Marshall. (See Chapter XX on Lincoln's Washington.)

St. Paul's Episcopal Church, Rock Creek Church Road and Webster Street, N.W., different from any church mentioned so far. Smaller, older. Much less visited. No Presidents on the roster. Yet I can't think of a single church with more exceptional surroundings.

St. Paul's is located in Rock Creek Cemetery (7 A.M.–sundown), a rolling, landscaped woodland of towering white oaks, some four centuries old, more than 100 types of evergreens, dogwood, and azalea to dapple the shadows in spring. And works of sculpture in this outdoor setting rank with the finest in any museum.

St. Paul's was established in 1719, when Colonel John Bradford donated one thousand pounds of tobacco and a "glebe" of 100 acres—a tract which remains almost intact today. In pre-Revolutionary days the prosperous church owned its own tobacco warehouse in Georgetown while its parish included Maryland counties north to the Pennsylvania border. In 1775, a red-brick church was started to replace the original frame chapel, but the Revolution interrupted. After two remodelings (the last in 1920), only ivy-covered walls remain from the pre-Revolutionary beginning.

The church, however, is a charming little place with its tall-arched windows, square central tower, and gold cross atop the steeple.

Burials have been made here since the church first took possession of the property nearly two and a half centuries ago. Graves include those of David Burnes, one of the city's four original landowners; Montgomery Blair, Abraham Lincoln's friend who owned Blair House; Elisha F. Riggs, former partner of W. W. Corcoran and founder of the Riggs Bank; Alexander Shepherd, territorial governor of the District of Columbia in the 1870s, and John Marshall Harlan, Supreme Court Justice from 1877 to 1911.

But to see the most impressive monuments and memorials, follow this route:

From the church, follow the road west to the small, tree-banked lake. Note the elaborate Carrara marble Leiter sarcophagus (L-24) of Levi Leiter, a wealthy merchant, and the tomb of Thomas Nelson Page, diplomat and author (L-26). Turn right into section B and observe the memorials to Samuel H. Kauffmann (B-11), a portrayal of Shakespeare's Seven Ages of Man from *As You Like It;* Peter Force, once mayor of Washington (B-7); Crosby Noyes, editor of the Washington *Evening Star* (B-10); Admiral Sidney Staunton (B-12). One of the greatest is the sculpture over the tomb of banker Charles M. Ffoulke (B-19), Gutzon Borglum's "Rabboni" ("My Master," in Galilean), the figure of Mary Magdalene emerging from the empty tomb of Christ.

In a grotto of holly trees and shrubs, almost screened from view, you reach the Adams Memorial (E-16), carved by Augustus Saint-Gaudens, which the critical Alexander Woollcott called "the most beautiful thing ever fashioned by the hand of man on this continent." It was commissioned by Henry Adams, author and historian, on the death of his wife in 1885. (Later he was buried in the plot, too). The bronze, shrouded figure of a woman seated on a granite boulder has no title. Saint-Gaudens deplored the popular name of "Grief"; he said that if it had to have a title he would prefer "The Peace of God that Passeth Understanding." John Hay, Henry Adams' intimate friend of Lafayette Square, described it so: "It is full of poetry and suggestion, infinite wisdom, a past without beginning, and a future without end, a repose after limitless experience."

Principal national churches, representing their denominations in the capital, and others of significance include:

National Memorial Baptist Church, 16th Street and Columbia Road, N.W., built jointly by Northern and Southern Baptist Conventions as a national memorial to religious liberty.

Metropolitan Memorial Church, the national church of Methodism, Nebraska and New Mexico Avenues, N.W., adjacent to Wesley Theological Seminary, on the campus of American University.

Luther Place Memorial Church, 1226 Vermont Avenue, N.W., erected in 1870 as a thanksgiving to God for "freeing our land from slavery and war." Lloyd Douglas, later a religious novelist, was its second pastor.

National City Christian Church, 14th Street and Thomas Circle, N.W., national church of the Disciples of Christ. James A. Garfield, Disciples minister and Congressman, preached to the congregation many times before he was elected President. This building, designed by John Russell Pope, was erected in 1930.

St. Sophia's Greek Orthodox Cathedral, Massachusetts Avenue and 36th Street, N.W., completed in 1955 at a cost of $2,000,000, the largest Greek Orthodox church in the United States.

St. Matthew's Cathedral, 1721 Rhode Island Avenue, N.W., cathedral church of the Roman Catholic Bishop of Washington, a red-brick, green-domed landmark.

Washington Hebrew Congregation, Massachusetts Avenue and Macomb Street, N.W., the strikingly modern new home of the city's oldest Reformed Jewish congregation, founded in 1852.

Adas Israel Congregation, Connecticut Avenue and Porter Street, N.W., handsome Conservative Jewish Synagogue built in 1952. Adas Israel grew out of the Hebrew Congregation in 1870.

Seventh Day Adventist Church, Takoma Park, Maryland, adjacent to the General Conference Building, world headquarters of the Seventh Day Adventists. Here, too, are the Washington Missionary College, Adventist Theological Seminary, and the Adventist publishing plant.

You may also wish to visit these religious centers:

National Catholic Welfare Conference, 1312 Massachusetts Avenue, N.W., eight-story building with a windowless stone front, accenting the bronze statue of Christ.

B'nai B'rith, 1640 Rhode Island Avenue, N.W., eight-story national Jewish cultural center. Ground-floor exhibit hall displays historic documents, paintings, and sculpture on Jewish contributions to American progress.

Methodist Building, 100 Maryland Avenue, N.E., headquarters of Methodist Commission on Chaplains and Board of Temperance. The inexpensive cafeteria is popular on Capitol Hill.

Chaplains Memorial Building, 122 Maryland Avenue, N.E., headquarters of the General Commission on Chaplains and Washington Office of the National Council of Churches. The building originally was a Capitol Hill mansion and many furnishings are preserved.

XIV *The Restaurants*

It is time we rest from all other pursuits and turn to the subject of food. Preferably good food, if possible.

The point is that Washington has been more of an "eating in" than an "eating out" city. Frankly, it has little culinary tradition in the same sense as, say, San Francisco. When you do go out you find that some of the better restaurants close at nine or ten, which to certain people is the time to start *thinking* about food.

However, don't get me wrong. The eating picture here may not be as exciting as in San Francisco, New Orleans, or New York, but you don't have to order a box lunch sent from Trader Vic's or Galatoire's either. As Washington emerges from its provincial shell, good food is emerging also. The worthwhile dining rooms, a few new and a few old, are doing very well—which proves there is hope—and are earning national reputations. Hotel dining is probably better than in most places, more gracious and inviting than at the typical big city business stop. And where else can you dine surrounded by so many statesmen, politicians, five per centers, six per centers, and twenty-six per centers?

A word about prices. You will find that food costs less here than in New York and many large cities. Pick your spots and you can eat well quite reasonably; for instance, the $3.50 Sunday buffet at the Sheraton-Park. As a general rule in Washington, you pay just a little more to eat well.

It is wise to phone for reservations, even though they're not always necessary. Fifteen per cent is about right for the tip.

Local specialties? Blends of seafood from Chesapeake Bay and vicinity; Crab Norfolk, for instance, crab bisque and soup, crab imperial. Also clams and the luscious Chincoteague oyster on the half shell. In spring, shad and shad roe from the Potomac.

Following is a list of restaurants and cafeterias where the food is above average or acceptable, the price within reason, and in some cases with atmosphere too. Because such relative words as "moderate," "expensive," and "dirt cheap" mean different things to different people, I have tried to suggest the amount of money you may expect to spend per meal. If your bill is higher, you have had one extra drink or the super dessert; if it's lower, you can afford another good meal!

French-and-American

The Colony, 1737 DeSales Street, N.W., ST 3-8165. Open noon to 11 P.M., except Sundays and holidays. This is currently at the apex of eating places in the capital; dignity and service match the excellent cuisine, with such specialties as Rock Cornish game hen Périgourdine, frogs' legs with shrimp sautées Provençale, and coq au vin. The Colony is colonized by the high expense account set. Cocktail lounge below the dining room is open 4:30 to 2 A.M., within easy shuttling distance of the Mayflower Hotel across the street. Luncheon $5, dinner $10.

LaSalle du Bois, 1800 M Street, N.W., RE 7-1124. Open noon to 11 P.M., except Sunday. Under same ownership as the Colony and equally popular. The "White House table," as they call it, is held till after 1 P.M., even on busiest days, for Vice-President Nixon or others of the inner circle. For a light luncheon, thin pancakes with sausage Normand are perfect. Luncheon $4.50, dinner $10.00.

Bonat's, 1022 Vermont Avenue, N.W., RE 7-3373. Open 11:30 to 3 P.M. for luncheon, until 10:30 for dinner, including Sunday. Bonat's, the poor man's Colony, is popular, crowded at lunch hour, but with plenty of dining rooms and a generous steak for $1.50. Walls are covered with interesting copies of oil paintings, cupboards of china and silver. Dinner $2.50.

French

Napoleon's, 2649 Connecticut Avenue, N.W., CO 5-8955. Open noon to midnight, Sunday 12:30 to 10 P.M. You can walk it snail-paced in three minutes from the Sheraton-Park or Shoreham hotels. And this is the place for escargot, as well as coq au vin or frogs' legs. Music in the cocktail room 9 P.M. to midnight. Dinner $8.

Chez François, 818 Connecticut Avenue, N.W., ME 8-1849. Open noon to 10 P.M., except Sunday. Cocktail hour starts 4:30,

5 P.M. on Saturday. Across Lafayette Park from the White House. Fine French cuisine at moderate prices. Luncheon $2.50, dinner $6.00.

Chez Odette, 3063 M Street, N.W.

France's, 1204 30th Street, N.W.

Cordon Bleu, 3125 M Street, N.W.

Rive Gauche, Wisconsin and M Streets, N.W.

Mostly American

Golden Parrot, 1701 20th Street, N.W., DE 2-7440. Open noon to 10 P.M., except Sunday. The Golden Parrot is worth the price just to see the interior. This elegant spot is a converted, or rather restored, old mansion of the '80s which once belonged to a Pennsylvania Railroad president. The lobby is paneled in hand-carved teakwood, the original dining room, now the cocktail lounge, in crotch mahogany. In the dining rooms—the Red, Grey, and Gold Rooms—are the original chandeliers and hand-decorated plaster ceilings. This was a tea room until 1950 when it was purchased by John and Hilda Goldstein. Now it ranks high in quality of food as well as décor. Luncheon, $3.50; dinner $7.

Water Gate Inn, 2700 F Street, N.W., DI 7-9256. Open 11:30 A.M. to 10 P.M., including Sunday. Almost in view of the Potomac, close to Arena Stage and the Wax Museum—at least until the Roosevelt Bridge changes things. Water Gate is decorated in Pennsylvania Dutch motif, features full servings of roast beef, hot popovers, apple cheese pie. Luncheon $2.50; dinner $5.

Town House, 1365 Wisconsin Avenue, N.W.

Billy Martin's Carriage House, 1238 Wisconsin Avenue, N.W.

Steaks and Chops

Duke Zeibert's, 1730 L Street, N.W., ST 3-1730. Open noon to midnight, Sunday 1 to 10 P.M. The Duke's specialties are roast beef, surrounded by pickles and brown bread. Luncheon reservations are advisable unless you're prepared to wait—as do many who rank Zeibert's tops in town. Duke is sort of the local Toots Shor, who looks like his own best customer. Or maybe it's the waiters who make the place; they're all characters, but lovable. Luncheon $3, dinner $6.

Goldie Ahearn's Charcoal Pit, Connecticut Avenue at M Street, N.W., DI 7-7700. Open 11:30 A.M. to midnight, except Sunday. There really is a charcoal pit, where you can see your steak or chops broiled. Goldie, the former boxer and fight promoter, is . . . well, a local Toots Shor type, too. Pictures of celebrities decorate the walls. Luncheon $3, dinner $6.

Blackie's House of Beef, 1217 22nd Street, N.W., FE 3-1100. Open 9 A.M. to 10:30 P.M., except Sunday. Blackie started the surge of new restaurants serving beef and nothing else, but his place is still out front, and keeps expanding. The atmosphere is attractive, basically unpretentious. At dinner hour wheels of blue cheese and crackers are passed around. The best buy is the $2.95 prime rib of beef, with baked potato, vegetable, and salad. You can try the New York sirloin, $4.50, but you'll never finish it. Luncheon $1.75.

Black Saddle, 709 18th Street, N.W., DI 7-5080. Three blocks from the White House, this is Blackie's with saddle and other Western decorations. Same menu as at the House of Beef.

Cannon's Steak House, 1270 5th Street, N.W., LI 3-8685. Open 7 A.M. to midnight (last order at 10:30), except Sunday. The Cannon family has been doing business in the Florida Avenue wholesale market twenty years or longer, and loyal fans vow they've never been disappointed nor found better steaks anywhere than the thick, onion-ringed specimens served here. Dinner $5.

Seafood

Harvey's, 1107 Connecticut Avenue, N.W., NA 8-1448. Open 11:30 A.M. to 11:30 P.M. This famous restaurant, two doors from the Mayflower Hotel, was started by the Harvey brothers as an oyster house in 1858 in a converted blacksmith shop. During the Civil War, President Lincoln, like thousands of Union soldiers and civilians, came to taste the new discovery, the steamed oyster; many Presidents have dined at Harvey's since. In recent times, the late Julius Lulley, who rose from wine steward to owner, created traditions and a loyal following of his own. Among his friends, you will still see J. Edgar Hoover at his usual table (first floor, left) almost every evening. The present owner, Jesse Brickman, is off to a healthy start in Lulley's large footsteps. Best for Maine lobsters, Bay crab, but also for prime beef. Luncheon, $2.50, dinner $5.50.

Hall's, 7th and K Streets, S.W., ME 8-8159. Open from 11 A.M. to 11 P.M. This wonderful old spot will probably have moved by now, to make way for the Southwest redevelopment, so check the address. Happily, Julie Hall plans to pick up the best of the physical interior—gaslights, mahogany bar, wall paneling, the unshamed painting of buxom Eve cavorting with Adam—and move them intact, with the atmosphere and waiters. If you're looking for a standard, quick meal, go elsewhere. Come to Hall's when you have time for drinks and good food (lobster to steak) in leisure. Luncheon $2.50, dinner $5.

Along the waterfront, seafood restaurants are, or will be shortly, uprooted to make way for progress. Wherever they may be, look for these:

Hogate's, largest on the waterfront, last at 9th and Maine Avenue, S.W., RE 7-3013. Open weekdays 11:45 A.M. to 9 P.M.; Sunday 1 to 9 P.M. Hogate's is the seafood name visitors know best. If plans materialize, the new Hogate's will be operated in conjunction with a major tourist attraction, a planetarium. Hogate's Arlington House is at 4001 Wilson Boulevard. Luncheon $1.75, dinner $3.

Also the Flagship, New England Raw Bar, Herzog's, and Cy Ellis, all of which were in the ancient but honorable and lamented Municipal Fish Market.

For Family Dining

The Hot Shoppes, a growing Washington institution of about 20 restaurants and 10 cafeterias at last count. Willard Marriott, a Utah Mormon, started here in the Depression with the curious concept (for then) of drive-in restaurants and curb service. Except for government cafeterias, more people eat at Hot Shoppes than anywhere. Most serve breakfast, lunch, dinner, snacks at all hours. Showpiece of the chain is the Sirloin and Saddle Room at the Marriott Motor Hotel, on the Virginia side of 14th Street Bridge, where in summer you can watch, through picture windows, swimmers in the pool, and in winter, skaters on the rink, as you eat. Another favorite Hot Shoppe: Fairfield Inn, at the new Marriott Key Bridge, in Rosslyn, Virginia, across Key Bridge. These two are open 6:30 A.M. to midnight. Largest downtown location is the cafeteria at 1621 H Street, N.W., open 11:15 A.M. to 2:30 and 4:30 to 8 P.M. For other locations, phone TU 2-2000. Luncheon for a family of four, $5.50, dinner $8.

Howard Johnson's is represented with twelve restaurants in the area, and 28 varieties of ice cream. If you're a fan of the chain, which extends from Maine to Florida, its restaurants here are open 7 A.M. to 1 A.M. Phone EX 3-5555 for locations. Luncheon for a family of four, $5.50, dinner $8.

German

Olmsted's, 1336 G Street, N.W., DI 7-2100. Open 11:30 A.M. to 11 P.M., except Sunday. Wonderful atmosphere and fine food. Owner James Brahms (who once had a share of Luchow's in New York) cultivates both. He says he and Winston Churchill have the same favorite cocktail, two-thirds brandy, one-third dry champagne, and dash of triple sec. In Olmsted's it is called The Churchill, naturally. The varied menu covers French as well as German dishes; you should enjoy the bouillabaise or filet mignon as well as the Sauerbraten and roast goose. Luncheon $3, dinner $5.50.

Bavarian, 727 11th Street, N.W., ST 3-5679. Open noon to 2 A.M., Saturday and Sunday to midnight. Drink Würzburger on tap with Sauerbraten and dumplings. German music nightly. $3.

Eight Twenty Three, at 823 15th Street, N.W., two blocks from the Statler Hotel, NA 8-7169. Noon to 1:30 A.M. Nürnberger specialties—Bratwurst, Sauerbraten, and music nightly. $3.

Old Europe, 2434 Wisconsin Avenue, N.W., FE 3-7600. Open 11:30 A.M. to 2 P.M. and 5 P.M. to 2 A.M., Sunday 1 P.M. to midnight. Out of the heart of the city, but worth the drive to savor the "Biergarten" atmosphere in the basement rathskeller. The musicians are reminiscent of Berlin's Hotel Adlon—and they frequently come from there. Try the Zwiebel Rostbraten; ask Otto or Hans to interpret, if necessary. Luncheon $2.50, dinner $4.50.

Italian

Roma, 3419 Connecticut Avenue, N.W., EM 3-6611. Open 11 A.M. to 2 A.M. daily. This thriving, lively uptown spot is at its best in summer when you can dine in the vine-covered outdoor garden and hear troubadours sing Italian melodies. Any time of year Frank and Anna Abbo offer a menu starting from spaghetti and manicotti, ranging to saltimbocca (beef filet and prosciutto) and concoctions like Rock Cornish squab with wild rice and Burgundy-marinated filet mignon with mushrooms. Luncheon $2, dinner $4.

Rocco's, 2637 Connecticut Avenue, N.W., HO 2-3868. Open noon to midnight. In that restaurant-full block between the Sheraton-Park and the Shoreham, Rocco's plush basement draws the gourmet. Specialties are the seafood aspect side of Italian cooking, lobster fradiavolo and clams posillipo, as well as steaks and chops. Luncheon $3.50, dinner $6.50.

Gusti's, 19th and M Streets, N.W., RE 7-0895. Open 11 A.M. to 2 A.M., Sunday 1 P.M. to 1 A.M. Mostly spaghetti, filling and inexpensive, but many other Italian dishes worth trying. For instance, brochetta: tender boiled beef skewered with tomato and onion. Luncheon $1.75, dinner $2.75.

Aldo's, 1143 New Hampshire Avenue, N.W., FE 7-2985. Open 11 A.M. to 2 A.M., to midnight on Sunday. You can make the antipasto alone do for lunch—but don't. Extend yourself for the Prati family cooking. In summer, lunch in the lovely arbor garden. Luncheon $1.75, dinner $2.75.

A.V., 607 New York Avenue, N.W., RE 7-0550. Open 11:30 A.M. to 4:30 A.M. The pizza (as well as lasagne and scallopini) palace where you can stop in for a late, late snack.

Mexican

La Fonda, 1637 R Street, N.W., AD 2-6965. Open 5 to midnight, Sunday 2 to 10 P.M. Besides tamale and enchilada dishes, La Fonda effectively represents Spanish and Cuban cuisines with paella and picadillo. It is popular with the Latin American embassy set. Dinner $4.50.

Chinese and Oriental

Genghis Khan, 1805 Connecticut Avenue, N.W., DE 2-1771, noon to 11 P.M., except Sunday. The décor here is purely modern and the clientele largely what is called "echelon" and expense account. The menu, Pan Asian, covers everything from Japanese to Javanese, with Indian curry too. Luncheon $4, dinner $10.

Yenching Palace, 3524 Connecticut Avenue, N.W., EM 2-6358. Open noon to midnight, Friday and Saturday to 1 A.M. It differs from most Chinese restaurants, since the cuisine here is out of North China, rather than Cantonese. $1.75 to $3.50.

Peking, 5522 Connecticut Avenue, N.W., WO 6-8079. Open 11:30 A.M. to midnight. Northern Chinese food at Chevy Chase Circle, with a popular downtown branch at 711 13th Street, N.W., open to 1 A.M. $1.75 to $3.50.

Cathay, 624 H Street, N.W., RE 7-3330. Open 11 A.M. to 3:30 A.M. Located in the middle of Washington's block-long Chinatown. Here's the place to listen to Chinese music on the juke box while eating egg foo yung. $1.50 to $3.

Japanese

Tokyo Sukiyaki, 1736 Connecticut Avenue, N.W., HO 2-7891. Open noon to 11 P.M. Even if you can't use chopsticks, be sure to eat in the Ozashiki Room, to watch the Japanese who do. Settle comfortably on a cushion to a low table and start with a sake cocktail, followed by misoshiro soup and chicken teriyaki or tempura (fried shrimp)—or both. $2 to $4.

Kosher-style

Rich's, 500 19th Street, N.W., ST 3-9829. Open noon to 9 P.M., for luncheon, cocktails, dinner. Near the Interior Department. Best for blintzes, large corned-beef sandwiches. $1.50 to $3.

Roumanian Inn, 815 13th Street, N.W., RE 7-6434. Open noon to 3 P.M. for luncheon, 5 to 9 P.M. for dinner; closed Monday. Continental as well as kosher-style, and one of the best moderate priced places in Washington. $1.50 to $3.

Hofberg's, 7822 Eastern Avenue, N.W., RA 3-5878. Open from 6:30 A.M. to 2:30 A.M. A combination restaurant, sandwich shop, delicatessen, and bakery—whether you want a bagel, hot pastrami, or pastry, you will be close to the source of supply. Fifty cents to $3.

Cafeterias

Sholl's, at three locations: 511 14th Street, opposite Willard Hotel; 1433 K Street, and 1032 Connecticut. Open 7 A.M. to

9 P.M., except Saturday and Sunday. Quick service and a full meal for 75¢.

S & W, 1425 G Street, N.W., (open 10:30 A.M. to 2:45 P.M. and 3:45 to 8 P.M.), opposite the Treasury Building, part of the well-known Southern chain.

YWCA, 17th and K Streets, N.W. Open 8:30 to 10:30 A.M. for breakfast, 11:30 to 2 P.M. for lunch, 4:45 to 7:15 P.M. for dinner. Closed Saturday, Sunday hours 11:30 A.M. to 4 P.M. Convenient location, pleasant atmosphere, good food.

Linda's, 1000 Connecticut Avenue, N.W., and six other locations. Open 7:30 A.M. to 4:30 P.M., closed Saturday and Sunday. Roast-beef sandwich with potato salad the specialty.

Cleaves, 1715 G Street, N.W., one block from the White House. Open 7 A.M. to 8:15 P.M., except Sunday.

National Zoological Cafeteria. Open 9 A.M. to 5 P.M. You can count on a wide choice of food when you visit the Zoo.

You are also welcome to eat in cafeterias at most government buildings. Forty of them, serving 45,000 lunches daily, are operated by Government Services, Inc., (GSI), a unique quasi-public firm. This is your chance to eat with Federal employees and share their atmosphere. Most cafeterias serve breakfast, 7 to 9:30 A.M. Lunch served from 11 A.M. to 1:30 P.M., costs from about 50¢ up. GSI also operates snack bars, good for a coffee break while you're touring the government buildings.

Of the cafeterias, these are the largest or most accessible:

Health, Education and Welfare (HEW), 3rd Street and Independence Avenue, S.W. The place for lunch when you tour the Voice of America.

United States Supreme Court, First Street, N.E.

United States Court House, 3rd Street and Constitution Avenue, N.W.

National Gallery of Art, 6th Street and Constitution Avenue, N.W.

Department of the Interior, 19th and C Streets, N.W.

Department of State, 21st Street and Virginia Avenue, N.W.

Hotel Dining

Carroll Arms, 1st and C Streets, N.E., LI 6-6800. This favorite on Capitol Hill has two restaurants, the Colonial Room specializing in steaks and chicken ($2.25 luncheon, $4.50 dinner), and the pleasant, lower-priced Garden Lounge for sandwiches and salads.

Congressional, 300 New Jersey Avenue, S.E., LI 6-6611. The Caucus Dining Room (luncheon $2.50, dinner $5) is the closest restaurant to the House Office Building.

DuPont Plaza, DuPont Circle and New Hampshire Avenue, N.W., HU 3-6000. The Crown Room is open for breakfast, luncheon ($2.25) and dinner ($4.00).

Jefferson Hotel, 1200 16th Street, N.W., DI 7-4704. The Monticello Room in this smaller, fashionable hotel, serves luncheon ($2.50), cocktails and dinner ($4.25).

Manger Hay-Adams, 16th and H Streets, N.W., ME 8-2260. The handsome, paneled Tudor Room is favored by businessmen with long lunch hours ($3) and those who enjoy the formal touch at dinner ($6). Try the Old English Tap Room, less expensive for either a short lunch or a long afternoon.

Mayflower, Connecticut Avenue and DeSales Street, N.W., DI 7-3000. Hotel Corporation of America, which acquired this distinguished Washington landmark from the Hilton chain, added something of merit in the new Rib Room. You pay well (perhaps $10) but eat well, too. The beef, carved alongside your table as you like it, is accompanied by salad, Yorkshire pudding, and Idaho potato with chives and sour cream. The Presidential Room, where you may see Perle Mesta or Gwen Cafritz or Harry Truman (who once signed the Maître d's guest book and added "Retired Farmer" after his name), features dining in the Continental manner; dinner-dancing 9–1 except Sunday. Other eating spots at the Mayflower are the Town and Country and the Men's Bar.

Roger Smith, Pennsylvania Avenue at 18th Street, N.W., NA 8-2740. The downstairs cocktail lounge was converted into the Steak House and they've been selling more cocktails ever since, along with tender, charcoal-broiled steaks. Luncheon $2.50, dinner $4.00. In summer, the Starlight Roof is a favorite spot for dining and dancing.

Sheraton-Carlton, 16th and K Streets, N.W., ME 8-2626. The Sheraton Room features excellent French cuisine and service. Prices are on the high side (luncheon $6, dinner $10). Almost every hotel has its prominent luncheon regulars who become tourist attractions after a while—look for John L. Lewis at the Carlton.

Sheraton-Park, 2660 Connecticut Avenue, N.W., CO 5-2000. The Carlton's uptown big brother, which spreads out over sixteen acres, has three attractive, practical eating rooms. Best for evening is the Colonial Dining Room, with candlelit, Williamsburg-like atmosphere and a varied, interesting menu stressing colonial dishes. Dinner is served till 10 P.M., à la carte till 1 A.M., with dancing until 1:30. The Sunday Colonial Buffet, of baked ham, kidney pie, and roast beef, complete with dinner music and atmosphere, is an excellent value at $3.50. The Sheraton-Park's Town Room, open for breakfast, lunch, and dinner, is a lower-priced coffee shop. The newest addition, the Terrace Patio, is a delightful summer oasis, overlooking the tennis courts and swimming pool. Try it for lunch, cocktails, or dinner under the stars; dancing from 9:30 P.M. to 1 A.M.

Shoreham Hotel, Connecticut Avenue and Calvert Street, N.W., AD 4-0700. The glamour spot for dining is the Blue Room, which imports talent like Celeste Holm and Edith Piaf from the supper-club circuit. Dining from 7, dancing from 8:15, with the show at 10:30 P.M. Tuesday through Saturday. Summertime, the setting moves outdoors to the Terrace. About $7.50. Cozier, less expensive and minus floor show is the Palladian Room, where Colonial-costumed waiters serve from rolling carts. Dinner from 6 to 10 P.M. Monday through Saturday, dancing from 10 P.M. to 2 A.M., to 1 A.M. on Saturday. The Garden Restaurant, the coffee shop, is open from 7 A.M. to midnight.

Statler Hilton, 16th and K Streets, N.W., EX 3-1000. The Embassy Room is the center of things for luncheon or dinner at Hilton's modern Washington hacienda. Roast beef and seafood are staples on the menu and the waiters love to carry flaming entrées and desserts. Luncheon $4, dinner $7.50. Dinner from 6 P.M., with dancing nightly, except Sunday, from 9 P.M. to 1:30 A.M. There are those, however, who prefer the adjoining thick-carpeted Veranda, enhanced by shrubbery and a picture-window outlook of 16th Street. It seems to be open always, starting with breakfast, then through lunch, cocktail hour, dinner by candlelight and for the final one at 12:30 A.M. Other restaurants at the

Hilton are the Lounge, which specializes in copper casserole dishes at luncheon, and the Coffee House, for breakfast, lunch, cocktails, and dinner.

Washington Hotel, 15th Street and Pennsylvania Avenue, N.W., ME 8-5900. The Sky Room is *the* room with a view. This rooftop restaurant looks out over the White House lawn, waist-high at the Washington Monument and across the parklands to Virginia. Be sure you have reservations for lunch ($3.50). Consider it for a breakfast stop in the morning or for afternoon cocktails; it's also open for dinner ($5.50).

Woodner Hotel, 3636 16th Street, N.W., HU 3-4400. At the Golden Steer, fronting on wooded Rock Creek Park, you can get a good steak dinner until 11 P.M. ($5). However, allow time for a cocktail at the Beverly Lounge.

For Cocktails on Sunday

The District of Columbia is dry on Sunday, except for light wine and beer; Virginia is wine and beer country every day. But you can have a drink with Sunday dinner at two fine restaurants in suburban Maryland. They're also in business during the week, of course:

Normandy Farm, Potomac, Maryland, OL 2-9421. Open from noon to midnight daily. Drive out River Road or Massachusetts Avenue eight miles past the District line. Decorations are French provincial, with a friendly open fireplace. The emphasis is on French cooking served with brioche and onion soup. Reservations are advisable on weekends. Dinner $4.50.

Olney Inn, Olney, Maryland, WH 6-5757. Open noon to 9:30 P.M., except Monday. Twelve miles north of Silver Spring on Route 97. Plantation-style restaurant of high quality. Fried chicken and beef dinners, with Sally Lunn bread, rum pie. Dinner $5. An especially good place for dinner when you're going to the Olney Theatre.

Nearby Virginia Restaurants

Charterhouse, Alexandria, FL 4-4400. Nine miles south on Shirley Highway (Route 350). The Rib Room (open 5 to 10 P.M. daily, noon to 10 P.M. Sunday) at this large new motor hotel is similar to the Rib Room at the Mayflower Hotel, both being under the same ownership. Prime ribs, with potato and salad bowl, $3. Come early, bring your bathing suit and swim in the pool. Coffee shop open 6:30 A.M. to 11 P.M.

Collingwood, SO 8-7944. On the Potomac five miles south of Alexandria, on the Mount Vernon Memorial Highway. Open mid-March through November, noon to 4:30 and 6 to 9 P.M., Sunday 1 to 9 P.M.; closed Monday. A handsome colonial mansion in the Mount Vernon tradition serving Southern fried chicken, Smithfield ham, spoon bread, and pecan pie. $2.75 to $4.25.

Penn-Daw, SO 8-7654. Three miles south of Alexandria on Route 1. Open 7 to 10:30 A.M. for breakfast, noon to 3 P.M. lunch, 5:30 to 8:30 P.M. dinner; Sunday 12:30 to 8:30 P.M. Thirty years ago when Cooper Dawson, Sr., opened this as a motor hotel with restaurant, Washingtonians enjoyed driving out in the country for a good meal of fried chicken or country ham. Everything in the area has boomed, including Penn-Daw, but Cooper, Jr., still serves the same fine Southern fare. Children especially welcome. $1.50–$3.25.

Seaport Inn, 6 King Street, Alexandria, KI 9-2341. Open 11:30 A.M. to 10:30 P.M. daily. Seafood at moderate prices is the specialty here, in the historic port section of Alexandria. $1.50 to $3.50.

XV *Hotels and Motels*

Hotels have been an important part of the Washington fabric ever since the city began, and slightly earlier. Lately, they have had to move over to make room for the motel boom—and are edging into it themselves wherever they can. But the hotel as an institution continues to fill a key role in the social and political life of the national capital.

The first establishment of note was Mr. Suter's pre-Revolutionary Fountain Tavern in Georgetown. It was supplanted in 1796 by the Union Tavern, later known as Crawford's Hotel, at 30th and M Streets, built by a syndicate at the staggering cost of $16,000. Anybody who was anybody, including most of Congress, tried to stay at the Union.

In time, however, hotels and boardinghouses (and bawdy houses) stretched the length of Pennsylvania Avenue from the Capitol to Georgetown. Probably the greatest in pre-Civil War days was the National, at 6th Street, built in 1827 by the Alexandria innkeeper and slave trader, John Gadsby. At this mammoth establishment (capacity almost 200 guests) Gadsby dared charge $1.25 for three meals a day and $3.50 for a bottle of liquor. But politicians, including Henry Clay, loved its grandeur and made it their headquarters. James Buchanan came to stay here before his inauguration but almost all the guests, including the President-elect, were stricken with water-poisoning and the National was nearly ruined.

Willard's, at 14th Street, dates back to 1818, and succeeded to first place among hostelries at the outbreak of the Civil War— even though it was considered really too far uptown. Much of the business of government was done in its passages and bars, and each morning a procession of celebrities could be seen break-fasting on fried oysters, steak and onions, pâté de foie gras, and blanc mange. Presidents Zachary Taylor, Millard Fillmore, and James Buchanan slept here, and it was Abraham Lincoln's quarters prior to his inauguration in 1861. It was here that General Grant received his appointment as lieutenant general in the Union Army, and in a room at the Willard, Julia Ward Howe composed "The Battle Hymn of the Republic."

The Willard, and later the New Willard, the present hotel built on the same site, continued as the center of things until recent years.

A great Washington hotel man of the old school was Harry Wardman, the Englishman. In 1916 he built the thousand-room Wardman Park far out on Connecticut Avenue, beyond anyone's concept of accessibility, and followed in ten years with the downtown Carlton, which to this day is immodestly expensive.

Unlike some cities, where the last new hotel was opened twenty-five or thirty years ago, Washington can point to four in the post-World War II period—Statler Hilton, Woodner, Dupont Plaza, Congressional—plus extensive additions to several others. Besides this construction, motels around the city have been adding new rooms at the rate of one thousand a year.

Even so, if you come here in spring, be sure you have a reservation. In summer, bear in mind that hotels offer family rates (often lower than those shown below) and free parking, while most motels have swimming pools.

The largest convention meeting room is Sheraton Hall at the Sheraton-Park, with a seating capacity of 3000; all the hotels, however, contribute to Washington's eminence as a convention center.

Following is a selected list of Washington's leading hotels, plus a representative group of outlying motor hotels:

Ambassador, 14th and K Streets, N.W., NA 8-8510. Restaurant and cocktail lounge. Indoor swimming pool free to guests. Close to shopping, theater districts. $12 to $18 double.

Carroll Arms, 1st at C Streets, N.E., LI 6-6800. Opposite Senate Office Building on Capitol Hill. Restaurant and cocktail lounge. $8 to $12 double.

Congressional, 300 New Jersey Avenue, S.E., LI 6-6611. Closest to House Office Building. A Knott hotel; restaurant and cocktail lounge. Pets allowed; children under 14 free in same room with adults. $12.50 double.

Dupont Plaza, Dupont Circle and New Hampshire Avenue, N.W., HU 3-6000. Attractive location off Dupont Circle. A modern hotel with a refrigerator in every room. Restaurant and cocktail lounge; garage. Children under 14 free. $13 to $14 double.

Fairfax, 2100 Massachusetts Avenue, N.W., HO 2-4480. A block west of Dupont Circle, on Embassy Row. Quiet hotel; some housekeeping rooms and family apartments. Very good dining room with children's menu. Free parking. Pets allowed. Children under 14 free. $12 double; family suite (2 adjoining rooms for four persons) $14 to $16.

Jefferson, 1200 16th Street, N.W., DI 7-4704. Just about the only one of its kind in Washington. A chic, medium-size establishment that reminds you of those hostelries in the East Fifties of New York. Well-appointed dining room and bar. $13 to $15 double.

Manger Hamilton, 14th and K Streets, N.W., DI 7-2580. A Restaurant and cocktail lounge. Close to shopping, theater districts. Children under 14 free. $12.50 to $15 double.

Manger Hay-Adams, 16th and H Streets, N.W., ME 8-2260. A hotel of distinction; many of its tastefully decorated rooms overlook Lafayette Park and the White House. Speaking historically, this is the site of the homes once occupied by John Hay and Henry Adams. Most convenient location to AFL-CIO and U. S. Chamber of Commerce headquarters. Excellent dining room and bar. $20 to $22 double.

Mayflower, Connecticut Avenue and DeSales Street, N.W., DI 7-3000. A great name among world hotels, and a great hotel. It opened in 1925 with spacious suites, a thousand richly furnished rooms, block-long promenade and more gold leaf in its adornments than any other building in America. Presidents and politics have been closely associated with the Mayflower. Presidents-elect Herbert Hoover and Franklin D. Roosevelt established themselves here and ex-President Truman, when in Washington, occupies a suite decorated especially for him. Visiting royalty and heads of state (including the Shah of Iran, King of Morocco, President of Germany) have entertained in the main ballroom. Three restaurants and bars. The hotel has survived changing ownership and now belongs to Hotel Corporation of America. Durable C. J. Mack, vice-president and general manager, has been with the Mayflower since it opened. $16 to $25 double.

Pick-Lee House, 15th and L Streets, N.W., DI 7-4800. If you have news for the Washington *Post,* you're almost next door. Good, moderate-priced coffee shop and cocktail lounge. $11.50 to $16 double.

Sheraton-Carlton, 16th and K Streets, N.W., ME 8-2626. The place to stay for that unhurried, pleasantly plush feeling and for service with a smile. Fine, fashionable dining spot. Sometimes I wonder how Harry Wardman, who built this little *basha* on 16th Street for the exclusive if not the snobbish, would feel today knowing the Laborers and Hod Carriers Unions had set their new headquarters next door. $18.50 to $22.50 double.

Sheraton-Park, Connecticut Avenue and Woodley Road, N.W., CO 5-2000. This is the uptown Sheraton branch and I must say that Washingtonians have finally been brainwashed out of calling it the Wardman Park, as it was known for years. Chief Justice Earl Warren lives here, as do enough members of the House and Senate for a quorum. The prize political resident, however, is former Senator Henry F. Ashurst, a very pleasant elder citizen who now prefers Washington to his native Arizona. You can reminisce with him on the Sun Porch. Dining room, coffee shop, cocktail lounge, plus swimming pool, free to guests, and tennis courts. Pets allowed. Everybody finds fun in riding the miniature diesel-type train, which commutes on rubber tires from one end of the 16-acre grounds to the other. $15 to $20 double.

Shoreham, Connecticut Avenue and Calvert Street, N.W., AD 4-0700. The growingest hotel in the city. The newest addition, a 100-unit motor inn, overlooks Rock Creek Park and is about 7 minutes drive from the Lincoln Memorial. Another new addition is the Olympic-size swimming pool. The word is that more motor-court rooms are in the works, along with a large convention hall. The old Shoreham cocktail lounge was so cozy you could look any blonde in the room straight in the eye, but in the new large one, called the Marquee, you can't tell whether she's a blonde or your secretary. There are four places to eat, five counting the snack bar. $17 to $20 double.

Statler Hilton, 16th and K Streets, N.W., EX 3-1000. This is really the heart of modern, business, expense-account Washington. It started in life as part of the Statler chain, which Conrad Hilton acquired lock and stock. When the government's anti-monopolists ruled he couldn't keep both this and the Mayflower, Hilton elected to relinquish the Mayflower. Eisenhower headquartered here as President-elect; so did General MacArthur when Truman recalled him from Japan; so did Comrade Khrushchev's Russian entourage (although he was at Blair House). The Statler Hilton is built along strictly modern, but commodious, lines both in its architecture and interior furnishings. It is close to Connecticut Avenue and the White House, and the limousines seem to run almost continually to the airport. Of course, the world will come to you at the Statler Hilton lobby, or in its four dining rooms. $18 to $24 double.

Tabard Inn, 1739 N Street, N.W., HO 2-1277. A different kind of hotel, usually discovered accidentally. It consists of three converted town houses, with large, tastefully decorated rooms. There's no elevator service, but the exercise up a flight or two will do you good. Only breakfast is served. $7 to $10 double.

Washington, 15th Street and Pennsylvania Avenue, N.W., ME 8-5900. Closest hotel to the Treasury Department and to the White House, which you can see from Sky Room. Cocktail lounge and coffee shop. John Nance "Cactus Jack" Garner lived here when he was Vice-President. $13 to $17.50 double.

Willard, Pennsylvania Avenue and 14th Street, N.W., NA 8-4420. Convenient location to the Federal Triangle and the shops on F Street. The Willard is steeped in history and tradition; note the plaque near the lobby in the block-long promenade commemorating the writing of "The Battle Hymn of the Republic." Dining room, coffee shop, attractive cocktail lounge and men's grill. Children under 14 free. $14 to $21 double.

Woodner, 3636 16th Street, N.W., HU 3-4400. A modern combination transient-residential hotel, off the beaten tourist path, overlooking Rock Creek Park. Good dining room and bar. $13 to $16 double.

MOTELS

About seventy-five acceptable to superb motor courts are located within a 15- to 20-mile radius of downtown Washington. I will not attempt to supply a complete list, but will indicate several of the most prominent, with a wide range in prices—all with swimming pool and room TV. Curiously, their seasonal peak differs from the hotels. Business is great for everybody in spring; motels do well in summer, with the family motoring trade, while the city hotels are off; but from autumn to early spring motels have their lightest period.

On the Virginia side—

Charterhouse, on U.S. 350 (Shirley Highway), nine miles from Washington, FL 4-4400. One of the largest (234 rooms), with five stories and a resort-like atmosphere. Lushly appointed, spacious rooms. Room service, valet, dining room of merit, and coffee house. Pets allowed. $12–$14 double. Another Charterhouse, part of the Hotel Corporation of America chain, is located in the District, near the entrance to the Baltimore-Washington Expressway. $13 to $18 double.

Arva, on U.S. 50, west of Arlington Memorial Bridge, JA 5-0300. Fine, modern motor hotel. Restaurant; some of its 118 rooms have kitchenettes. $12 double.

Iwo Jima, on U.S. 50, JA 4-5000. Restaurant, valet, laundry-room. $13.50 to $17 double. One mile from either Key Bridge or Arlington Memorial Bridge.

Marriott Motor Hotels, NA 8-4200 for both. The newest, at the south end of Key Bridge (Routes 29, 211), is the junior size with only 225 rooms. The older Marriott is reportedly the world's largest motor hotel (360 rooms). Just across the 14th Street Bridge from downtown Washington this superb, almost self-contained community has barber and beauty shops, laundry, swimming in summer, ice skating in winter. The restaurants at both motels are showplaces of the Hot Shoppe chain. Pets allowed. $15 to $25 double.

South Gate Motor Hotel, 2480 South Glebe Road, just off Shirley Highway, JA 4-4400. Kennels for dogs, 9-hole putting green; also a heliport, in case you're planning to drop in that way. Restaurant. Ask for a look at the bridal suite, even if you're not on your honeymoon. $12 to $15 double.

South of Alexandria, on U.S. 1, several good motels provide accommodations near Mount Vernon. Wagon Wheel and Mount

Vee both occupy landscaped, resort-like grounds, with swimming pools. Each about $12 to $16 double. Penn-Daw is older, well operated with fine food, no swimming pool. $9.50 to $10.50 double.

On the Maryland side—

In Town, two locations. U.S. 240, Bethesda, OL 4-1400, and just off U.S. 29, Silver Spring, JU 8-5801. Large, attractive rooms, with restaurant, room service. Pets allowed. $12 to $20 double.

Bethesdan, 5 miles north of Washington on U.S. 240, OL 6-2100. Near National Institutes of Health and Bethesda Naval Hospital. Pets allowed. $12 to $18 double.

Motel Park Silver, off U.S. 29, Silver Spring, JU 8-4400. Well-appointed rooms, several with kitchenettes. Pets allowed—but leave them out when you come to complimentary Continental breakfast. $12 to $14 double.

XVI *Life after Dark*

For sheer noise and neon, Washington yields night-life honors to New York, Newark, Jersey City, Baltimore, and several points south and west. Presently, however, it is catching up, despite the traditional patterns of private entertaining.

Now there are more places to go and more headline performers to see. They don't earn as much or stay as long as they do at Las Vegas, but here they don't lose it back at the gaming tables, either. And speaking of gaming tables, there aren't any (that I know of).

Of late there has been a trend to home-grown, or at least home-based, night life, at smaller, intimate *boîtes*, not quite avant-garde but with candlelight and talent. Charlie Byrd, the classic guitarist at the Showboat, is the showpiece in this department.

Why has Washington been so apparently circumspect all these years? Discretion is undoubtedly one factor, as far as the higher echelons are concerned. I can recall seeing a bachelor Supreme Court Justice courting in the genteel confines of the Statler's Embassy Room and the Vice-President and his wife dancing at the Mayflower's Presidential Room, but I doubt you will ever see a political figure with a blonde at his side in public.

Of course, as in most cities, you can find anything you want, from the placid to the exotic, if you look for it. The difference is that in Washington you have to know where to look.

For sociality on the mild side, attend the functions of your state society, a unique type of Washington institution composed essentially of Federal employees, both men and women, from the same state. Congressmen and Cabinet members show up too. Most state societies hold four or five dances yearly, starting with the Congressional reception in January. The big whingding is the George Washington Birthday Ball, held by the Conference of State Societies. Watch the newspapers for dates of these functions, or phone your Congressman's office for the name of your state society's secretary.

Servicemen are welcome at the Saturday night dances at the air-conditioned USO-Lafayette Square Club, 719 Madison Place, N.W., and at the Penthouse, 17th and K Streets, N.W.

A good bet for servicemen is to stop at the office of the Armed Services Hospitality Committee, Room 27A, Old Post Office Building, 12th and Pennsylvania Avenue, N.W., for information, guidance and a copy of the excellent 24-page booklet, *Summer Fun in the Washington Area.*

Girls, heed this serious note: when you're unescorted, go home by 10 P.M. and read a book. This town is not always safe at the late hours. Sometimes even a police officer is attacked in the dark. Lawlessness was so acute in 1959 that one Congressman proposed calling out the Marines to supplement the undermanned police department patrols. Fun is fun but stay with the lights, the crowds, and your friends.

Drinking habits are slightly peculiar in Washington bars. You cannot drink standing up. You cannot carry a drink from one table to another—ask the waitress and she'll do it for you. Weeknight drinking hours last until 2 A.M., until midnight on Saturday. On Sunday only beer and light wines are sold.

There is a buzz of after-hour, or pre-dawn, activity. If you're still awake, check with a cab driver, exercising caution. He may have some interesting information. Waterfront Baltimore is the red-light district for the nation's capital.

Whiskey prices, in bottles at Washington's 400 retail stores, are the lowest in the nation. Prices are fixed by competition, not by law. To show how well off you are buying it here, following are recent comparative prices between the District of Columbia and Trenton, New Jersey, on four principal brand names:

	Trenton	*D.C.*
Black & White	$ 6.44	$ 4.81
Smirnoff	4.25	2.99
Seagram 7	4.79	3.28
Old Grandad	6.59	4.99

Following is a list of some Washington night spots. The 15 per cent tipping rule applies in most.

FLOOR SHOWS, WITH DINNER-DANCING

Casino Royal, 14th and H Streets, N.W., NA 8-7700. Open nightly with two dance bands and three floor shows, 8:15, 10:30, and 12:30. An attractive room with such vocal performers as Hi-Lo's, Bobby Darin, and Josh White. Cover charge $1.00, minimum $3.00. The menu is both American and Chinese.

The New Lotus, 727 14th Street, N.W., NA 8-0600. Open nightly. Cocktails from 4 P.M., with dinner to 9:30 P.M., late supper until 2 A.M., Sunday dinner 4 P.M. to 1 A.M. Also weekday luncheons 11 A.M. to 3 P.M. There is a $4 minimum after 8:30 P.M., but you get a good run for your money. As the old Lotus, this was a modest night club. Under its new owners, the David Brothers, the redecorated Lotus opened with Sammy Davis, Jr., and has been following with other Hollywood headliners since.

Champagne Room, 1304 F Street, N.W., ME 8-1061. Ameen David's is the newest of the trio of centrally located night clubs. Minimum $3.00. Dancing nightly 8:30 to 2 A.M. Two shows, 9:15 and 12:15, Monday through Saturday. A beautiful room featuring top recording stars and Broadway comics.

Embassy Room, Statler Hotel, 16th and K Streets, N.W., EX 3-1000. Dancing 9 to 1 A.M. Frequently brings in name femme stars like Hildegarde, Celeste Holm.

Blue Room, Shoreham Hotel, Connecticut Avenue at Calvert Street, N.W., AD 4-0700. Dancing 8:15 to 12:45 Tuesday through Saturday. Celeste Holm, Edith Piaf, and other glamorous ladies, have been here, too.

ENTERTAINMENT—DANCING

Old New Orleans, Connecticut Avenue at 18th Street, N.W., RE 7-7284. In the Sazerac Room, downstairs *boîte,* there is dancing every night except Sunday until 1:30 A.M., and usually a girl singer doing two shows nightly. A favorite of the Latin American embassy set. Creole and Continental dishes.

The Flame, 1631 Connecticut Avenue, N.W., AD 4-0300. Cocktail music 4:30 to 6:30. Dancing till 2 A.M. Monday through Saturday at this newish, attractive uptown supper club. The food (shishkebab a specialty) is good and moderately priced. Open for lunch 11 A.M.

DANCING, NO ENTERTAINMENT

Presidential Room, Mayflower Hotel, DI 7-3000. From 9 P.M. to 1 A.M. except Sunday (cover $1.50). An elegant spot with Sidney's music (but this doesn't mean Sidney—like Lester Lanin, he has several bands).

Colonial Room, Sheraton-Park Hotel, 2660 Connecticut Avenue, N.W., CO 5-2000. Dancing to trio music (9:30 P.M. to 1:30 A.M.) in an attractive, candle-lit room with cheek-to-cheek atmosphere. Stop for a drink across the lobby at the Gilded Cage, a cozy bar with everything, including waitresses, in Gay 90s motif.

Palladian Room, Shoreham Hotel, Connecticut Avenue at Calvert Street, N.W., AD 4-0700. Dancing to the music of Sande Williams, a popular Shoreham fixture; from 10 P.M. to 2 A.M. Monday through Friday, cover charge $1.00; from 10 P.M. to 1 A.M. on Saturday, cover charge $1.50 (closed during summer months). The Palladian, refusing to be overshadowed by the Blue Room, has a stanch, enthusiastic following.

STRICTLY FOR JAZZ

Showboat Lounge, 2477 18th Street, N.W., DU 7-9895. This is the home concert hall of Charlie Byrd, probably the greatest American guitarist playing today. He's an admirer of Segovia and sounds it when he turns to serious music, and combines it with jazz. He and his trio play from 9 P.M. to 1:30 A.M. nightly.

Bayou, 3135 K Street, N.W., FE 3-2897. Open 7 P.M. to 2 A.M. Tuesday through Friday; to midnight on Saturday and Sunday. An off-beat location more or less under the Whitehurst Freeway, with music strictly from Dixieland by Wild Bill Whelan and his Dixie Six. With pizza on the side.

BARS WORTHY OF NOTE

Town and Country, Mayflower Hotel, Connecticut Avenue and DeSales Street, N.W. If you require proof that Washington's women are attractive, and chic, report here around sundown. Have a late lunch at the Men's Bar and you're only a revolving door away from the cocktail hour, which may last well past dinner.

Beverly Lounge, Woodner Hotel, 3636 16th Street, N.W. A friendly cocktail bar in a semiresidential hotel, where distaff tenants sometimes stop for a tall one after a day at the office and improve matters no end.

Cafe Lorraine, Lafayette Hotel, 823 16th Street, N.W. An intimate, well-decorated spot in an older hotel finally undergoing renovation. Favorite with association people.

PIECE DE RESISTANCE

The Gaslight Club, 1020 16th Street, N.W., DI 7-4141. Open 11 A.M. to 2 A.M. Monday through Friday, Saturday from 4 P.M. to midnight. Admission is $75, for membership and a gold key to the front door, and the drinks are $1.50 each. It's worth the price, too, if your expense account can stand it. This is the most elaborate pub in the city, a converted three-story town house opposite the Statler Hilton, furnished in the gaslight era—gaslights included. This new celebrity hangout is presided over by Rear Admiral Robert Archer and Frank Judge (an alumnus of the National Press Club bartending school) for the Chicago-New York Gaslight Gang. The waitresses are called Gaslight Girls and every one, as they say, is a "living doll."

The National Headquarters
of the American Red Cross...

XVII *A Woman's World*

Women of all types adore and adorn Washington. Career women.
Unmarried but hopeful women. Rich, leisured women. Beautiful
women. Social climbing women. Accomplished party-givers and
partygoers.

There also are some who don't like Washington at all and would
prefer to be home in comfort in the Middle West or the Near
East, free of protocol and politics, which are practiced in female
circles here as a fine art.

Washington's women are immensely influential. This is true
everywhere, as any married man knows, but in Washington their

influence is exerted on the course of government. On Capitol Hill, there are now about twenty Congresswomen, plus a host of wives on their Congressional husbands' staffs. The ladies of the Washington press corps have not one club, as do the men, but two. As reporters they are no shrinking violets in competing for top stories and headlines. The society pages are well read and uniquely significant in national and even international affairs, because of the role of the diplomatic colony.

Capital society has a certain ritualism, tradition, and archaic caste, based on protocol or precedence, yet without the pure blue-blood limitations found in other cities. There are four distinct social sets—residential, Congressional, diplomatic, and military— with the White House the pre-eminent shrine. The most significant functions are those held at the White House and the First Lady, whether she cares to wear the crown or not, is the Madame Queen of Social Washington.

Since the days of Dolly Madison, sumptuous dinners and receptions have been characteristic of the scene. Women have vied with all the determination of a Presidential candidate for the first place in unofficial entertaining. Presently the ribbons are worn by Mrs. Perle Mesta, the "hostess with the mostest." Mrs. Mesta possesses rare social talent; although she contributed to the Democratic cause (and was rewarded with an ambassadorship to Luxembourg), she transcended politics in the succeeding Republican administration. A truly bipartisan achievement. Her nearest rival in the Democratic days, Mrs. Gwendolyn Cafritz, never quite succeeded in pulling the same switch, although still a formidable Foxhall Road hostess nonetheless. A social priestess without political portfolio is Mrs. Merriwether Post May, one of the world's richest women (Post cereals), whose late ex-husband was Ambassador Joseph Davies. With her present husband, steelman Herbert May, she commutes about in their private propjet airliner, although her social headquarters remain in Washington. Mrs. Polly Guggenheim, widow of the copper millionaire, also ranks very high on the social ladder; her 20-acre estate, Firenze, is among the city's private showpieces. Then there are socialites of an intellectual bent, like Mrs. Robert Woods Bliss of Georgetown, who with her husband presented Dumbarton Oaks to Harvard University as a research center and comes to work there almost daily, and Mrs. Robert Low Bacon, who occupies the imposing red-brick house at 1801 F Street, where two Chief Justices of the Supreme Court, John Marshall and Melville W. Fuller, lived during their respective lifetimes.

While café society is not on the heavy side, there are periods of the year when eligibles and their wives can be entertained almost every night, at cocktail and caviar soirées and dinners tendered by embassies, lobbying organizations, and expense accounters who have learned this is the best way to a man's ear.

Protocol rules at many such functions. Simply stated, it determines who sits next to whom on the basis of rank. If you find yourself at the foot of the table you may conclude you have minimum rank in those circumstances . . . but rank enough to be invited.

Protocol applies rigidly to womanly affairs. The wife of the Vice-President ranks next to the wife of the President, followed by wives of the Chief Justice, retired Chief Justice, widows of former Presidents, wives of the Speaker of the House, Secretary of State and other Cabinet members in the order in which their departments were established.

This entire business becomes exceedingly complex when different groups are brought together. It's easy enough to say a Senator's wife outranks a Congressman's; but how about the wives of an ambassador, a general, an assistant secretary, and a socialite? And where does the naval attaché of Peru rate in relation to the cultural attaché of Pakistan? These are not merely people, you see, but place cards. Shuffle and reshuffle, but deal from the top.

The last word on the subject is the Protocol Office of the Department of State, relied on by everyone in Washington, from the White House down, when foreign diplomats and U.S. officials are involved. One day, as Mrs. Edith Helm, who served for many years as social secretary at the White House, recalls, the Protocol Office was confronted by a flustered hostess. She had invited two friends to assist at a party, one to pour tea and the other to pour coffee. But since she was anxious to honor the ranking guest with the more important beverage, which had precedence, she asked, tea or coffee? The answer: tea and coffee have equal status.

The unofficial social arbiter is Mrs. Carolyn Hagner Shaw, a society writer who went on to create news. She publishes the Green Book, officially the Social List of Washington ($15 the copy). It is not a social register like New York's Blue Book, but a compilation of 4500 key government officials and nonofficials socially acceptable. The 126-page Green Book also includes Mrs. Shaw's "table of precedence," and pointers on correct social form. As a subscriber you may ask Mrs. Shaw for her counsel on arranging small dinners and other procedural questions of import. There is also the matter of when to leave calling cards: Just ring the doorbell once a year for the President, Vice-President, and other ranking officials, suggests Mrs. Shaw, then leave your card with the maid and go quietly. "It wasn't exactly like you told me," a Congressman's wife called and said excitedly to Mrs. Shaw. "The maid didn't answer the door. It was Mrs. Nixon. She didn't have a card tray; she had a baking pan. She asked me to come in and I sat on the kitchen stool while she finished her cake. We started talking about our recipes and our children and I'm sorry, but I stayed more than an hour!"

The moral of the story: being yourself, if you're given a chance, may be the best kind of protocol, after all.

Another popular consultant on doing things right in Washington, especially if you have a daughter Coming Out, is Mary-Stuart Price, the public relations director at the Sheraton-Carlton. Mary-Stuart arranges the Debutante Cotillion, a Coming Out ball for a group of girls every Thanksgiving.

The social world aside, there are points of interest in Washington that appeal especially to women. Among these are:

National headquarters and garden of the American Red Cross, 17th and D Streets, N.W. (8:30–4:30, Monday through Friday). The Memorial Building contains exhibits, stained-glass windows designed by Louis C. Tiffany, and statuary, including a bust of the Czechoslovakian patriot, Dr. Alice Masayrk, by Ivan Mestrovic. The azalea around the Red Cross building are as pretty as any in Washington in spring.

Daughters of the American Revolution, 17th and C Streets, N.W., (10–3 weekdays), a block from the Red Cross. The new D.A.R. Museum (1950) is a "must" if you appreciate antiques. This distinguished collection of early Americana includes rare furnishings, silverware, china, crystal, pewter, associated with

George Washington, Paul Revere, Patrick Henry, John Hancock. The portrait of Martha Washington, by E. F. Andrews, matches the one he painted for the East Room of the White House. The State Rooms are furnished to reflect periods before 1830. The Virginia Room, for instance, has Hepplewhite chairs, blown glass, Thomas Jefferson's Sheffield silver candlesticks. If you're a D.A.R. member, you may tiptoe into the library to check your genealogy; the volumes here are probably the most extensive in the country.

The new Educational Center of the American Association of University Women (completed 1960), 2401 Virginia Avenue, N.W., (9–5, Monday through Friday). The glass-enclosed lobby is the setting of sculptured mahogany panels depicting famous American women from Anne Hutchinson, the religious pioneer, who was banished from the Massachusetts Bay Colony in 1638 to Amelia Earhart the aviator who perished in the Pacific in 1937. A feature of the building is a lounge for visiting A.A.U.W. members; the restaurant is open to them for luncheon.

You can also attend fashion shows in Washington almost every day in the week, at the leading department stores and hotels. These are held between 12 and 2 P.M. in almost every case. Much of the modeling is done informally with the models walking among luncheon tables and giving the vital statistics—price, sizes, colors—about the clothes they're wearing. The current schedule follows but check the fashion pages in the Sunday papers for changes and special events:

Daily (including Saturday)—Garfinckel's Tea Room, a pleasant place for a feminine luncheon—men are not excluded.

Daily—Presidential Room, Mayflower Hotel. Conducted by Evelyn Barton Brown, Tuesday–Saturday, conducted by Jelleff's on Monday.

Tuesday—Shoreham Hotel, Garden Restaurant.

Tuesday evening—Embassy Room, Statler Hotel, 8–9 P.M., conducted by the Hecht Company.

Wednesday—Rib Room, Charterhouse, 1–2 P.M.

Also during luncheon hour in three rooms at Sheraton-Park— Town Room, Terrace Lounge, and Colonial Room.

Thursday—Normandy Farm, Potomac, Maryland.

Friday—Sheraton-Carlton.

Saturday—Willard.

XVIII *The Overseas Guest*

Having been a foreigner once or twice myself, and a confused foreigner at that, in large cities of other countries, I can sympathize with overseas visitors in Washington.

They may not really need sympathy. Not that Washington is necessarily simpler than other places, but foreigners seem to have a facility for preparing themselves to travel so much better than we do. This applies not only to the superficial things, like learning the exchange rate between penny and piaster, but in understanding something about our history, way of life, and government.

When Nikita Khrushchev had tea at the Capitol with the Senate Foreign Relations Committee, he looked the Senators straight in the eye and identified them individually by their speeches in the *Congressional Record,* which he had been following for months. But millions of Americans come to Washington without knowing the names of the Senators from their own state or the Congressman from their district.

Likewise, foreigners display an incredible knowledge of Washington or Lincoln or the Civil War battlefields. Yet some Washingtonians—people who live in the city—endure for years without ever entering the National Gallery of Art or the Smithsonian Institution. Of course, it may be natural; our attitude changes when we go abroad. Who would think of going to Europe without visiting the Prado, the Louvre, and the British Museum?

Let us say that now you are here from another country, traveling for pleasure, study, or business, or serving officially for your government. You will find Washington an international city. Several thousand foreigners live here, stationed at embassies or with United Nations agencies. The city is accustomed to hearing different languages and to seeing every manner of dress (your native costume is always appropriate). The differences between your homeland and the United States—whether in customs, dress, language, or currency—will be only minor problems.

The reception accorded you by our government and by the average people you meet will be hospitable and courteous. American characteristics are informality and easy friendliness. In addition, we know the best way to represent the American concept to the world is to let you see how we live our daily lives and practice our form of self-government. The best and the worst, uncensored, are yours to explore.

Overseas visitors react to Washington in many different ways. They may be delighted or disappointed. Or both. You may feel we do not quite have the philosophy or appreciation of living which people in some countries cultivate so well. And certainly if you look twice at our official version of contemporary architecture you will conclude that it lacks the creativeness and daring being shown abroad.

On the other hand, if (as most visitors do) you have first stopped in hurried, harassed, preoccupied New York, Washington will be a welcome and restful relief. The tempo is slower, the flavor and design are cosmopolitan. Washington was, after all, planned by the European Pierre L'Enfant, and foreigners heartily appreciate his broad tree-lined boulevards and parks.

To speak specifically, the following pointers and practical suggestions should help to eliminate confusion and to deepen your perception of our national capital:

Hotels—For general information, addresses and rates, see Chapter XV. Of the major hotels, two give special attention to overseas visitors. One is the Statler Hilton, part of the Hilton International chain. This hotel has a list of cab drivers who speak foreign languages; when you want to go sightseeing ask the assistant manager to engage one for you. The Sheraton-Park Hotel has a special International Manager, Joaquin Tristani (who speaks French, Spanish, Portuguese, Italian) to assist you, as well as four bilingual room clerks and twenty-five bilingual waiters who can take your orders in French, Spanish, German, Russian, Hungarian, Polish, Arabic, Lithuanian, Danish, Yugoslav, Dutch, and Turkish.

If you prefer a smaller, more Continental hotel, the Jefferson or Tabard Inn, both attractively furnished and comfortable, should prove to your liking.

If economy is a prime requisite, these modest hotels cater to foreign vistiors at reasonable rates (about $4.50 single to $7 or $8 double): Admiral, 2131 O Street, N.W.; Emery-Georgian, 1812 G Sreet, N.W.; National, 1808 I Street, N.W., and Presidential, 900 19th Street, N.W.

Generally speaking our hotels are larger than foreign hotels and consequently less apt to provide the personalized service you may expect. A request for tea served in your room in the morning is often not understood, so arrange for it the night before. Do *not* place your shoes outside your room for polishing, since such automatic service is not provided. When you register or "check in," ask for the "check out" time (usually between 3 and 6 P.M.) so you will not be charged for an extra day. If you want to keep the room for a few hours longer, call the desk.

There is no service charge added to the bill at hotels or restaurants so you are expected to add a tip (*pourboire*). Bellboys who carry your luggage in a first-class hotel are given 25¢ for one bag or for two small ones; 50¢ to 75¢ for two or three bags. If you stay one week or more it is proper to leave a one-dollar tip on the dresser for the chambermaid.

Other tipping pointers—In restaurants, leave 15 per cent of the total bill on the table. No need to tip at cafeterias or drugstore luncheon counters. Tips in taxis vary from 10 to 25 per cent, but none is necessary for a short ride. Guides at public buildings do not accept tips, but will appreciate your spoken thanks. Guides on sightseeing buses do accept tips.

Restaurants—For restaurants serving your national dishes, see Chapter XIV. However, try a variety of American dishes—not all of it is uninspired by any means.

The normal meal hours are: breakfast, 7 to 9:30 A.M.; lunch, 11:30 A.M. to 2 P.M., and dinner, 6 to 8:30 P.M. Though afternoon tea is not customary, the midmorning and midafternoon "coffee break" has grown to be almost as cherished an institution in Washington offices as pay day.

The choicest, and usually most expensive, main course at dinner is steak or prime ribs of beef. Southern specialties of the Washington area are Virginia ham and fried chicken; seafood is another local favorite.

Two inexpensive American "delicacies" are the "hot dog" (a type of sausage in a long, soft bread roll) and the "hamburger" (beef patty in a round bread bun). The hamburger claims a higher culinary standing, with elaborations ranging to the cheeseburger and the superburger.

Meat is generally ordered rare, medium or well done. But if you want it rare, as in England, you specify "very rare." If well done, ask for an "outside cut" of beef. Medium is hard to come by and may take some discussion.

Cafeterias are generally least expensive and informal. You pick up tray, napkin, and silverware at the start of a long counter, then push it over a railing while choosing foods from a series of cases before you. At the end of the line a cashier totals your charges and either accepts payment or gives you a ticket to be paid on the way out. Then you carry your tray to a table, remove the dishes and eat your meal, often accompanied by any other diner who wishes to sit in an empty seat. Drugstores have counters for quick breakfasts or a light lunch. Prices are low, service is fast.

Getting around the City—Streetcars and buses are the adventurous forms of perambulation and the surest way to come in contact with our average people. Raised platforms in the middle of the street are for boarding streetcars; "bus stops" are indicated with round signs on iron standards. You board at the front door and place coins amounting to 20¢ in the coin box beside the driver. If you do not have the correct coins, the driver will give you change; this may include a "token," a dime-sized coin with a hole in it, which you put in the box for your fare. It is best not to ask the driver to change paper currency of the larger denominations.

When you cross streets, hesitate at the curb and watch other people going in the same direction; they give more certain guidance than the traffic signals.

Public toilets are called "rest rooms." They are located in public buildings, office buildings, hotels, restaurants, gasoline stations. But separate rooms are always provided for men and women (marked MEN or WOMEN; LADIES or GENTLEMEN); there are no public rest rooms of the type found in other countries.

Shopping—An interesting place to shop, whether you need clean shirts, clothing, or gifts, is a department store, something like a bazaar under one roof. Prices are clearly marked on the label; there is no bargaining. Incidentally, if you do need a traveling shirt, try a Dacron washable, which you can wash yourself and hang to dry overnight.

The four principal medium-priced department stores in Washington are: Woodward & Lothrop, 11th and F Streets, N.W.; Kann's, 7th Street and Pennsylvania Avenue, N.W.; Lansburgh's, between 7th and 8th at E Street, N.W., and Hecht's, 7th and F Streets, N.W.

Many drugstores carry a wide selection of articles other than medicines, too. In this respect they differ from the usual pharmacy or apothecary, although they do have pharmacy departments.

Exchanging Currency—I suggest the Foreign Department at the main branch of Riggs National Bank, 1503 Pennsylvania Avenue, N.W., which handles money matters for most embassies and visiting heads of state like Queen Elizabeth and King Ibn Saud. Riggs personnel can handle drafts, letters of credit, and currency exchange for about one hundred countries. This famous bank has been cashing checks and keeping deposits for all kinds of citizens, from Presidents down, for more than a century. Hours are 9 A.M. to 2 P.M. Monday through Thursday, 9 A.M. to 5 P.M. on Friday. Other banks also render foreign services.

International Friends and Countrymen—The surest place to meet countrymen is at your own embassy or legation. To locate the address and telephone number, look in the Yellow Pages under "Embassies and Legations."

You may also want to call at the office of your national airline or steamship company. Those located in Washington include: Cunard Line, 914 15th Street, N.W.; French Line, 734 15th Street, N.W., and Holland-America Line, 914 17th Street, N.W.; Air France, 1518 K Street, N.W.; Alitalia, 1001 Connecticut Avenue, N.W.; Brazilian International and TSA, 1006 Connecticut Avenue,

Luxuriant tropical vegetation and tropical birds in the patio of the Pan American Union...

N.W.; British Overseas Airways Corporation, 1124 Connecticut Avenue, N.W.; Japan Airlines, 1008 Connecticut Avenue, N.W.; KLM, 1001 Connecticut Avenue, N.W.; Lufthansa, 1000 Connecticut Avenue, N.W.; Sabena, 1005 Connecticut Avenue, N.W., and Swissair, 1000 Connecticut Avenue, N.W.

The largest group of international residents in Washington is the Chinese. Many of the 3500 have moved outside Chinatown, which extends along H Street from 5th to 9th, Northwest, but a hard core of several hundred still remains on the old ground. The two centers of Chinatown are the long-time rival, but presently peaceful, tongs, On Leong, 620 H Street, and Hip Sing, 503 H Street.

Two official international organizations have their headquarters in Washington: the International Monetary Fund and International Bank for Reconstruction, H Street from 18th to 19th Streets, N.W. Flags of their 68 member nations are on display at the entrance. Each of these agencies has loaned more than $4,000,000,-000, the Bank on long-term development projects like railroad and dam construction, the Fund in extending short term credits to nations temporarily in need of foreign exchange to pay for imports.

The Pan American Union, 17th Street and Constitution Avenue, N.W., (9–4:30, 9–12 Saturday, free guided tours), headquarters of the Organization of American States (OAS), should be visited by anyone from, or interested in Latin America. This Spanish-style marble villa houses the "United Nations of the Western Hemisphere." The patio on the first floor is a fragment of Latin America in Washington, with exotic tropical plants and palms and a macaw fluttering and screeching about in the upper leaves. Also on the first floor are the travel division, a shop selling Latin American records and handicrafts, and the art gallery. On the second floor be sure to see the Hall of Americas, decorated with Tiffany crystal chandeliers and stained-glass windows. It is used for international conferences, diplomatic receptions, and entertainment. Ask for the schedule of free concerts given by Latin American performers. Behind the building, the landscaped Aztec Garden is the setting of outdoor summer concerts.

Most of the offices of the Pan American Union are located in its new (1949) Administration Building, in a triangular plot at Constitution Avenue between 18th and 19th Streets. Secretary of the Interior Harold Ickes, the "Old Curmudgeon," opposed construction of this building, charging it would mar the view of his Interior Building—and it wasn't built until after his resignation from office. Simon Bolivar Plaza, a landscaped park centered around a statue of Bolivar the Liberator now lies between Interior and the Pan American Administration Building.

If you are participating in a program sponsored by a U.S. government agency, you are welcome to join in the activities of the Washington International Center, 1630 Crescent Place, N.W. This unique institution was established in 1950 at government request, but is operated by the American Council on Education, a private, co-operative group, staffed largely by volunteers. The Center offers guided bus tours of the city, lectures, and discussions by technical experts on various phases of life in the United States, and social gatherings.

Another excellent group is the International Crossroads Breakfast, which meets every Sunday at 9 A.M. at the Young Men's Christian Association (YMCA), 1736 G Street, N.W. It has attracted visitors from 109 countries since it started during World War II. For 60¢ you are served a typical American breakfast of juice, bacon and eggs, toast and coffee, followed with a discussion led by an educator, Congressman, scientist, or professional man.

Leisure Activities—Washington churches welcome foreign visitors. St. John's, on Lafayette Square, conducts Protestant services in French on Sunday afternoons at 4:30 P.M., except during the summer, with a social gathering after services the first Sunday every month. A social club, Le Foyer, open to anyone interested in French, meets at St. John's at 8 P.M. the second Thursday of each month.

The Meet Americans Club (membership $1) holds informal get-togethers Friday evenings starting at 8 P.M. at the Atlantic Coast Conference Club, 1349 E Street, N.W.

Through such groups you are quite likely to be invited into an American home—the best place to see us as we really are. Very few families have servants, so anticipate informality. If you're invited for dinner, don't worry about differences in table customs. When in doubt, simply say to your hosts, "I hope you don't mind if I follow your lead."

Try to see a sporting event. When you go to Griffith Stadium to a baseball game (something like cricket), get in the spirit of things by eating hot dogs and shouting epithets at the umpires. Reading a newspaper through the game or listening to a portable radio are considered marks of the serious enthusiast.

Travel to the surrounding countryside for a picture of our suburban and rural life. Unless you're sure you understand our rules and regulations, avoid driving except in the company of an American. Consider taking a tour with one of the sightseeing bus companies to Gettysburg or Colonial Williamsburg. If you are adventurous, ride by train to Richmond, then travel by bus to see the University of Virginia at Charlottesville, founded by Thomas Jefferson, and return from there to Washington.

Unfortunately, international visitors are not exempt from embarrassment and discomfort in racial practices south of Washington. Race and color barriers are encountered at many hotels, motels, restaurants, public places, and most churches. There is no legal segregation in the city of Washington, nor is any countenanced by the Federal government, but this separation lingers in the South, and to a degree in the North. As I said, I've been confused in large cities abroad. However, I can't remember being turned away from any door—and, with most Americans, I hope for the day when you may say the same here.

XIX *Children by Ages and Stages*

Most of the activities and places recommended in this book have been child-tested. By my own youngsters, that is. They've shared in the research of monuments, memorials, parks, museums, government buildings, fishing streams, picnic grounds, weekend trips.

They and all children raised in these parts are a lucky bunch. First, because they are sitting in on history. Second, they have at their fingertips national landmarks which are only mental images to youngsters elsewhere. And third, Washington is capital of the Children's World, almost as though L'Enfant and his successors had them in mind.

Except for night life, there is nothing here you cannot do with your children. Even in the evenings, a family group can spend its time to advantage at the Lincoln Memorial, Lincoln Museum, National Archives, Library of Congress, and one or two other points we will come to presently.

The secret to sightseeing fun with youngsters is to gear the schedule to their capabilities and not to the adults'. The younger they are the shorter their attention span. They can walk less, need more rest; on reaching a saturation point, they rebel against discipline, history, and education, and crave romping room and the most juvenile-slanted pursuits.

Feed a balanced fare. Compromise your tastes to meet your youngsters'. Dragging children on a grown-up holiday guarantees a miserable time for everyone. Speaking of feeding, get in early to cafeterias or restaurants (noon for lunch, six for dinner), so your family has no wait for service. Take advantage of picnic areas in the parks, where you eliminate restaurant restlessness and the children can work off steam.

Choose your activities and objectives by age groups. For example, with children under five, your best bet is to live with the outdoors; this age can't tolerate being cooped up. Visit such places as:

*One of the Washington
Zoo's most popular new attractions
is Dzimbo, the baby elephant...*

Tidal Basin, for a ride on the Swan Boat (25¢ for 15 minute ride). Five- and six-year-olds will enjoy the pedal boats (75¢ an hour).

Lincoln Memorial, about right for their sightseeing depth. Then let them romp alongside the Reflecting Pool.

National Aquarium, in the Commerce Department.

National Zoological Park, in the wooded heart of Rock Creek Park (grounds open till dark, buildings open 9 to 4:30, Saturday and Sunday to 5; half hour later in summer). You can reach it either on Rock Creek Parkway or on Connecticut Avenue to

Hawthorne Street. The Zoo has been administered with a flare of showmanship since it was established in 1890 with its first head-keeper a Barnum & Bailey Circus alumnus.

For thirty-one years, until his retirement in 1956, the personality of the Zoo was shaped by its director, Dr. William Mann. He developed it as a happy place, where animals live longer than in the wilds and births are not infrequent—including a giraffe and a rare, beautiful snow leopard, first of its kind born in the Western Hemisphere. Another indication of how the animals are cared for: when the tusks of Ashoka, the Indian elephant, grew so close together he could hardly raise his trunk to feed himself, the elephant keeper, Roger McDonald, fashioned him a set of braces rather than saw off the tusks.

Because this is *the* National Zoo, it receives notable specimens and gifts from foreign and domestic potentates. Buffalo Bill once sent three American elk. Smokey Bear, the children's fire-fighting hero, was brought as a cub from a New Mexico national forest; but he's a big one now. Another bear, named Teddy, was presented to the Army as a mascot by the citizens of Berlin in 1957. He did so well he was promoted to Pfc, but then did what many soldiers have wanted to do—he bit the sergeant and went AWOL. This caused great consternation in Berlin and when he was captured, the Army, though it still loved him, transferred Teddy to the Washington Zoo.

Feeding hours are: monkeys, 9:30 A.M. and 3 P.M.; lions and tigers, 1:30 P.M., except Sunday; bears and sea lions, 8:30 A.M. and 3 P.M.; birds, 2 P.M. The cafeteria at the Zoo is a good stop for your lunch.

All the above places are in the Northwest section. In the Northeast, Kenilworth Aquatic Gardens is a favored children's spot where they can watch frogs, toads, and birds at close range.

For youngsters of about six to nine years, you can visit all these with such additional stops as the Smithsonian, Capitol, Washington Monument, FBI, Archives (try the treasure hunt for your state display case), National Gallery of Art (start them young; rent a Lectour radio aid—a good game, helping them to absorb art), White House, Arlington Cemetery, Marine Memorial, and Mount Vernon.

But don't press this age group too hard either. Give them chances to play and visit these two wonderful, painlessly educational attractions:

Rock Creek Nature Center, in its new $200,000 headquarters near the Upper Rock Creek Park Stables, reached via Military Road and Ross Drive (Saturday 9:30–5:30, Sunday 1–5:30; open on other days to groups by appointment—phone RE 7-1820, ext. 2557). Here is the ideal place to start learning about outdoor America. Youngsters not only look at the glassed-in beehive and live reptiles, but play with electric-quiz games and do-it-yourself devices relating to plants, animals, nature hobbies. A miniature planetarium in a 150-seat auditorium depicts the wonders of the heavens at a level of child understanding.

The submarine USS *Drum*, which you can board at the Naval Weapons Plant, through the gate at 11th and O Streets, S.E. (8:30 to 3:30 daily, but you must first call Submarine Division, LI 7-5700, ext. 2094, two days in advance for clearance). The *Drum*, a veteran of the Pacific war now used by the Naval Reserve, is berthed permanently at the historic Anacostia River pier. The main gate, at 8th and M Streets, was built in 1805 under supervision of famed architect Benjamin Latrobe. This installation was known as the Washington Navy Yard and later as the Naval Gun Factory. All the Navy's World War II guns—including the huge 16-inchers—were made here. Now the emphasis is on missile launching devices. Along with the *Drum*, you may see other ships at Pier 5.

As children pass the ten-year mark, they become ready for exploring and educational experiences. And by the time they reach fourteen, they are apt to *know* just what they want to see. However, you might suggest, gently, to the culture-minded the Phillips Gallery, Library of Congress, National Symphony, and the Sunday afternoon opera.

Of special interest to young scientists is the IBM Space Computing Center, 615 Pennsylvania Avenue, N.W. (Monday through Friday, 9–5), the satellite tracking center, with displays and movie. And, of course, the Smithsonian. Encourage youngsters at this questioning, alert, learning age to look for answers in government agencies off the beaten tourist paths. Ranking authorities in many scientific fields—archaeology, geology, aeronautics, the space field, forestry, meteorology, nuclear power, medicine —are employed by the Federal government. Your Congressman's office or the Greater National Capital Committee will help you locate the proper bureau.

The Naval Observatory, Massachusetts Avenue and 34th Street, N.W., is a "must" in astronomy. (Monday through Friday, 9–5, tours at 2 P.M. Night tours at 8 and 9 P.M., Tuesday, Wednesday, Thursday during week of the full moon. For night tours, write six weeks in advance to Superintendent, U. S. Naval Observatory, Washington 25, D.C., or phone DE 2-2723, ext. 17. Minimum age, 12). The Observatory ranks with Greenwich in the field of time; fundamental positions and motions of heavenly bodies are charted by telescope for determining precise time, and for devising air and sea navigation tables. The night tours are exciting, amid astronomers at work; and you get to look through the 26-inch photographic telescope.

Or, for another area of interest, your family can tour several of Washington's communications media. One is the Voice of America, from which radio broadcasts are beamed all over the world.

Two of our daily newspapers offer guided public tours. The oldest, the *Evening* and *Sunday Star* (founded 1852), occupies the newest building (1959), 225 Virginia Avenue, S.E. (9:30–5, Monday through Friday). In this modern, five-story plant with 9 acres of floor space, you see all phases of production, from the city desk and the news room to the huge presses which use enough paper in one week to extend a five-foot-wide strip from Washington to Tokyo. Best time: from 10:30 A.M. to 4:30 P.M., when the presses are more likely to be running.

The Washington *Post,* now the city's largest paper, occupies a new building, too (1951, expanded 1960), at 15th and L Streets, N.W. (tours 10:30–5, Tuesday through Friday, 9–12 Saturday; phone RE 7-1234, ext. 207). The *Post* had more editorials quoted in the *Congressional Record* than any other newspaper in the country, and is the home paper of Herblock, the great editorial artist, and other talents.

The Scripps-Howard Washington *Daily News,* 1013 13th Street, N.W., will arrange tours by appointment; call DI 7-7777 and ask for the promotion department. Ernie Pyle's desk and chair, each bearing a small brass plaque, are still in use in the city room. Scripps-Howard correspondents for 19 papers work on the third floor; while they are too busy for "sightseeing" visits they would be glad to see anyone from their home towns who might have real stories for them.

These three newspapers impart the sense of Washington as a city, a distinct personality in its own right, as well as the center of national affairs.

You can visit a television station, too—WRC-TV, Washington headquarters of the National Broadcasting Company, 4001 Nebraska Avenue, N.W. (by appointment Monday through Friday, phone EM 2-4000). President Eisenhower dedicated the studios in a live color telecast in 1957. You will see the control rooms, newsroom, color studios, and learn how direct pickups are made from the White House and Capitol.

A worth-while new attraction with family appeal is the National Historical Wax Museum, 500 26th Street, N.W. (open 9 A.M.– 9 P.M., admission 75¢, children under 12, 50¢), depicting events in American history with life-size figures made of vinyl plastic, a more realistic material than wax. Beginning with the landing of Columbus, scenes dramatically re-created include Pocahontas saving John Smith; Davy Crockett at the Alamo; the discovery of gold in California; Lee and Grant meeting at Appomattox; the assassination of Lincoln, and the Yalta Conference. The Hall of Great Americans presents life-like figures of John Marshall, Oliver Wendell Holmes, Andrew Jackson, Dolly Madison, Eleanor Roosevelt, and others.

Teen-agers, or anyone, will find plenty of interest at Washington's colleges. Few realize it, but the capital is a center of higher education, drawing from the talents of government leaders and serving the government in many research projects. Following are the six area colleges:

George Washington University, 20th and G Streets, N.W., the only college where the President of the United States is within walking distance of an honorary degree. George Washington hoped there would be a university at the seat of government and left

50 shares of stock in the Potomac Canal to get things started. The stock wasn't worth much, but the idea was—and the first graduation in 1824 was attended by President Monroe, Secretary of State John Quincy Adams, Henry Clay, General Lafayette, the Supreme Court, the House and Senate. Never has a graduating class, anywhere, been so thoroughly honored. In recent times top Navy officers, including Admirals Nimitz and King, sat through a course on atomic energy taught by Dr. George Gamow, then on the GW faculty.

The campus centers around the landscaped triangular Yard, although it spills all the way to the hospital at George Washington Circle. From a visitor viewpoint, the University Library probably holds most interest with the full-length Gilbert Stuart portrait of Washington, art exhibits and the Wright Collection of Washingtoniana. Lisner Auditorium plays a large part in the city's cultural life, as the scene of recitals, opera and dramatic performances.

Margaret Truman attended GW and received her degree ('46) while her father was in the White House. She was driven daily in a large Cadillac, but insisted on stopping at least two blocks from the college and walking the rest of the way; the Secret Service men brought up the rear.

Georgetown University, 37th and O Streets, N.W., the tradition-rich first Catholic college in the United States. It was founded by the Rev. John Carroll (later the first Archbishop of Baltimore) in 1785, with 60 students, one building, and an acre of ground. Today its campus on the Georgetown bluffs above the Potomac is full of historic landmarks: Old North Tower, dating to 1795; a pair of cannon from the *Ark* and the *Dove,* which brought English settlers to Maryland in 1634 in search of religious freedom, and the grounds in front of Healy Hall, where the 69th New York Regiment, the "Fighting Irish," bivouacked en route to the First Battle of Bull Run (Manassas) in the Civil War.

Global minded Georgetown is attended by students of many nations—and different religions. Its Foreign Service School, founded by Father Edmund A. Walsh, has been a training ground for diplomats since 1919. A new feature of the Foreign Service

Georgetown University, Georgetown and the Key Bridge, from the Virginia shore of the Potomac River...

School is a multilingual conference room, similar to that at the United Nations, equipped with interpreters, booths and headpieces for simultaneous translation. You can see it on the East Campus, 35th and N Streets, N.W.

Of scientific interest: the Seismic Observatory, in a vault under the Maguire Building, and the Astronomical Observatory, where Washington's true meridian was determined in 1850 (phone FE 7-3300 to arrange evening observation).

Catholic University, 4th Street and Michigan Avenue, N.E., its 30-plus buildings spreading across 140 acres adjacent to Soldiers' Home. The university was established in 1889 with the patronage of Leo XIII as "a national center of Catholic culture." About half its buildings are owned by seminaries and religious orders, while the National Shrine of the Immaculate Conception serves as the University Church. The Shrine excepted, the most prominent building is the Romanesque-style Mullen Memorial Library, containing 800,000 volumes, an important source of Biblical material. Franklin D. Roosevelt received his honorary LL.D. at exercises in the gymnasium attached to the library.

Besides its religious schools, CU has important science and art departments. At the Arctic Institute you can see displays of plants, fossils, minerals, and Eskimo artifacts. The Nuclear Reactor, in the Mechanical-Aeronautical Engineering Building, is one of the few in colleges; it was obtained through an Atomic Energy Commission grant. The Department of Speech and Drama produces plays and playwrights (Leo Brady, Walter and Jean Kerr).

Howard University, 2400 6th Street, N.W., flanked by Soldiers' Home and Griffith Stadium. Established at the end of the Civil War with Federal appropriations, it has since trained one-fourth of all Negro lawyers, half the physicians, surgeons, dentists. Though primarily for Negro students, Howard attracts others as well; its reputation overseas has drawn students from thirty foreign nations.

The university was named for Major General Oliver Otis Howard, one of the founders and an early president. Ivy-covered Howard Hall, once his home, now provides music classrooms. But the 55-acre campus is lately bursting out with modern buildings, reflecting its marked advancement under Mordecai W. Johnson, its first Negro president.

Founders Library (8 A.M. to 10 P.M., except Sunday) contains one area devoted entirely to books, manuscripts, clippings, and artifacts relating to Negro life. Another, the recently acquired Channing Pollock Theatre Collection, consists of 5000 volumes, pictures, and scrapbooks on the American stage. The Gallery of Art, on the first floor, exhibits both modern and pre-Columbian art.

American University, Massachusetts and Nebraska Avenues, N.W., a Methodist-supported institution founded in 1893 and dedicated by President Woodrow Wilson in 1914, is only now coming into its own. Its tree-lined, 75-acre campus on the site of a Civil War fort, is booming with construction and new ideas. Among the major additions which you can visit: Radio-TV Building, completed in 1954, where students operate their own closed circuit station (WAMU); School of International Service, completed in 1958, and the Wesley Theological Seminary, which moved here from Westminster, Maryland, in 1958.

American U. also has a downtown center, but its growth is concentrated on its expansive campus off Ward Circle, adjacent to the Metropolitan Methodist Church, the national church of Methodism.

University of Maryland, at suburban College Park, Maryland, known as a football power though it started (in 1856) as a land-grant Agriculture School and the College of Agriculture is still a major component. Newness abounds across its 350-acre campus, which really *is* a college park. The academic showpiece is the $2,500,000 library, completed in 1958 (8:45 A.M.–5 P.M., Monday through Friday, 9 A.M.–1 P.M. Saturday), with a capacity of a million volumes; a browsing room of 2000 books; ten listening booths in the phonographic section, and a map room with 10,000 maps. Other elements of newness: the brick, colonial-steepled Memorial Chapel, completed in 1952, with individual chapels for three separate faiths; streamlined barns and dairies of the College of Agriculture; a supersonic wind tunnel of the College of Engineering. You will have no trouble spotting 40,000-seat Byrd Stadium, where the main course is given on football Saturdays.

There is oldness, too, at College Park, too fine to overlook: Rossborough Inn, erected in 1798 as a principal stop on the post road from Boston, New York, and Philadelphia. Later it was a social center of southern Maryland and Washington. When the Agriculture School was chartered by the Maryland legislature in 1856, the 31-room inn became its first building.

A note about school groups: Some years ago, during a short but very happy career as a Gray Line sightseeing guide, I observed that two kinds of visitors appear to enjoy Washington most: foreign-born Americans and high-school students. The foreign born no doubt because they comprehend the substance of personal liberty and come here to manifest their appreciation; the high-school students because, while they cannot feel it in the same sense, they are quite willing to learn.

This is the place to learn; the whole city is a classroom. In my time, students arrived only in throngs, but now they constitute what seems an endless multitude—they are delegations from 15,000 schools coming by bus, train, chartered plane from all over America. They total nearly a million a year, but the best part is they *want* to come, and if the senior-class tour to Washington has become standard procedure in every high school, so much the better.

Many aids and activities are available exclusively to school groups. The most important is provided by the School Service Department, Greater National Capital Committee, 1616 K Street, N.W., which answers questions and helps develop schedules to use every minute fully and well. This agency helps direct school groups to acceptable hotels and sightseeing operators offering special rates.

A number of doors will open to a school group, providing you plan and write ahead. For example:

Any member of Congress, unless he has something really pressing on the floor or in committee, will meet with his young constituents in his office.

The Department of State conducts current events forums, or "briefings," on U.S. foreign policy for groups up to 200, any weekday except Tuesday morning. These include a talk by a career officer and a question-and-answer period.

The National Education Association invites teachers and principals to visit its headquarters and to bring along any students planning a teaching career. (See Chapter V.)

The National Symphony Orchestra holds a five-week Music for Young America series April and May. (See Chapter XI.) And what better way to spend an evening?

If I had a young friend of serious bent coming here I would suggest he prepare himself with independent reading of a broad nature into the ways of Washington and our government. Favorites of mine are *White House Profile* by Bess Furman; *Thank You, Mr. President* by Merriman Smith, and *Profiles in Courage* by John F. Kennedy, as well as those quoted in the last chapter of this book. For the Civil War period: *Reveille in Washington* by Margaret Leech, and Carl Sandburg's one volume biography of

Abraham Lincoln. I would also suggest he expose himself to Mark Twain's *The Gilded Age*.

And while on the subject of school tours, Colonial Williamsburg, 150 miles from Washington in neighboring Virginia, conducts a comprehensive program for more than 1000 groups a year coming from as far as Alaska. This program has become so popular that in 1956 it was expanded from a single general tour to four tours, each related to the age, grade level (starting with the fourth), and curriculum of the class.

Now, at Williamsburg, trained escorts are provided to interpret the various tours, and a wing at Williamsburg Lodge is normally assigned to overnight school groups. The best time to visit—and this holds true of Washington as well—is during the fall and winter months; at least during these periods you have the advantages of reduced rates and freedom from congestion. Spring is the prettiest season, but also the most crowded.

As an educational institution at heart, Colonial Williamsburg considers part of its mission the preparation of pre-visit materials for classroom use. Books, pamphlets, films, and film strips are sent to a school as "briefing" material, and further follow-up activities are generally encouraged. For information, write: Tour Office, P.O. Box 627, Colonial Williamsburg, Williamsburg, Virginia.

XX *Lincoln's Washington*

Like a thief in the night, or so his opposition charged, Abraham Lincoln arrived in Washington on February 23, 1861, to become the sixteenth President of the United States.

At first he had refused to end his long tour from Springfield, Illinois, by entering the capital incognito. But in Philadelphia his friends insisted he would endanger his life by going through hostile, Southern-sympathizing Baltimore unless he did so in secrecy. Telegraph wires were cut to prevent information leaks and the few people aware of Lincoln's whereabouts were fitful until they received the code message, "Plums delivered, nuts safely." They knew then he had reached the B & O Station at New Jersey Avenue and C Street, N.W. (at the corner of the Capitol grounds), and was established at the old Willard Hotel on 14th Street.

This was not Lincoln's first experience in Washington. He had been here earlier as a rather inconspicuous single-term Congressman elected in 1846. But almost from the day of his arrival as President-elect the sense and spirit of Lincoln have pervaded the national capital in a timeless, ineradicable way. The landmarks associated with his life speak more fully with the passing years. They're everywhere—the White House, the Capitol, Pennsylvania Avenue, and other places less known. Actually, the time of Lincoln and the Civil War are not so long ago. Scarcely a century.

The city was still unattractive and incomplete. Streets were unpaved, swampy during rainy weather and dusty when it was dry. Most private buildings gave the impression of crudeness and insignificance. Even then gardens and long rows of trees added a certain pleasant aspect and Washington looked like a large rural village. Its population was 75,000.

In less than two weeks after his arrival, on March 4, Lincoln rode to his inaugural with President James Buchanan. The Civil War was clearly imminent and Washington was almost overrun by Southern sympathizers. In this climate, the inaugural pro-

Keen on witnessing combat at close range, President Lincoln would unwittingly expose himself to danger at Fort Stevens...

cession drove swiftly down Pennsylvania Avenue nearly hidden by a military escort, while troops stationed on housetops with pointed rifles watched the thronged sidewalks. At the east front of the Capitol, before a crowd of 30,000, a cordon of soldiers was drawn tight around the inaugural platform. Cadaverous, 83-year-old Supreme Court Chief Justice Roger B. Taney delivered the Presidential oath. The spreading structure of the Capitol formed a grotesque background, with gaunt derricks and steel braces rising upward to the unfinished dome. The statue of Freedom, waiting to be hoisted atop the dome, stood on the lawn.

The war began the following month. To the Union, Washington was a symbol that must be held at all costs. To the Confederates it was the supreme prize—and for the next four years they threatened it almost continually. The city was filled with troops. At one point some slept in the East Room of the White House. On Capitol Hill, drums beat, feet tramped, and guns clanked in marble halls. Churches and mansions, converted into hospitals, were filled with the wounded and dying. Before long there were

5000 prostitutes (and 450 registered houses), plus many more in Georgetown and Alexandria.

In 1861, President Lincoln took up summer residence at Soldiers' Home. Ten years earlier the government had purchased the gray stucco summer place of banker George Washington Riggs and 500 wooded acres as a residence for retired soldiers. Lincoln renamed the main building, in which he stayed, Anderson Cottage in honor of Captain Robert Anderson, the commander of Fort Sumter when it was fired on. It is still known by this name. You can reach this Lincoln landmark, the first summer White House (later used by Presidents Hayes and Arthur) through the Park Road entrance to Soldiers' Home.

In the restful seclusion of Anderson Cottage, Lincoln arrived at many grave decisions about the war, and in 1862 prepared a draft of the Emancipation Proclamation. He would normally spend the day at the White House, then ride here, three miles beyond the city limits. Walt Whitman, who observed him en route with a cavalry escort at Vermont Avenue near L Street, wrote that, "Mr. Lincoln on the saddle generally rides a good-sized, easy-going gray horse, is dressed in plain black, somewhat rusty and dusty, wears a black stiff hat, and looks about as ordinary in attire as the commonest man." Lincoln, in fact, embarrassed by the clatter and rattle of sabers, dismissed the cavalry, preferring to ride unattended. The Army then assigned an infantry escort of the Bucktail Brigade, which he found easier to live with; when Mrs. Lincoln was away he would invite the captain to share his quarters.

Earthworks were erected around the Capital until a 34-mile interlocking circuit was completed in 1863. It consisted of 68 inclosed forts and batteries with 800 cannon and 100 mortar, with 20 miles of rifle trenches between the main works. "The city, with its girdle of encampments, presents a superb scene," exulted a balloonist after a reconnaissance under the auspices of the Smithsonian Institution. Although Washington was within grasp several times, the strength of the field fortifications repelled invasion.

The only direct attack on Washington occurred in 1864, when General Jubal Early struck suddenly from the north before undermanned Fort Stevens, off 13th Street near Silver Spring. At the time there were barely 10,000 troops in Washington, where

36,000 were needed, but all available aid had been rushed to General Grant in a determined effort to capture Richmond. On July 12, Lincoln came to witness the Fort Stevens engagement. He was constitutionally fearless, and on this occasion drew to his full height at the parapet to survey the enemy lines. "Get down, you fool!" shouted a young, angry, and terrified lieutenant colonel of the 20th Massachusetts Volunteers by the name of Oliver Wendell Holmes. The reply, Lincolnesque and calmly stated, was, "I am glad you know how to talk to a civilian."

The Union defenders were as much concerned with the President's safety as with fighting the Confederates. "Mr. President," General Horatio Wright finally insisted, "I know you are commander of the Army of the United States, but I am in command here and as you are not safe where you are standing I order you to come down." Lincoln smiled and acquiesced, although he persisted in standing up from time to time. This was the only battle in American history where a President of the United States was present and exposed to fire.

Jubal Early's Confederate troops were driven back but not until 72 Union soldiers were killed and 207 wounded. On Fort Drive today you can see the earthworks and restored palisades of Fort Stevens, now part of National Capital Parks. A bronze plaque marks the very spot where Lincoln stood at the parapet. Forty of the Union dead, mostly from New York and Massachusetts, are buried in Battleground Cemetery, a half mile northeast of the fort; this is our smallest national cemetery.

Abraham Lincoln was a prayerful man. His devotion to God enabled him to endure and prosecute the war on its principles, with compassion for his enemy. He and his family regularly attended New York Avenue Presbyterian Church, now called the "Lincoln Church," on the triangular plot at the corners of New York Avenue, H and 13th Streets, N.W. Mr. Lincoln liked to walk alone the two blocks from the White House to attend the midweek prayers, but found he was less likely to cause disruption by sitting unnoticed in the minister's study with the door partly open to the adjoining lecture room. Both he and the minister, Dr. Phineas Gurley, kept his attendance a secret; but one snowy evening two boys of the church discovered the mysterious tall stranger's identity by following his large footprints to the White House.

The church was organized in 1803 and the first building on this site erected in 1820. John Quincy Adams was the first President to join, but Andrew Jackson, William Henry Harrison, Millard Fillmore, Franklin Pierce, James Buchanan, Andrew Johnson, Benjamin Harrison—and, of course, Mr. Lincoln—were to follow. The present building, erected in 1951, follows the classic, steepled lines of its predecessor. The Lincoln Pew, seventh from the front on the right, is marked by a silver plate. New pews have been so designed that Lincoln's could be joined and installed in exactly the same position it occupied in his time. The Lincoln Parlor enshrines the first draft of the Emancipation Proclamation in Lincoln's own handwriting, which he discussed with his friend, Pastor Gurley. Of contemporary interest: Dr. Peter Marshall, author of *Mr. Jones, Meet the Master,* was a pastor here from 1937 until his death in 1949.

Lincoln, who had arrived in Washington almost at the outbreak of the Civil War, died as it ended. With Lee's surrender to Grant at Appomattox Court House, Virginia, on April 9, 1865, the fighting and dying on the battlefield yielded to the future of living. But Lincoln had a scant five days to live, until the morning of April 15.

His last day was full. In the morning of April 14, 1865—it was Good Friday—he had breakfast with his son Robert, a captain on Grant's staff; kept several appointments, and met with his Cabinet. During the afternoon he and his family took a long carriage ride to the Washington Navy Yard, on the Anacostia River. It was one of his favorite haunts; as an old river man and inventor, he felt at home around the Yard and followed developments in ordnance closely. After dinner, he visited the War Department in the Winder Building, at 17th and F Streets, a block from the White House. (This building is still standing and in use by the Government.)

Later, President and Mrs. Lincoln departed for the theater. The National was his favorite playhouse; he had been to that theater at least a hundred times. But tonight the Lincolns were attending Tom Taylor's comedy *Our American Cousin* starring Laura Keene, at Ford's Theatre, 511 10th Street, N.W. It was among the country's finest theaters, seating nearly 1700, and was less than two years old. Originally, the Lincolns had planned to

attend the play with General and Mrs. Grant, but during the afternoon the Grants sent word they could not go, and in their place
the President invited two young friends, Miss Clara Harris, a
New York Senator's daughter, and her fiancé Major Henry Rathbone.

When the Presidential party entered the threater, the orchestra
interrupted the performance to play "Hail to the Chief." The
audience rose to cheer, the President smiled and bowed in appreciation. The party occupied a large double box above the
left of the stage, the President sitting in a black walnut rocking
chair placed there specially for him, with Mrs. Lincoln on his
right and the young couple on a sofa.

Meanwhile, John Wilkes Booth, the demented actor, and his
eerie band craved the center of attention. Booth had been staying
at the National Hotel, four blocks away, but at 10:15 P.M. he was
standing outside Lincoln's box. As the third act was nearing its cur-
tain, he rushed in and at close range fired a single-shot derringer
at the President's head.

Mr. Lincoln slumped in his chair, unconscious. Major Rathbone
clutched at Booth, but the killer slashed him with a dagger
and leaped over the rail to the stage. "Sic semper tyrannis!" (Thus
always to tyrants), Booth shouted before dashing through the
wings and out the stage door to his horse in the alley and a flight
down Pennsylvania and Virginia Avenues into Maryland.

Mrs. Lincoln's screams of terror turned Ford's into a scene of
pandemonium and confusion. Three doctors in the audience entered the box and examined the President. The bullet had entered
above the left ear and was lodged behind the right eye. He could
not ride over the cobblestone route to the Executive Mansion,
they agreed, but must be carried gently to the comfort of the nearest bedroom. The President was lifted down the stairway into 10th
Street. Across the street from the theater a man with a lighted
candle beckoned from a doorway. It was 516 10th Street, the red-
brick rooming house run by a Swedish tailor, one William Petersen, and here Abraham Lincoln came to die. He was laid on the
bed of a roomer named Willie Clark. Robert Lincoln and the
Cabinet were sent for. During the long vigil Mrs. Lincoln moaned
and sobbed and fell in a faint so prolonged the physicians ordered
she not be allowed in the room. At 7:22 A.M. the next morning,

Saturday, Lincoln breathed his last. Secretary of State Stanton reportedly approached the bed and said, "Now he belongs to the ages."

Tenth Street, between E and F, the scene of Lincoln's last hours, is a nondescript, if not shabby, little street today, shared by history and cut-rate appliance shops. The Lincoln Museum, administered by the National Park Service, in the old Ford Theatre building (9–9 daily; 12:30–9 Sunday), has little left of the original interior; there is no semblance of stage, balconies, or seats, although a movement is underway to restore the theater, at least partially. It does contain a great collection of Lincolniana, assembled largely by a single private citizen, the late Osborn H. Oldroyd. He spent 66 years, starting in 1860, in acquiring 3000 objects that trace the life of Lincoln from birth to death—furniture, photographs, his father's Bible, letters and documents, books from his law library, Currier & Ives lithographs, exhibits of the Lincoln-Douglas debates and the Presidential campaign, the war years and the assassination.)

The three-story, green-shuttered Petersen House, officially called the House Where Lincoln Died (9–5:30 daily, Sunday 12:30–5:30) has recently been restored by the National Park Service. In the front parlor, the horsehair sofa, brought from the Lincoln home in Springfield, is in the same location as the one occupied by Mrs. Lincoln during the death vigil. The one original item in the room where Lincoln died is the pillow on which his head rested; the spool-type walnut four-poster, chairs, floral-striped wallpaper and the other items are accurate reproductions.

The body of the assassinated President was carried to the White House and death masks were made (now on display at the Lincoln Museum). First he lay in a new black suit in the State Guest Room; on Tuesday he was moved to the East Room, where thousands came to pay their tribute. At services here the next morning, Dr. Phineas Gurley said, "His noblest virtue, his grandest principle, the secret alike of his strength, his patience and his success was his abiding confidence in God and in the final triumph of truth and righteousness through Him and for His sake." Then, under cloudless blue skies, Lincoln's coffin headed a mournful procession of 30,000 down Pennsylvania Avenue to the Capitol, where he became the first to lie in state in the Rotunda. On Friday,

April 21, one week after his assassination, he left Washington for burial in Springfield, accompanied by the smaller coffin of his son Willie, who had died three years earlier and until then was buried in Oak Hill Cemetery, Georgetown.

The Civil War finale was enacted in Washington in a two-day burst of glory the following month. It was the Grand Review, the greatest pageant of the war, the greatest parade in our country's history. Here they marched, 140,000 strong, bearing the banners of 2000 battlefields. The first day came the Army of the Potomac, 60 abreast from curb to curb, 80,000 troops, saber-clashing cavalry, artillery, infantry, marching through Pennsylvania Avenue's dusty clouds from early morning to night. The crowds roared lovingly, wept, threw flowers. This was Washington's own army; it had protected and saved the capital with fortifications and with the sacrificing of thousands at Manassas, Antietam, Gettysburg. General George G. Meade rode at their head. Phil Sheridan was missing; he had been rushed off to the Mexican border. Golden-haired 25-year-old George Armstrong Custer was hatless after a near-catastrophe when his horse was frightened by a floral wreath tossed at the corner of 15th Street.

The next day came another mighty host, Sherman's army, fresh from its conquest of half a continent, bearing the battle flags of Shiloh, Vicksburg, Atlanta, Chickamauga, Carolinas. These troops were less formal than the Army of the Potomac, these Western men in broad-brimmed hats instead of regulation caps, wearing just enough blue uniform to show they were Union soldiers. Tall, sinewy Sherman rode at their head, with one-armed Oliver Howard and John A. Logan, the greatest volunteer general, at his sides. As he topped the rise of the Treasury Department, turning the corner of 15th Street, Sherman looked back. He had been in the reviewing stand at the White House the previous day and wondered whether his troops would suffer in comparison with the Army of the Potomac. He saw them taking long swinging, cadence-free steps; they strode rather than marched. But they were a proud, bold Army. Today the towering equestrian statue of Sherman (facing weathered Alexander Hamilton at the Treasury's classic south entrance) stands near the place where he turned in his saddle to glance backward.

In the crowded reviewing stand were Andrew Johnson, heavy-jowled and red-faced, the new President; stoop-shouldered, bearded U. S. Grant; generals, Congressmen, Supreme Court Justices. Only one man was missing—Abraham Lincoln. Yet, even in absence, his spirit was strongly felt in Washington the two days of the Grand Review, as it probably will be forever.

XXI *Tomorrow's Capital*

The new Washington is an exciting city of changing dimensions. Developments now underway are so extensive that by the mid-60s our national capital will be vastly different from the late '50s.

But will the city be better as well as bigger and newer? Probably so, in most respects. Judge for yourself. Have a look at the changes in process; in a sense it's like watching the stage settings of history as they change. Take an interest in the shape of things. Too few people do, and yet everyone agrees that Washington should symbolize free America at its finest.

Within the city proper, the most dramatic phase of the emerging new Washington revolves around destruction and replacement of the old, blighted slums—worse than in most cities. The place to see this is in the Southwest area. Here the Redevelopment Land Agency, a Federal bureau, has been directing the greatest urban renewal project ever undertaken.

The area of the "New Town in the City" covers 556 acres, which the Land Agency has been purchasing parcel by parcel for a total expenditure of $75,000,000. The next step, block-by-block demolition, may still be under way during your visit. At times, parts of the Southwest have resembled the aftermath of an air raid. A total of 5000 structures are being demolished and 4500 families relocated.

As you travel through the Southwest, you'll see new apartments, from low cost to luxury; new-type row houses or "maisonettes" in the landscaped "super blocks"; new Federal office buildings, new commercial offices and tourist landmarks—in various stages of development. It is all scheduled for completion in late 1964 or 1965, though much of it will be ready in 1961. Following is a suggested route for you to follow:

Starting from the Health, Education and Welfare (HEW) Building at 4th Street and Independence Avenue, S.W., drive south on 4th Street. Federal Office Building No. 6 is due for completion in mid-1961. Take note of the Capitol Park Towers, at H Street, a 400-unit showplace apartment with private gardens, tree-lined walks, reflecting pool and shopping facilities, surrounded by town houses. The Town Center, a six-block square shopping and social development, starting at I Street (due for completion in 1962) is one of several Southwest projects of William Zeckendorf's Webb & Knapp Corporation. On N Street, across Town Center, near Fort McNair and the National War College, are a group of historically important houses built before 1800 as a suburban development in which Lawrence Washington, George Washington's brother, was a partner. The most prominent element is Wheat Row, four handsome three-story row buildings sometimes called Washington's first apartment house. Others are the Law House, Washington-Lewis House, Barney House.

Turn right to Maine Avenue and drive along the mile-long waterfront, much loved even in its late run-down days for its seafood restaurants and fishing boats along the wharves. The new waterfront, one of the last phases of Southwest redevelopment (1964 or '65), will have sailing marinas, an elevated shoreline drive, restaurants, possibly a planetarium. Perhaps the best part is the plan for sewage treatment so it will no longer be dumped into the Washington Channel.

At 10th Street, you will reach the Mall, a broad, super-boulevard sweeping north to Independence Avenue and the Smithsonian Institution. L'Enfant Plaza, a $50,000,000 Webb & Knapp project off the Mall, will include a World Communications Center, a 1000-room hotel, restaurants, a theater, and office buildings. Our Plaza will exceed in size, if not in height, New York's Rockefeller Plaza, and it should be at least as beautiful.

Newness will be evident elsewhere in the city; many of the changes (Capitol, New State Department, Mall, Executive Office Building) are described in other chapters. Foggy Bottom, the once marshy land between New State and the Potomac, is the site of Columbia Plaza, a rising $20,000,000 development of plush apartments and row houses. Nearby, the $60,000,000 National Cultural Center, designed by Edward Stone, with halls for opera, symphony, and drama, will be erected on the banks of the Potomac (facing Theodore Roosevelt Island), and a memorial to Franklin D. Roosevelt will be placed in West Potomac Park. Both

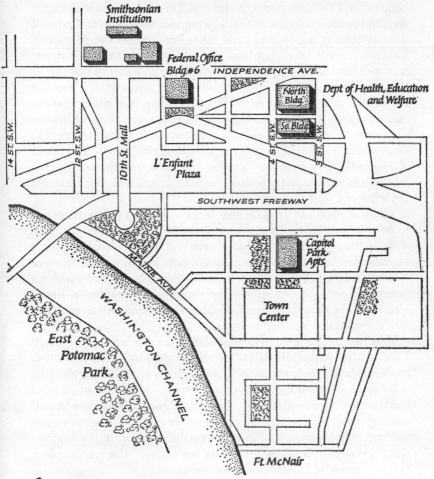

Smithsonian Institution

Federal Office Bldg. #6

INDEPENDENCE AVE.

North Bldg.

Dept of Health, Education and Welfare

So. Bldg.

14 ST. S.W.

12 ST. S.W.

10th St. Mall

4 ST. S.W.

3 ST. S.W.

L'Enfant Plaza

SOUTHWEST FREEWAY

Capitol Park Apts.

MAINE AVE.

WASHINGTON CHANNEL

Town Center

East Potomac Park

Ft. McNair

The Southwest Redevelopment Area

of these, being financed by public contributions, are likely to be finished in the middle to late '60s.

You will travel over new roads and bridges, in the Southwest and throughout the Washington area. The Southwest Freeway is due to be the first completed link (spring 1962) of the new Inner

Loop around the downtown periphery. The Circumferential High-way, to broaden the picture, will swing in a 58-mile circle around the city so that a trip that now takes one hour—from Maryland to Virginia—will take about 20 minutes in 1962. Before long we may also have a $500,000,000 subway or suburban rail system.

Metropolitan growth is incredible. Washington, which was not even listed among major cities fifty years ago, now ranks seventh in size among metropolitan areas, with a population of nearly 2,000,000. Within thirty years the metropolitan population will double and some experts predict we will really be part of a super "Chesapeake and Potomac" city of 9,500,000, encompassing Baltimore, and ranking only behind New York, Los Angeles, Chicago, Philadelphia, and Detroit.

These figures are frightening to anyone who takes time out to think about them. Can the area absorb so many people in so short a time? Can Washington remain a city of beauty and a symbol of national dignity and orderliness in the face of tremendous pressures to build? Growth is one thing, but growth without control or plan, or regard for the planners, is another—a lesson which should have been learned from the consequences of L'Enfant's dismissal.

This recalls the sequence that started at the end of the Civil War and led to modern Washington developing as the beautiful, modern place we know today. After the war, Washington had once again become a sleepy country town. Flocks of geese and herds of swine, cows, horses, sheep, and goats found forage and running room in the streets. An English visitor thought he was visiting a cardboard city. "It is impossible to remove the impression," he wrote, "that, when Congress is over, the whole place is taken down and packed till wanted again."

Many members of Congress were indifferent and willing to move the capital to St. Louis, which pledged to spend millions, as cities now bid on a baseball franchise. When Western cities supported the St. Louis offer, Eastern cities responded by agreeing that a new capital site would indeed be a good idea.

At this dangerous juncture, Alexander R. Shepherd, the leading plumber in town and a friend of President Ulysses S. Grant, appeared on the scene. As vice-president and executive officer of the Board of Public Works from 1871 until he became Governor of the District in 1873, "Boss" Shepherd pushed through an improvement program which brought the city 180 miles of paved streets and more than 200 miles of sidewalk, 3000 gas lamps, schools, churches, attractive homes instead of the old barrack-like wooden huts, the planting of 25,000 shade trees, and filled up the cursed Tiber Canal. In ten years Shepherd transformed the dusty, muddy city into freshness and charm.

It was not this simple, of course. Shepherd had more power than L'Enfant and at least as many enemies. He was an imperious man, who frightened and antagonized the property owners. He overspent his appropriations, provoking court suits and a Congressional investigation. In 1876, after he had placed the District heavily in debt, he decided to follow the course of wisdom by departing for Mexico. Partly as a result of his mistakes, Congress deprived the District of any semblance of self-government. But Shepherd left a heritage in many ways as great as that of the original city planners.

At the turn of the century came the McMillan Commission, with its plan for redefining the Mall and for public buildings surrounded by open spaces. The McMillan Commission did something else; it recognized the role of the artist in the design of the city. The Fine Arts Commission was established in 1910 to evaluate private buildings and parks concerning height, appearance, color, and materials; later a planning agency, presently called the National Capital Planning Commission, was created. These two commissions operate on low budgets from Congress and are much harassed, yet they have contributed much to preserving the precious qualities of the city.

For example, when it was proposed to rezone 16th Street from Lafayette Square to Scott Circle and extend the height limitation from 90 feet to 110 feet, the Fine Arts Commission noted that "Inasmuch as it is the principal approach to the White House, any lowering of the architectural standards of the treatment of this or any other section of 16th Street would only serve to cheapen and commercialize one of the most important streets in Washington." Similarly, in dealing with Georgetown, the Commission declared that "To allow commercial interests to invade historic Georgetown would be deplorable. The residents of these historic houses with their adjoining gardens have made substantial investments in order to preserve the charm and distinguished character of this section. It represents an important movement in the preservation of our national heritage."

There are no such controls, however, in the suburbs, even where they are only a bridge's length away and clearly seen from Washington. As you tour the outlying areas, you will find some very attractive communities but also a host of mass-production settlements which do not promise much for tomorrow's landscape.

There is another problem Washington, or rather the nation, must solve, if the capital is to be a proud representative of life in a democracy. The city suffers a freakish form of government. At first, in 1802, it was governed by a mayor, appointed by the President, and an elected 12-man city council. Later it was made a territory, with an appointed governor and an elected assembly. But since 1878, when the Shepherd era ended, it has been neither city nor state, but a disenfranchised District, with less autonomy than either Puerto Rico or the Virgin Islands. The city administration today is headed by three commissioners, of limited power, appointed by the President, but Congress is the city council. The House and Senate District Committees are composed almost entirely of freshmen members who switch to some other committee as soon as they build enough seniority. Once Senator Wayne Morse was relegated to the District Committee as "punishment" for failing to follow his party line; it was the worst possible form of exile, but Senator Morse surprised both Congress and the city by showing substantial interest in Washington problems.

Every American should show some interest in the national capital. It is right to enjoy and appreciate the city as it is now, but the more people express concern for its orderly development the better and more attractive it will be in its greatest period of expansion.

XXII *Six Suggested Tours from Washington*

TOUR 1: George Washington's Home Ground— A One-Day Tour
(60 Miles)

Come across to the Virginia side of the Potomac River and head for the countryside. It may be slowly vanishing, but it still holds lovely woodlands and gardens, shrines of heroes and history from the Jamestown colony to Woodrow Wilson. This is also the home country of Smithfield ham, fried chicken, and old-fashioned Southern hospitality.

Start with George Washington's domain, in northern Virginia, just south of the capital. Mount Vernon, where he lived and died, is the high point, of course, but don't limit your sights. Visit the places where he met with his friends and family, where he worshiped, marketed, belonged to a Masonic lodge and volunteer fire company. All these are within a pleasant hour's drive of the District. Later, if you have more time, you can follow the Washington trail farther south to his birthplace, the farm where he supposedly threw a coin across the Rappahannock and the home he built for his mother (see Tour 2).

From Washington, cross the 14th Street Bridge and follow the Mount Vernon Memorial Highway to Alexandria. You can spend at least an hour to advantage in touring this historic town, founded in 1749 and once a flourishing seaport, where the earliest streets bear such names as King, Queen, Prince, Princess, Duke, and Royal. The three principal points to see are Christ Church, Carlyle House and the National Masonic Memorial, all associated with George Washington. A number of fine old houses, of Colonial and early Federal architecture, are open to the public during Historic Garden Week in April and on special tour days in spring

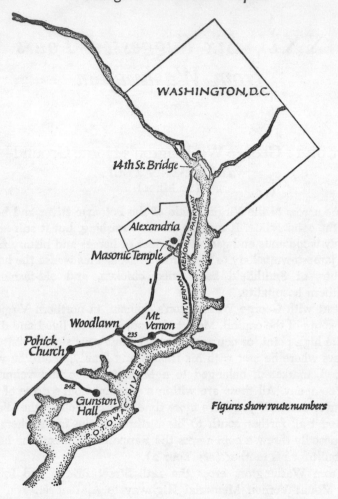

WASHINGTON, D.C.

14th St. Bridge —

Alexandria

Masonic Temple

MT. VERNON MEMORIAL PARKWAY

Woodlawn

Mt. Vernon

235

Pohick
Church

242

Gunston
Hall

POTOMAC RIVER

Figures show route numbers

and fall. But any day is suitable for a drive or stroll through the
Old Town section. Here is a suggested route:

Start on Washington Street (which Washington surveyed as a
young man) at the intersection with Oronoco Street. Robert E.
Lee lived at 607 Oronoco and prepared for West Point at the
Hallowell School next door at 609 Oronoco. The white frame build-
ing across the street, 429 N. Washington, is the home of John L.
Lewis.

Visit Christ Church, Washington and Cameron Streets (9–5 daily), where Washington was a vestryman (pew number 60) and Lee a later pewholder (number 46). The pulpit, canopy, and communion table were in this handsome church in Washington's time.

Turn left on Wolfe Street into Old Town, the section near the river, where you will see entire blocks of restored Colonial and Federal homes and their brick-walled gardens. The Presbyterian Meeting House, at South Fairfax Street (9–5 Monday through Friday, Saturday to noon), was built in 1774 and attended by many of Washington's friends. The Unknown Soldier of the Revolutionary War lies in the churchyard. The parish home, in the rear on Royal Street, is an early flounder-type house.

North just off Fairfax Street are Gentry Row, composed of stately town houses in the 200 block of Prince Street, and Captains Row, the cobblestoned 100 block of Prince Street. Visit the old Apothecary Shop, 107 S. Fairfax Street, (10–5, free) where Washington, "Light Horse Harry" Lee and others had their prescriptions filled, and Ramsey House, at the corner of King Street, the rebuilt house of Alexandria's first and only lord mayor, now the City Clerk's office. Here you are two blocks from the old port; if it's near lunch or dinner hour, stop in at the Seaport Inn (see Chapter XIV).

Carlyle House, 121 N. Fairfax Street (10–6 daily, 30¢, children 20¢) was the city's first great mansion. In 1755, General Braddock met with the five royal governors to plot the French and Indian campaign (Washington as an aide was present, too), and then marched from here to his death near Pittsburgh. George and Martha Washington attended social gatherings in the Blue Room, now restored and furnished.

Turn left on Cameron Street, back toward Washington Street. Stop at Gadsby's Tavern, at the corner of Royal (10–5 daily, 25¢, children free), a famous eighteenth-century inn and drinking place. It was Washington's headquarters when he was a colonel of the Virginia Militia and he attended his last birthday celebration here before his death. That year, 1799, he reviewed the Alexandria troops from the steps, told them, "Fall out, men, and go home, the wars are over." Gadsby's still serves as a meeting place for Alexandria groups and late each summer the up and coming Little Theater performs eighteenth-century plays in the coach yard. Soon the Theater will be in its own home several blocks away.

Note the house at 611 Cameron Street, the home of "Light Horse Harry" Lee and his family, including son Robert. From here you may wish to drive to the Friendship Fire Company, 107 S. Alfred Street (9–4:30 daily except Sunday) to see the little fire engine George Washington brought from Philadelphia for his own company.

The National Masonic Memorial, at the west end of King Street, a 333-foot temple of questionable architectural merit (modeled after an ancient Egyptian lighthouse, in case you wonder), contains a replica room with original furnishings of Masonic Lodge No. 22, over which George Washington presided as master. Among the notable items in the Memorial (9–5, free) are the trowel which he used in laying the cornerstone of the Capitol; his bedroom clock that was stopped at the moment of his death, and a bronze statue, dedicated by President Truman, a Mason, on Washington's Birthday, 1950.

Fifteen miles south of Washington you will reach Mount Vernon. The Memorial Highway is the perfect approach, preserving within its narrow right of way undisturbed woods and marshes. The loveliest time of year are the months of April and May, when trees and shrubs—crabapple, forsythia, dogwood, redbud, wild azalea—burst into bloom. General Washington knew and loved this entire terrain. He owned most of the land beyond Little Hunting Creek, at the southern boundary of Alexandria, and within his vast estate of 8000 acres laid out all the roads, divided plantation tracts, and directed improvements.

Plan at least an hour at Mount Vernon (9–5, March 1–October 1, 9–4, October 1–March 1, 75¢). If you enjoy a high-class luncheon, stop en route at Collingwood; for a less expensive luncheon the Little Hatchet Tavern, adjoining the estate, will do nicely. Get set for crowds. Mount Vernon is thoroughly loved and there is hardly a day in the year when you can commune privately with the spirit of George and Martha Washington. If there is such a day it comes in winter—which is not too bad a season, either. Avoid weekends, if possible, and try to get here early, before the crowds.

George Washington once wrote an Englishman that, "No estate in United America is more pleasantly situated than this." But it was he who made it so. The original portion of the building dates from 1742. It was modest in size, a story and one-half high. Washington inherited the property from his older brother, Lawrence, ten years later. At first he was away fighting the French and Indians but after marrying the widow Martha Custis in 1759 he started expansion of the house. "The whole plantation, the garden, and the rest prove well that a man born with a natural taste may guess a beauty without ever having seen its model," a European guest of Washington's later described Mount Vernon. "The General has never left America; but when one sees his house and his home and his garden it seems as if he had copied the best samples of the grand old homesteads of England." In evidence, the piazza, extending the length of the building, was his concept, although the design of its columns are of English origin.

By all means, make the most of the piazza vantage above the river. While you walk through the mansion you will be part of an endless single file observing, or rather glimpsing, all too briefly. You will see the room in which Washington died, the dining room, parlor, library, his clothing, wine bottles, the key to the Bastille presented him by Lafayette, and intimate reminders of his home life with Martha Washington. On the piazza, however, you can enjoy the estate in leisure. And as you look over the outbuildings— the stables, kitchen, coach house—walking down to the tomb of George and Martha Washington, appreciate the outdoors of Mount Vernon. Originally there were five farms on the estate and George Washington, between his wars and the Presidency, was among the most progressive farmers of his day. He practiced crop rotation and once was awarded a silver cup for raising a prize donkey.

Washington was an enthusiast of trees and gardens. His diary contains frequent references to the grading of the central lawn area and the transplanting of young trees and shrubs from the adjacent woods to the "Shrubberies" and "Wildernesses" which border the broad expanse of lawn on each side.

The flower garden and kitchen garden symmetrically placed on each side of the bowling green follow his design, and the boxwood hedges have been growing since his day. The kitchen garden has been restored, with vegetables, fruits, and herbs based on Washington's writings and the weekly reports of the gardener. For a worth-while souvenir, stop at the museum to purchase seeds, slips, or a boxwood plant; they're inexpensive, pleasant reminders of Mount Vernon.

The mansion and estate have been restored and are maintained by the Mount Vernon Ladies Association, an organization founded by Miss Ann Pamela Cunningham of South Carolina, who noted while she rode by on a river steamer in 1853 that the place was going to seed. She first appealed to Congress to buy it, but without success. The money to purchase Mount Vernon from the Washington heirs was raised by public contributions and it was acquired in 1858.

On leaving Mount Vernon, follow Route 235 for three miles to Woodlawn Plantation, the historic mansion of Nellie Custis, Martha Washington's granddaughter, and her husband, Major Lawrence Lewis, George Washington's nephew (10–5 in summer, 10–4:30 in winter, 75¢, children 25¢). The site for the mansion was selected by General Washington; he set aside 2000 acres of his estate as a wedding gift to the young couple, who were married February 22, 1799. Nellie and her brother, George Washington Parke Custis, both were raised at Mount Vernon as the President's adopted children. Major and Mrs. Lewis lived at Mount Vernon until Martha Washington's death in 1802, then moved to their new home.

Woodlawn was designed at Washington's request by Dr. William Thornton, the first architect of the Capitol. The view from the portico of the rose-red Georgian mansion toward the river and Mount Vernon is still one of the area's best, despite the commercial growth along Route 1, directly below. In the middle distance you can see George Washington's stone grist mill.

Although old as a house, Woodlawn is new as a point of interest. For many years it was out of Washington family ownership and in 1948 was vacant and almost barren inside. Since 1951 it has been administered by the National Trust for Historic Preservation and beautifully furnished with original and period items. The gardens have been restored by the Garden Club of Virginia, with traditional serpentine roads, paths, blooming flower beds, and rose parterres.

George Washington attended church most frequently at Pohick Church, at least before the Revolution. He was a vestryman twenty years, when the church was in its early frame building, now gone, and in the "new" brick building on Route 1, six miles below Mount Vernon (9–5 daily). He and his friend and neighbor George Mason of Gunston Hall, the author of the Bill of Rights, disagreed on locating the site; to resolve it, Washington, the trained surveyor, spot-checked the parish, drew a map showing roads, houses and distances, and claimed this point was the nearest to most members. Then he helped by drawing an elevation plan for the builders. He owned two pews (28, 29), as did George Mason (3, 4).

The church interior was shattered during the Civil War, when it was used as a cavalry stable. But today the restoration of the attractive interior is almost complete. Although Pohick is within metropolitan Washington, it is still a country church at heart. Drive down for the Country Fair one Saturday in early autumn, when the parish ladies sell preserves, embroidery, and apple butter, serve Brunswick stew and barbecued chicken, and the men operate an old-fashioned turkey shoot.

Often on Sundays the Washingtons would meet at Pohick Church with George Mason and would return to dinner at one or the other's house. The principal "highway," however, was the Potomac, and on other occasions Washington would come downriver to visit Mason in a barge rowed by six men in livery.

To reach Gunston Hall now, turn off Route 1 to Route 242, near Occoquan. This is one of Virginia's great houses (9:30–5 daily, 75¢, children 25¢) and a worthy companion piece to Mount Vernon. It was built for Mason by William Buckland, a remarkable, self-taught craftsman. From the outside, the brick Georgian house is graceful but not overwhelming. But the interior, with its richly decorated Chinese Chippendale dining room and Palladian drawing room, is one of the most impressive of the colonial era. From the east door of the house a view of the Potomac is framed by towering 200-year-old boxwood hedges nearly 12 feet high, with formal gardens on both sides.

The visit to Gunston Hall, administered by the National Society of Colonial Dames, is an introduction to the spirit of George Mason, patriot and Revolutionary. He was author of the Fairfax Resolves (the first statement defining the rights of the colonies), the Bill of Rights, and the Constitution of Virginia. Although he was a delegate to the Constitutional Convention of 1787 in Philadelphia, Mason refused to sign the Constitution because it failed to provide for the abolition of slavery or safeguard sufficiently individual rights.

TOUR 2 : Fredericksburg and Williamsburg— A Three-Day Tour
(375 Miles)

This trip can easily be an extension of the day at Mount Vernon and environs, if you travel on Route 1. Or you can start directly for Fredericksburg on the Shirley Highway from Washington.

The components of these three days are: history where it was written, a little off-beat travel, and an introduction to Tidewater Virginia. If you are headed for Virginia Beach or Nags Head, you can visit at least one or two of the high spots en route. For a longer circle tour of Virginia, drive west from Richmond for the Blue Ridge Mountains.

Fredericksburg, like Alexandria, is closely linked with George Washington and his family, and with James Monroe. It was also the focal point of four major Civil War battles, being halfway between the two capitals of Washington and Richmond; it changed hands seven times and endured some of the fiercest action of all time. First, drive down shaded Lewis Street to Kenmore, the Georgian mansion of Washington's sister, Betty, and her husband, Fielding Lewis (9–5, 75¢, children 45¢). Chippendale furniture, detailed plaster cornices and ceilings make this a colonial treasure house. Besides the tour of the house, you'll be served tea and gingerbread in the old brick-floored kitchen. From Kenmore, drive to Charles Street to see the neat little clapboard house which Washington bought and gave to his mother, and where she died (9–6, 50¢), then to the law offices of James Monroe, containing furniture which he used in the White House (9–5:30, 30¢).

Near the southern end of town, the Battlefield Park Museum is filled with mementoes of the battles of Fredericksburg, Chancellorsville, Wilderness, and Spotsylvania, as well as a battle map

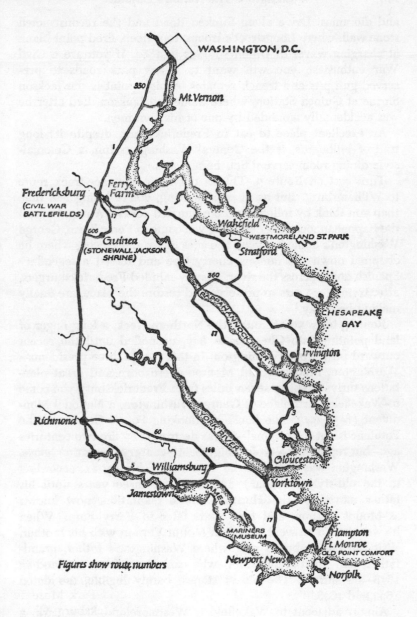

WASHINGTON, D.C.

350

Mt. Vernon

1

Fredericksburg
(CIVIL WAR
BATTLEFIELDS)

Ferry
Farm

17

606

Wakefield

3

WESTMORELAND ST. PARK

Guinea
(STONEWALL JACKSON
SHRINE)

Stratford

360

RAPPAHANNOCK RIVER

CHESAPEAKE
BAY

17

3

Irvington

YORK RIVER

Richmond

60

160

3

5

Williamsburg

Gloucester

Jamestown

Yorktown

JAMES R.

17

MARINERS
MUSEUM

Hampton
Ft. Monroe
OLD POINT COMFORT

Newport News

Norfolk

Figures show route numbers

and dioramas. Drive along Sunken Road and the reconstructed stone wall, where Longstreet's troops, four deep, fired point-blank at charging waves of Union soldiers in 1862. If you are a Civil War enthusiast, you will want to follow park roads to preserved gun pits and trench remains. A high point is the Jackson Shrine at Guinea Station, where Stonewall Jackson died after he was accidentally wounded by one of his own men.

An excellent place to eat in Fredericksburg, despite its long trail of billboards, is the General Washington Inn, a Colonial-style dining room serving Southern dishes.

Turn east on Route 3. This is not quite the race-track route to Williamsburg. But as in most touring, you're losing less time than you think by following the unhurried course. A mile beyond the Rappahannock River crossing you come to Ferry Farm, George Washington's home between the ages of six and eleven, where he chopped down the famous cherry tree and tossed a legendary Spanish dollar across the river. History-minded Fredericksburgers, after trying for years to preserve and restore the place, are finally making headway.

Route 3 takes you through the Northern Neck, a long finger of land pointing into Chesapeake Bay, unspoiled until the recent outward push from Washington. In this region three presidents—Washington, Madison, and Monroe—were born and great plantations thrived. Thirty-seven miles from Fredericksburg you come to Wakefield, birthplace of George Washington, a National Monument (8–5, 25¢). The house overlooking Pope's Creek and the Potomac is not the original—it was destroyed by fire two centuries ago—but represents a typical eighteenth-century plantation house. Washington was born here in 1732 (on February 11, according to the old-style calendar) and lived for three years until his father moved to the Hunting Creek Plantation, now known as Mount Vernon, and four years later to Ferry Farm. When he was sixteen he went to live at Mount Vernon with his brother. Visit the family burial plot where Washington's father, grandfather, and great-grandfather—who came here from England in 1656—are buried. The oldest stones, barely legible, are dated 1690 and 1696.

Almost adjacent to Wakefield is Westmoreland State Park, a very good summer spot with cabins, tent and trailer campgrounds fronting on the Potomac. Stratford, the plantation home of the Lees of Virginia (9–5, 75¢, children 25¢), is a few miles beyond. The austere brick mansion, five years in the building by Thomas Lee, is a Virginia classic, now completely furnished and fault-lessly maintained by the Lee Memorial Foundation. Four genera-tions were born here, including two signers of the Declaration of Independence, Richard Henry Lee and Francis Lightfoot Lee; Washington's compatriot, "Light Horse Harry" Lee and, best known of all, Robert E. Lee. Plantation luncheons (ham and biscuits) are served in the office wing during summer months.

The road to Yorktown is an historic route through the bright-leaf tobacco country. At Irvington, the Tides Inn is one of the country's finest smaller resorts, complete with golf, swimming, tennis, and yachting on the bay—an ideal place to spend a week at leisure—($34–$44 per day, double with meals). Cross the new Rappahannock River Bridge (toll, 75¢). In mid-March to mid-April you will see thousands of daffodils in bloom around Glouces-ter; what the tulip is to Holland, Michigan, the daffodil is here.

By late afternoon you will cross the York River Bridge (toll, 75¢) to the Virginia Peninsula, the compact corner where York-town, Williamsburg, and Jamestown are linked by the Colonial Parkway. If it is early and light enough, do Yorktown now. Here you can follow the course of battle leading to Washington's crown-ing victory in 1781, which ended the Revolution. Drive past the Swan Tavern in the village to Lord Cornwallis' headquarters, where a cannon ball is still embedded between gabled windows, to the Park Service Visitors Center. From the observation deck, the field of action on the battlefield comes into view. The Americans and French had moved in from three directions to bottle up Cornwallis' entire army: Admiral De Grasse by sea, Lafayette from the west, Washington and Rochambeau from the north. You can see the British earthworks; the reconstructed French battery; the site of Washington's field headquarters, and Redoubt 10, stormed by a bold young officer named Alexander Hamilton.

Tip for seafood: Nick's Pavilion, under the York River Bridge. No history, but plenty of fresh fish from the bay and ocean.

The thirteen-mile trip to Williamsburg along the Parkway is one of America's prettiest drives, with greensward and the river on your right, woodlands on your left. Know your plans in Williamsburg before you get there; too many visitors arrive without sufficient idea of the range in accommodations, the attractions (especially the free ones)—or even the history of the place. There are many motels in and around the town. If you want to stay within the restored area and price is no object, the Williamsburg Inn ($18–23 double) is a superb resort-type hotel, with swimming pool, tennis courts, golf course, and a dining room to remember. If price is a consideration, your best bet is the pleasant Williamsburg Lodge ($9–$13 double), whose guests are entitled to use facilities at the Inn. For the real Williamsburg flavor, stay at restored cottages operated in connection with both Inn and Lodge, and slightly lower priced. Rates generally are dropped a little in summer at the Inn, winter at the Lodge.

The place to begin your sightseeing is the Information Center, to see the wonderful free 35-minute film, *Williamsburg—Story of a Patriot*. It carries you back to the first permanent English settlement at Jamestown Island in 1607, the founding of Williamsburg in 1633, and its golden era as Virginia's capital from 1699 to 1780. After the capital was moved to Richmond, Williamsburg declined. It dozed until 1927, when John D. Rockefeller, Jr., became interested in the city and began a restoration project which has cost $60,000,000 and is still going on. If you want to do Williamsburg thoroughly, purchase a combination ticket ($3; students and military, $1; children under 12, free) for admission to the seven principal buildings, including the Governor's Palace, the Capitol and Raleigh Tavern. Individual tickets are sold, too (Palace, $1.50, others, 75¢ each).

Don't overlook the excellent admission-free buildings: historic Bruton Parish Church, erected around 1712; the Wren Building, at the College of William and Mary; the Abby Aldrich Rockefeller Folk Art Collection, the Archaeological Museum and the restored craft shops (bakery, milliner, wigmaker, printer, silversmith).

For an economy luncheon eat at Chowning's Tavern, a reconstructed alehouse on Duke of Gloucester Street. But you ought to splurge one evening for a memorable dinner at King's Arms (English mutton chops with a tankard of ale, topped off with green-gage ice cream), Christiana Campbell's, or the Williamsburg Inn.

It is only ten miles over the Parkway from Williamsburg to Jamestown; you should be able to tour the highlights of the area in about two hours. At Jamestown Island (50¢, children free), where three small ships touched land to begin a new epoch in history, you can walk through the excavated "New Towne" and, at the west end, inspect the ivy-covered Old Church Tower where Pocahontas was baptized and married—the only standing vestige of the original settlement.

Nearby Jamestown Festival Park ($1, children 50¢) re-creates the original scene, complete with tri-cornered stockaded village, built by Captain John Smith and his fellow settlers, and replicas of those three small boats, which you can board at the mooring.

Jamestown, Williamsburg, and Yorktown are so prominent that most visitors overlook the rest of the peninsula. A great mistake. Try to visit these two places (both admission-free), at least:

Mariners Museum, on the James River in Newport News (9–5 daily, Sunday 2–5), a great collection of the sea—models, boats, prints, art, china, furniture—in a 700-acre park.

Fort Monroe, at Old Point Comfort, facing the bay at the tip of the peninsula, the only eighteenth-century moated fortress still in use (as headquarters of the Continental Army Command). You can see the casemate (8–5 daily) within this massive citadel where Jefferson Davis was imprisoned after the Civil War.

Heading to Richmond, there are two routes: the expressway, if you're in a hurry, and Route 5, the James River route, which I prefer. It leads through pine woods, dappled white in spring with dogwood, passing great plantations of another era. Stop at Berkeley (8–5, $1), tastefully restored by its present owners, Malcolm and Grace Jamison. It was the home of two Presidents, William Henry (Old Tippecanoe) Harrison and Benjamin Harrison, and during the Civil War served briefly as General McClellan's headquarters.

The approaches to Richmond are lined with battlegrounds—Seven Pines, Cold Harbor, Fort Harrison, Seven Days—now preserved in a National Battlefield Park. Cold Harbor, in June 1864, was probably the most harrowing; in thirteen days the Union lost 12,700 men—7000 of whom fell in ten minutes. Finally Grant was forced to swing south to Petersburg, chasing Lee from there to Appomattox.

Richmond, the old, proud high temple of the South, is almost a neighbor of the national capital (about two hours distant via the direct route), and Washingtonians should really know it better. It exudes history and tradition, but has a modern personality.

Entering from Williamsburg, stop at white-framed St. John's Church, 24th and Broad Streets (10–4 daily, conducted tours after Sunday services), where fiery Patrick Henry delivered his "Give Me Liberty or Give Me Death" oration before Washington, Jefferson, Richard Henry Lee, and other members of the Virginia Convention. Then drive downtown to Capitol Square, an interesting contrast to Capitol Hill in Washington. The Capitol is *the* building designed by Thomas Jefferson after the Maison Carrée at Nîmes, responsible for the widespread classic influence in Federal and state architecture. In the rotunda stands the celebrated life-size statue of Washington by Houdon. The Confederate Congress met in the old central part and a bronze statue of Robert E. Lee stands on the spot where he accepted command of the Virginia troops in 1861.

Lee and the Confederacy appear on all sides of Richmond. The Lee House, 707 East Franklin Street, which he occupied after Appomattox, is now headquarters of the Virginia Historical Society (10–4, Monday through Friday, free). Lincoln came here right after the war's end. The Confederate Museum, 12th and Clay Streets, Jefferson Davis' White House, contains thousands of war relics (9–5 daily, Sunday 2–5, 30¢, children under 12, free). Monument Avenue, lined with statues (Jeb Stuart, Lee, Stonewall Jackson, Jefferson Davis, Commodore Matthew Maury), leads to Battle Abbey, Boulevard and Kensington Avenue (10–4, Tuesday through Friday, 2–5 Saturday, Sunday, 30¢), containing battle flags, murals, arms, and equipment of the Confederacy.

Richmond could stand several more distinctive dining rooms. In town, the best is probably the Raleigh Hotel on Main Street, the politicians' rendezvous. Early in the century, as Rueger's, it was Richmond's elite stopping place; its food, notably steaks and seafood, have never been surpassed.

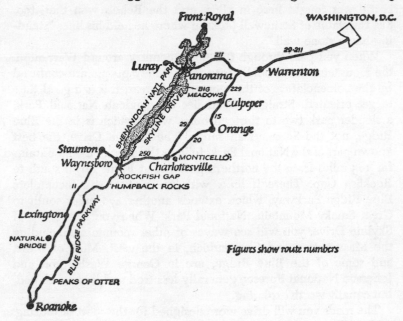

Figures show route numbers

TOUR 3 : The Mountains and Shenandoah Valley—
A Four-Day Tour
(510 Miles)

Westerners have a tendency to downgrade our southern Appalachians as mere foothills. That is, until they see for themselves that our mountains are wooded green clear to the peaks, with fine fishing, riding, hiking, flora and fauna. The heart of the Blue Ridge range is only two or three hours' drive from Washington and that is another point surprising to many vistors who come here with the misconception that we live in lowland surrounded by endless lowland.

From Washington, drive west on Routes 29-211. In the summer of 1861 thousands of Union soldiers and civilians streamed the other way over this road, back to Washington, in panicky retreat from the First Battle of Manassas (Bull Run, as the Yankees call it). Stop at the National Battlefield Park; another important battle was fought here in 1862—and the Rebels won that, too. See the statue of Stonewall Jackson where he held his lines "standing like a stone wall."

When you pass through the horse country around Warrenton, the mountains come boldly into view. Many people are confused by the nomenclature of the recreational areas; this is a good time to get oriented. Straight ahead lies Shenandoah National Park, a slender park two to thirteen miles wide, which is in the Blue Ridge, not the Shenandoah range. The Skyline Drive, the best known part of the National Park, follows the crest of the mountains for 105 miles from the northern gateway at Front Royal south to Rockfish Gap. There it links with the newer, still incomplete Blue Ridge Parkway, which extends another 470 miles south to Great Smoky Mountains National Park. When you get on top of Skyline Drive, you will see waves of other mountains, including the Massanutten and Shenandoah, in the west. Most of these, and some of the Blue Ridge, are in George Washington and Jefferson National Forests, generally less trod and less developed, but equally worth exploring.

The roads you will drive were designed for the sport of touring, with parking overlooks and visitor centers along the way. Plan it leisurely—your speed limit is lower in the mountains, anyway.

A word to hikers. The Appalachian Trail, extending 2000 miles from Mount Katahdin, Maine, to Mount Oglethorpe, Georgia, crosses the heart of our nearby national parks and national forests. Write the Appalachian Trail Conference, 1916 Sunderland Place, N.W., Washington, D.C., for information on its guidebooks and use of the shelters along the Trail (50¢ per night for members).

At Panorama, or Thornton Gap (elevation 2304 feet), Route 211 intersects Skyline Drive. Eight miles beyond, at Luray, the Mimslyn Hotel, an attractive older place (but with a new swimming pool so it's now a "modern motor inn") is a good stop for restful weekend and good food. The Luray Caverns (8–8, April through October, 9–5 in winter; $1.80, children 5 to 12, 90¢) is an undergound fantasyland with stalagmites, stalactites, and folded draperies in shades from deep brown to star-white. If you haven't seen the bigger western caves like Mammoth and Carlsbad—and even if you have—the one-hour Luray tour is well worth the admission, particularly since the recent installation of the stalacpipe "organ," an incredible instrument developed by Leland Sprinkle, a Washington scientist; it plays tunes with electronically controlled hammers striking several hundred rocks.

From Panorama, turn south on Skyline Drive (entry fee, 50¢ car and passengers) and follow the crest along gently curving roadway through woodlands ranging up to 4000 feet elevation. To the east are the foothills of the Piedmont Plateau, to the west the patchwork green and brown fields of Shenandoah Valley. This is a three season park, flowering in spring, cool in summer and foliage-colored in autumn (the peak is usually between October 10 and 20). Excellent, but limited, accommodations (motel-type lodge and cabins, $7–$12 double) are available at three locations, Skyland, Big Meadows, Lewis Mountain. Skyland, the largest, has the most activities: evening talks by the Park Naturalist, weekly square dancing in summer, saddle horses ($2 an hour). Reservations are advisable in summer; write Virginia Sky-Line Company, Luray, Virginia. An easy, but wonderful trail, riding or hiking, ascends the slopes of Stony Man Mountain, perhaps the most prominent landmark in the Park. The most extensive campgrounds are at Big Meadows.

More than twenty kinds of fish inhabit park streams: brook trout in the cooler headwaters, suckers, bass and sunfish farther downstream. President Herbert Hoover enjoyed fishing on the Rapidan River. His old cabin retreat is now part of a Boy Scout development.

At the southern terminal of Skyline Drive, turn west for an excursion into Shenandoah Valley—and plan to pick up the Blue Ridge Parkway on the way back. By all means, mark the birthplace of Woodrow Wilson (9–5 daily, 50¢, children 25¢) in Staunton—or Stan-ton, as they pronounce it locally—as a must. The substantial Greek-revival brick house was a manse and his father a Presbyterian minister when Wilson was born here December 28, 1856. Today it contains furnishings and a wealth of former possessions of the late President and his family. For a man who influenced the course of recent history, Woodrow Wilson is comparatively little known, and this is the place to meet him as an individual rather than in the pages of a history book.

Lexington, south on Route 11, is another very worth-while stop. And all its attractions are admission-free. At Washington and Lee

University, the Memorial Chapel (9–4) is a shrine to Robert E. Lee, who became president of the university after the Civil War. It contains the family tomb of the Lee family; a museum display of thousands of memorabilia, and the recumbent statue of the Confederate leader. Only a mile away, the Virginia Military Institute preserves an historic campus and buildings where cadets have trained since 1839. During the Civil War, the entire corps fought at the Battle of New Market, north in the valley, and helped repel the Yankees. The Trophy Room features the World War II collection of alumnus George C. Marshall. Retreat parades are held 4:15 P.M. Monday and Friday during the school year. Stonewall Jackson, who rose from a mild-mannered VMI instructor to Lee's strong right arm, lived at 8 East Washington Street, now refurnished with his personal items, and with prints and pictures relating to his career (8–6).

Natural Bridge (9 A.M.–10 P.M., $1.80, children 60¢) supports Route 11 and would be visible from the road except for the fence in the way. The best time to visit the erosion-formed 215-foot-high stone arch is in the evening when the "Drama of the Creation" is presented with recorded narration, music, and colored illumination. If you would like to see an acre-wide souvenir counter vending a multitude of trinkets, doodads, and knicknacks, the Natural Bridge has it.

Roanoke is the logical place to turn the tour loop, although if you have more time there's a great deal of interest in the mountains of southwestern Virginia. The Hotel Roanoke, a resort-like hotel ($10–$14 double), and its dining room are outstanding. To drive down from Washington and stay here can make a weekend in itself.

Start your return on the Blue Ridge Parkway, designed purely for recreational motoring, free of billboards and commercial traffic. Now, with completion of the James River Bridge, you can drive all the way on the Parkway to Rockfish Gap. In some sections it runs along a very narrow crest, opening magnificent views on both sides; stop at the overlooks so you can really take in the landscape. A favorite recreation area, the Peaks of Otter, about 30 miles above Roanoke, is the site of a new 40-unit motel ($10 double) and restaurant, as well as modern campgrounds and fine mountain trout fishing. Boating and swimming are easily managed at nearby Bedford County Park.

Farther north, at Humpback Rocks, the Parkway has assembled an Appalachian highland farm, the Charlie Carter place, as it might have been fifty or one hundred years ago, complete with wild grapevine from which jellies were made and the snake-rail fence enclosure.

From Rockfish Gap, the Parkway's northern terminal, turn east across the rolling hills and apple orchards of the Piedmont Plateau to Charlottesville, Thomas Jefferson's town, where his spirit is still strongly evident. First stop at the University of Virginia, which he founded as "an academical village." From the pantheon-like rotunda, the university still appears as Jefferson laid it out, with the two colonnades of student quarters facing each other across a terraced lawn and the serpentine wall behind the West Lawn. Walk to Number 13, West Range, to see Edgar Allan Poe's old room.

This was the University that Jefferson saw through the telescope from his mountainside plantation, Monticello. Drive through Charlottesville and up Carter's Range on Route 53 to see this great house (8–5, $1). It is full of Jeffersonian innovations. He loved architecture, but couldn't resist gadgetry. Among his inventions here are a dumbwaiter running from wine cellar to dining room, disappearing beds, one-arm lunch chair, and a big clock that records the hours, days, and rings bells on the roof— it still works. This was his dream house, bordered by gardens, commanding a view of the city and the Albemarle countryside. Note the simplicity of his gravestone and his own epitaph:

HERE WAS BURIED

THOMAS JEFFERSON

AUTHOR OF THE DECLARATION OF INDEPENDENCE, OF THE
STATUTE OF VIRGINIA FOR RELIGIOUS FREEDOM AND
FATHER OF THE UNIVERSITY OF VIRGINIA.

Jefferson's friend, James Monroe, lived at the crest of the next hill at Ash Lawn, (7–6, 75¢), restored and furnished and noted for its box hedges.

Signs of Presidents are almost everywhere in these parts. The short way back to Washington is via Route 29. However, if you would like to visit James Madison's hearth, and enjoy a pleasant drive, take Route 20 through Orange. Montpelier, his beautiful home, lies five miles west. The house is not open, but the graveyard, where James and Dolly Madison are buried, may be visited.

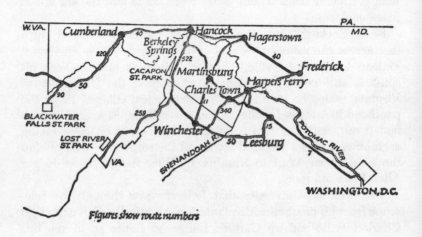

Figures show route numbers

TOUR 4: West Virginia's Panhandle—
A Three-Day Tour
(220 Miles)

West Virginia is a new place to go, or at least a newly discovered place, almost in Washington's backyard. Within two to four hours' driving lie surprisingly unspoiled state parks, with family-styled lodges and cabins, lake swimming and boating. And speaking of Washington, you can bathe in his (George's that is) favorite spa, which is probably as good as ever, and inexpensive.

The Eastern Panhandle, the closest part of West Virginia to the capital, is so named because of its shape, squeezed in like a handle between the boundaries of Maryland and Virginia. This little corner has had more than its share of history, sometimes toned with disaster. Thomas Jefferson admired it. So did John Brown, who picked Harpers Ferry as capital of his abortive mountain republic. Once the Civil War began, the armies charged back and forth until they left poor Harpers Ferry in ruins.

Start from Washington by crossing the Potomac and following Route 7 to Leesburg, a lovely spot in its own right whenever you're looking for a half-day or one-day trip. The Laurel Brigade Inn is a good luncheon or dinner stop. From Leesburg follow Route 9; just before you reach the state line, watch for the turn-off to Harpers Ferry on Route 671, a 15-minute time-saver.

Harpers Ferry, a reddish-gray hillside town, faces the confluence of the Shenandoah and Potomac Rivers, surrounded by the converging green hills of Maryland, Virginia, and West Virginia. Thomas Jefferson, after looking over these rushing waters and steep gorges, wrote, "This scene is worth a voyage across the Atlantic." Today the town is still and quiet, clearly a vestige of the past. But in the 1830s it was a key point on the route of the Chesapeake & Ohio Canal and the hard-competing Baltimore & Ohio Railroad. It was also the site of a great rifle works (producing a thousand rifles and muskets a month) and a Federal arsenal.

These brought John Brown and his followers here in 1859. Hoping to arm the slaves and establish a free state, on the night of October 16 they captured the arsenal and held several hostages, including Colonel Lewis Washington, a great-grandnephew of George Washington. Within two days they were driven to refuge in the engine house, the storied John Brown's Fort, and finally surrendered. His rebellion appears now as a curio in history, yet fiery abolitionist Brown forced the nation to realize the slavery issue was inescapable.

For the half-mile walking tour of Harpers Ferry National Monument, start at the old arsenal paymaster's office, now the Visitor Center and Museum. Follow the markers to the original site of the engine house, then up stone steps to Harper House Row, named for Robert Harper, who once operated a ferry across the Potomac, and to the heights of Jefferson Rock, from which Thomas Jefferson overlooked the scene. Later, drive up steep-graded Washington Street to Storer College, a Negro school founded after the Civil War (now closed), and where John Brown's Fort stands. The fort is surprisingly small, just a story and a half, twenty by thirty-five feet. Plans are to move it to its original site near the station and the river.

Drive on Route 340 to Charles Town, where several Washingtons, including George's brother Charles, had their homes. At the red-brick county courthouse stop to see the room, still in use, where on October 27 the trial of John Brown began. He was convicted and, on December 2, John Brown sat on his coffin riding to the gallows. His last reported words, on a peaceful, hazy morning in the West Virginia hills, were: "This is a beautiful country."

In case you're a racing enthusiast, meets at the ¾-mile Turf Club track are usually held in spring, summer, late fall. If you prefer old homes and gardens, an annual tour is sponsored by the Garden Council in late April or early May, a pretty time when apple orchards burst into bloom, along with redbud, dogwood, and wildflowers.

North through Martinsburg and around the rim of the Panhandle, Route 9 leads to Berkeley Springs, a spa since Colonial days when it was known, simply and properly, as Bath. George and Martha Washington not only came to take the waters, but he purchased two lots of land. In the nineteenth century it was a worldly rendezvous of celebrities and political figures out from Washington, but like so many other places it declined with the Civil War and never regained its luster. Today it is a pleasant village of 1500.

The springs flow at a rate of 2000 gallons per minute. The mineral content is considered almost identical with the water at Warm Springs, Georgia. Operated by the West Virginia Board of Control, the baths include steam and Roman baths (sunken pool holding 300 gallons of water), and a few variations. Try one; it's relaxing and refreshing. You can also swim in the spring-fed pool with a constant 74-degree temperature. The Park View Inn, adjoining the springs, has modern rooms ($16–$19 double with meals) and excellent American cooking.

Ten miles south on Route 522 lies Cacapon State Park, in a 5000-acre mountain forest, the most accessible, from Washington, of West Virginia's 21 state parks. Cacapon (pronounced ca-caypon) has a six-acre lake for boating, fishing and swimming; 24 miles of scenic trails for hiking and horseback riding; picnic grounds and playgrounds; tennis courts, and a golf driving range.

The 50-room Lodge ($11 double) is probably the best place for a couple to stay. There are evening social programs and summer square dancing. Thirty housekeeping cabins of varying sizes nestled in the woods are ideal for family vacationing, especially where your budget is a factor. They range from $10.50 a night for two to four persons (or $34.50 a week) up to a deluxe cabin for eight at $36 (or $105 a week).

West Virginia has other state park areas worth considering, farther from Washington, but still within six hours driving. Lost River State Park, in an isolated spot (ideal for jangled nerves) across the Shenandoah Mountains from Virginia, has twenty-two housekeeping cabins, swimming pool, tennis courts, nearby bass and trout streams. Blackwater Falls State Park offers accommodations in a luxurious new mountain lodge and 25 deluxe cabins; lake swimming, boating, hiking, and riding. Plus the sight of amber-colored Blackwater River plunging over its 60-foot ledge and then winding through a forested canyon.

Most of these lodgings are open all year, but are in greatest demand for summer use. Write for reservations far in advance (applications for nonresidents are accepted after February 15) to the Division of State Parks, Charleston 5, West Virginia.

Returning from the Panhandle, you can make a circle tour through Winchester, at the northern end of Shenandoah Valley. The Apple Blossom Festival is held here each spring (Thursday and Friday nearest May 1) when apple orchards for miles around are usually in bloom.

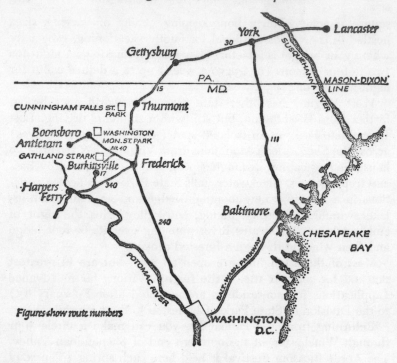

Figures show route numbers

TOUR 5 : Frederick and Gettysburg—
A Two-Day Tour
(160 Miles)

In our era of mobility, Gettysburg, the scene of the greatest
battle of the Civil War, is almost irresistible as an object of pilgrimage. It lies only 80 miles from Washington and half the route
is a new Interstate Expressway. The Maryland countryside you
pass through bears close examination too. It contains the most
accessible campgrounds from the national capital, mountain towns,
scenery, and history.

Notice that at one point you will be very close to Harpers
Ferry (22 miles from Frederick). You could easily combine this
tour with Tour 4 by crossing the Potomac River on Route 340.

For the direct approach to Gettysburg, take Route 240 (Interstate 70) past the new Atomic Energy Commission headquarters at Germantown into Frederick, where you can spend an hour, or longer, in worth-while, leisurely sightseeing.

On July 9, 1864, General Jubal Early, after extracting $200,000 in ransom from the town of Frederick, headed for Washington with an army of 23,000. He was met three miles south and engaged in the Battle of Monocacy before going on to Fort Stevens and almost invading the Capital.

Four places to see in Frederick are:

The monument marking the grave of Francis Scott Key in Mount Olivet Cemetery, one of the few places where the American flag is never lowered, on South Market Street.

Roger Brooke Taney House and Francis Scott Key Museum, 121 S. Bentz Street (10–noon, 2–4:30, contributions accepted), the home of Supreme Court Chief Justice Taney, who wrote the Dred Scott decision. It contains furniture and memorabilia of Taney and Key (who were brothers-in-law, Mrs. Taney having been Francis Scott Key's only sister, Anne).

Court House Square, surrounded by eighteenth- and nineteenth-century dwellings and law offices, and flavored with the past. Lafayette was entertained in the red-brick Ross House, on the north side.

Colonial Barracks, at the south end of the beautifully landscaped grounds of the Maryland School for the Deaf, on South Market Street, built by Hessian prisoners in 1777, later a hospital during the Battle of Monocacy.

Look over the Catoctin Mountains west of Frederick. You can camp in two unusual state parks. One is Washington Monument State Park, on the heights above Boonsboro. From the 34-foot stone monument, built in 1827 as a memorial to George Washington, the view extends to the Potomac River and the two states (Virginia, West Virginia) on the other side. Gathland State Park, on South Mountain, near Burkittsville, has a newly developed campground adjacent to the stone memorial arch erected to the memory of Civil War correspondents by George Alfred Townsend, a celebrated nineteenth-century journalist and author who once lived here. These parks are about nine miles apart on the Appalachian Trail; you can start youngsters in hiking by dropping them off at Washington Monument and picking them up at Gathland.

A notable historic point in this Maryland corner is Antietam National Historic Site, where an intense and bloody day-long battle (three generals were lost on each side) was fought in 1862. Though neither side won, Lee was turned back from his northward thrust. The tour route, starting at the Hagerstown Road, follows the course of battle almost chronologically from Hooker's opening artillery fire at dawn to Lee's withdrawal around dusk. In that single day 23,000 men were killed or wounded.

From Frederick, turn north on Route 15. Cunningham Falls State Park adjoins the wooded Catoctin area, where Franklin D. Roosevelt established his Shangri-La as a retreat from wartime Washington and later, renamed as Camp David, used by President Eisenhower. The state park has campgrounds, shelters, hiking trails, excellent trout and fly fishing.

Now, Gettysburg. Its significance in history was the "testing and survival of the Union under fire." But as you tour these sacred fields the greater issue becomes reduced to simple human terms of sacrifice, desperation, and courage. Here, on July 1, 1863, the great battle began, involving 170,000 Confederate and Union soldiers. From many points in the National Battlefield Park, you can reconstruct the sequence of action, aided by 2390 monuments, markers, and tablets. And you can stand where, a few months after the battle, Abraham Lincoln stated the American creed for eternity.

In the course of your tour, don't overlook the scope or the damage of the new battle of Gettysburg, in which commercial development—motels, spreading subdivisions, souvenir stands, beer parlors, automobile graveyards—is advancing in strength against rather weak defense lines. The tragedy is that local interests in Gettysburg and national interests in Washington, which could do so much to preserve the battlefield boundaries from intrusion, have thus far done so little.

To appreciate Gettysburg fully, you should tour in company with a licensed guide ($4.00), starting at the cannon that fired the opening shot on the Chambersburg Road.

Lee and the Confederates had finally brought the war to Northern soil and at this point the opposing armies collided. With the guide, you'll drive to the Eternal Light Peace Memorial on Oak Hill, where the first day's action shifted, then along Seminary Ridge, which became the Confederate line. Here are stirring memorials like the North Carolina Monument, one of Gutzon Borglum's early works, and the classic Virginia Monument, showing Lee astride his horse, Traveler.

Look out over the cannon, still in place, across the open field to the Union line at Cemetery Ridge. The third and decisive day opened with a blazing two-hour artillery duel. But it was only a prelude to the Confederates' daring gamble: the thrust of 15,000 men, headed by Pickett's division, across the open fields to pierce the Union center. One hundred men reached their goal and fought hand-to-hand to the death—but the others were forced back or fell.

While you're at Seminary Ridge, be sure to climb the lookout tower for a view of the 500-acre farm of President Eisenhower. Then drive through the Peach Orchard and Wheat Field to Devil's Den and Little Round Top, a principal vantage point on the sixteen-mile route.

Now the road leads along the Union line, to the huge Pennsylvania Monument and the stone wall called the Angle, or the high water mark, the crest of Pickett's Charge. Nearby is the statue of General George C. Meade, the Union commander who proved more than a match for the seemingly invincible Lee.

From here you enter the iron gateway of the National Cemetery, dedicated in autumn of 1863, when thousands came to hear Edward Everett's two-hour eulogy, followed by Lincoln's brief remarks. The President's words were almost lost in the closing hymn and benediction.

Another principal point is the Cyclorama (admission 30¢), a tremendous circular painting re-creating Pickett's Charge, which the National Park Service has scheduled to move from a building outside the Park into a new visitor center and museum.

Stay at the Hotel Gettysburg ($6–$13 double) in Lincoln Square. In the evening stroll the town square; one landmark, the Wills House is now a museum (admission 50¢). For a final hour with the battle, visit the Gettysburg National Museum (50¢, open till 9 P.M.) on Route 134, featuring an electric map and relic collection.

If you have another day and want to make a circle tour, drive east to Lancaster and York, the country of the Amish, the "plain people," who drive in horse and buggy and scorn modern conveniences; they are, nevertheless, industrious, prosperous farmers. Lancaster is also the heart of the Pennsylvania Dutch country, where German is spoken. Stop at the Willows, east on U.S. 30, for typical dishes like Schnitzel, shoofly pie, souse, and Schmierkäse.

This way, you can return through Baltimore. Pause long enough there at least for a Maryland crab dinner at Miller Brothers' downtown or their Kingsville Inn on Route 1. Baltimore has many sights, and is worth a visit on its own. Fort McHenry National Monument is where Francis Scott Key saw the flag aloft after a 25-hour bombardment in the War of 1812 and was inspired to write "The Star Spangled Banner." The Peale Museum contains historical portraits, and a collection of prints, models and paintings of clipper ships. And only an hour away from Washington, you can see the great Baltimore harbor, the country's second largest, filled with vessels headed to and from distant ports.

TOUR 6: Annapolis, the Bay and Ocean— A Three-Day Tour
(330 Miles)

The Atlantic Coast and the great inland sea called Chesapeake Bay are so close you could leave Washington after breakfast and be swimming in the surf or fishing for striped bass before lunch. Yet the Bay and Eastern Shore are in many respects worlds away, enriched with a certain flavor of isolation, oldness, and the sea.

This country is loved and shared by yachtsmen; fishermen (sport and commercial); landed gentry; antiquarians; hunters; tobacco, tomato, and chicken farmers; and the wild ponies of Assateague. And vacationers, of course.

Start on Route 50 to Annapolis, the State Capital and home of the U. S. Naval Academy, known to Navy men everywhere as "Crabtown-on-the-Bay." Annapolis is more than Navy, but an eighteenth-century city of brick-paved sidewalks, attractive Colonial houses and the scene of important events in history. As early as the 1600s, it was a seaport and center of political life.

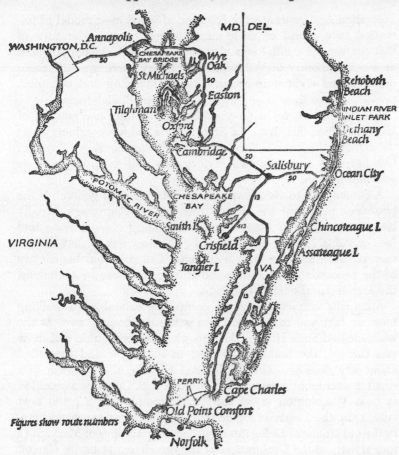

Figures show route numbers

Once it was even the National Capital and here, in 1783, George Washington appeared before Congress to resign as commander in chief. The State House, where Congress met and Washington took his leave, today is the oldest building still in use by any state legislature.

Few Americans realize the dramatic, significant events that took place in Maryland. In 1634, soon after the landings at Jamestown and Plymouth Rock, two small ships, the *Ark* and the *Dove*, landed at southern Maryland near St. Mary's City, where they established their capital and adopted the Religious

Toleration Act, guaranteeing freedom of worship—a model of toleration in a world of religious bitterness. Before the turn of that century the capital was moved to Annapolis, which flowered as a contemporary of Williamsburg. Today there are still about one hundred eighteenth-century houses standing and occupied, probably more than in any other city except Philadelphia.

The best place to begin your tour is at the headquarters of Historic Annapolis, Inc., 64 State Circle, which conducts tours throughout the year and particularly during Heritage Week in October; but any time this civic group will provide guidance and information.

A choice time to visit Annapolis, or Maryland in general, is the two-week period of the House and Garden Pilgrimage, usually late April and early May, when outstanding old mansions and "sea captains' houses" are opened by their owners so that visitors may see rare antiques and heirlooms. The principal beneficiary of the proceeds is the Hammond-Harwood House in Annapolis, the architectural gem of the state.

Annapolis' attractions are so compactly assembled a walking tour can take you to most of them within an hour or two. At the white-domed State House (daily, 9–5), an official guide will show you through the building, erected in the 1770s and expanded about fifty years ago. The old Senate Chamber, about the size of a small theater lobby, was where the entire U. S. Congress assembled to hear Washington reject all "public employments"; the next year, 1784, the Treaty of Peace with England was approved here. In the old House of Delegates chamber are paintings of Maryland's four signers of the Declaration of Independence (Charles Carroll of Carrollton, William Paca, Thomas Stone, Samuel Chase).

Walk down Maryland Avenue to the Hammond-Harwood House at King George Street (10–5 weekdays, Sunday 2–5, $1), preserving the flavor of the eighteenth century, with rich paneling, ornamented mantels and cornices, period furnishings and oil paintings. It was built by one Matthias Hammond, a man of means who lavished so much attention on the refinements of his new home that he lost his fiancée. Directly across the street, the Chase-Lloyd House was begun in 1769 by Samuel Chase, signer of the Declaration of Independence.

From here walk, or drive, through the main gate of the Naval

Academy. It, too, is steeped in history. It was founded as a training school for Naval officers in 1845 and is a great attraction for visitors, open from 9 A.M. to 7 P.M. daily, although buildings close at 5 P.M. (no admission charge). The well groomed yard is crammed with exhibits and relics, classrooms, laboratories, docks, basins, ships.

All activity radiates from Bancroft Hall, the world's largest college dormitory, actually a self-contained city, with its own post office, stores, barbershop, tailor, and a tremendous mess hall accommodating the entire brigade of midshipmen at one sitting. The newest building, the mammoth Gymnasium and Field House, provides enough area under cover for all 3600 middies to practice mass calisthenics and drills. In contrast, the somber crypt of the Academy Chapel contains only the marble sarcophagus of John Paul Jones, founder of the U. S. Navy.

On Wednesdays you get an extra dividend between 3:30 and 4:10 P.M.—the colorful dress parade on Worden Field. There is a grandstand for visitors and you can take all the photographs you wish. Second-best marching shows are Chapel formation Sunday mornings at 10:15 and the noon-meal formation in front of Bancroft Hall any weekday at 12:10 P.M., 12:30 on Sunday.

There is another eminent educational institution at Annapolis, which almost every visitor unfortunately overlooks. This is St. John's College, on College Avenue, known for its "100 Great Books" Curriculum. Much older than the Academy, St. John's was chartered in 1784, but can trace its history, as King William's School, to 1696. It has old buildings, but also the new $2,000,000 brick-and-glass Francis Scott Key Memorial Hall (Key was graduated in 1796), which contains a celestial observatory and 600-seat opera hall.

Probably the best place to stay at Annapolis is one of the motels on Route 50, like the modern Charterhouse, complete with swimming pool ($14 to $16 double). The Treadway Maryland Inn, downtown ($10 to $14 double), was built in the 1770s, but has modern conveniences (air conditioning, plumbing, elevator). For Maryland specialties, lobster pie and crab imperial, try the moderately priced Cruise Inn on State Circle, the Red Coach or the Academy's old rendezvous, Carvel Hall.

From Annapolis, start out one morning for the Eastern Shore

across the gleaming steel, 7.2-mile-long Chesapeake Bay Bridge
(toll $1.25 for car and driver, 25¢ for additional passenger, maxi-
mum $1.50), completed in 1954 at a cost of $45,000,000. Here you
get some impression of the magnitude of the bay, a tremendous
body of water extending 195 miles from the Susquehanna River
south to the open sea at Hampton Roads. With all its estuaries the
total tidal shoreline is 5100 miles; the surface area of these waters
is nearly four times the area of Rhode Island and the drainage
system covers nearly 65,000 square miles, almost equal to all of
New England. Its fishing is superb, for striped bass, hardhead,
perch, sea trout, spot, and about 200 other species.

The bridge has ended forever the isolation of "the Shore," yet
there are still many out-of-the-way, and a few primitive, corners;
little disturbed fishing villages on waterways and bays, and
architecturally rich estates with names like Troth's Fortune,
Crooked Intention, King's Prevention. The Shore, flat as Holland,
is part of the Delmarva Peninsula, shared by Delaware, Maryland,
and Virginia, from north to south.

As you follow Route 50 to the coast, stop to view the Wye Oak,
a huge tree more than 400 years old, and the tiny one-room
schoolhouse almost under its spreading branches—no longer in
use but furnished as it was in 1720. Nearby, the Wye House, a
showplace on the annual Garden Pilgrimage, has been lived in
by the same family, the distinguished Lloyds, for nine generations.

Easton, once the "East Capital of Maryland," is now a popular
social rendezvous, particularly at the Tidewater Inn ($9 to $15
double), a colonial inn of the Williamsburg type. My favorite
town, tiny Oxford, lies ten miles off to the southwest on Route
333. It was founded as a port three hundred years ago where the
Tred Avon flows into the Choptank (which flows into the bay);
today it is still known to yachtsmen everywhere for the workman-
ship of its boatyards. In summer, the waters offshore are filled
with white-sailed yachts, oyster and fishing boats of every de-
scription. Overlooking the Tred Avon is the pleasant Robert Mor-
ris Inn ($7 to $8 double), owned and operated by Mr. and Mrs.
Victor Pelle, former New Yorkers who decided they preferred
this life—and who can blame them?

You can find even more remote corners. Cross the Tred Avon
on the small ferry, which has been in operation since the early

1700s; the ten-minute crossing is a pleasant interlude in motor travel through history. Then proceed to off-the-beaten-track boating and oystering villages like St. Michael's and Tilghman Island.

Stay on Route 50 if you're eager to reach the ocean. The highway ends at Ocean City, the eastern terminal of a route that spans the continent to San Francisco. This is Maryland's only seashore resort and therefore the closest, about three-hours' driving time, from Washington. North on the Delaware side are smaller resorts at Bethany Beach and Rehoboth Beach.

In these waters a fisherman can catch marlin, bluefish, sea bass, porgies, flounder. For an exciting fishing experience, rent a boat, a tall outrigger with flying bridge ($100 a day for four or five persons), and head for the marlin grounds at famous Jack Spot 23 miles southeast or the Baltimore Canyon 45 miles out. If you bring back a dolphin, that isn't bad, either.

Ocean City has a clean sand beach and a boardwalk. The track at Ocean Downs offers harness racing in August. The newest sports addition is the 18-hole, $200,000 Golf and Yacht Club on Newport Bay.

Accommodations are not inexpensive during the summer, especially at the new motor hotels where you can expect to spend $15 to $22 double—that is, when you get a room. If you insist on waiting until the last minute, phone either the Chamber of Commerce (Atlantic 9-7184) or the Town Information Center (Atlantic 9-6130). They will help locate accommodations for you.

Delaware has developed beach camping areas, including one at Indian River Inlet, at the northern end of the Ocean City island. Camping rates are $12 weekly, $40 per month. For information, write State Highway Department, Dover, Delaware.

For the inveterate off-beat traveler, Crisfield, according to the one and only Aubrey Bodine, is the most colorful spot in the Chesapeake country and Tangier and Smith the most picturesque islands in the bay. They are south of Route 50 via Routes 13 and 413. Bodine has been taking pictures that are works of art for the Baltimore *Sun* these many years; if you want a worth-while memento, acquire his book of 220 photographs, *Chesapeake Bay and Tidewater*. Ten dollars a copy, and a bargain.

Crisfield, which calls itself the "Seafood Capital of the World," has a main street that is in reality one long wharf lined with weathered frame buildings leaning at odd angles. Much of the lower town is built on millions of tons of oyster shells, which leads the natives to explain, "We shipped out the oysters and live on the shells." The ancient ferries *Island Belle* and *Dorleena* sail to Smith Island ($1 round trip) and Tangier Island ($1.50 round trip) respectively. These two islands, almost in the center of the bay, and untouched by the modern world until recently, are replete with unusual customs, language, and mode of living. Prepare to stay overnight since the ferries make only one trip daily at noon. Rates are modest, no higher than $7 a day including meals. You can get information and call ahead for reservations in private homes at the restaurant on the Crisfield docks.

Chincoteague Island, on the Atlantic side, the home of those enormous, succulent oysters, is the scene of an old and honored festivity, a roundup of wild ponies, the last Wednesday and Thursday in July. The herd, which according to one legend are descendants of shipwrecked Spanish horses, now numbers about 300 and lives on Assateague. Men in boats and on horseback make them swim the 400-foot channel to Chincoteague, where they are penned and sometimes auctioned off.

These places are really not as remote as they sound. If fact, you can follow Route 13 to the tip of Cape Charles and take a ferry to Old Point Comfort or to Norfolk, and thus complete a wide loop around Chesapeake Bay.

XXIII *Washington without Oratory*

Think of Washington without its oratory. As the city of people, with all the shadings and subtleties they evoke, people who live here because they want to and like it. This is a softer, truer picture than the usual one of sheer monumentality and big government.

There is a place, perhaps, for oratory and rhetoric. As on July 4, 1851, when Daniel Webster, the old master, held a vast assemblage spellbound while the cornerstone was laid for the Capitol extension. In the course of the ceremony, a message, signed by Mr. Webster as Secretary of State, was deposited beneath the stone. It ended with this call to eternity:

"If, therefore, it shall be hereafter the will of God that this structure shall fall from its base, that its foundations be upturned, and this deposit brought to the eyes of men, be it known that, on this day, the Union of the United States of America stands firm; that their Constitution still exists unimpaired, and with all its original usefulness and glory, growing every day stronger and stronger in the affections of the great body of the American people, and attracting more and more the admiration of the world. And all here assembled, whether belonging to public life or to private life, with hearts devoutly thankful to Almighty God for the preservation of the liberty and happiness of the country, unite in sincere and fervent prayers that this deposit, and the walls and arches, the domes and towers, the columns and entablatures, now to be erected over it, may endure forever! God save the United States of America!"

A noble message, indeed. But I think I still prefer a little less certainty and a little more sense of mystery in appreciating the Capitol, or the city, or even the endless process of democracy. For examples of what I mean, following are excerpts from writings of six men who express their devotion to Washington and reveal gentle but exciting aspects of our capital and its meaning. As is often right, it may be best to let others have the last word. I hope yours will join these:

"The genius of the Potomac lies in its balance. It is a microcosm —it has been called a micro-chaos—of the nation. Lying between the ocean and the mountains, between the North and the South, its balance is epitomized in the profusion of plants, trees, birds, and wild life. On a foggy spring day the sea gulls are seen on the White House lawn; the mountain goldfinches rise in tiny yellow clouds along Rock Creek; and on a quiet evening in Lafayette Square you may find a small white owl. The foxtail pine of New England and the southern sweet gum flourish equally. The balance of nature is faithfully reflected in the very climate, the landscape, and the activities of man. Within a hundred miles of Washington can be found in miniature nearly every aspect of the nation.

"In its history the Potomac has been colored by the East and the West, the South and the North, and both the river valley and its principal city have become a cross section of the nation."

Frederick Gutheim, in *The Potomac* (1949)

"Washington is perhaps the most beautiful springtime city I have ever seen. It has space, it has air, it has light—a soft and extraordinary April glow that seems to hover just above your head as you stroll the side streets. The city appears to have more trees than Paris, and all the many dozens of parks and circles and squares and malls are alight with geraniums and azaleas, with plum and quince and crab-apple blossom. Coming out of your hotel in the early morning, you turn the corner onto one of the great avenues, and your heart is lifted by Washington's great white distances, by the subtlety and sweep of the genius of L'Enfant, the city's designer.

"Forget the crowds and the Kodaks and the conventions; this is Washington's time of year. In the morning, the Government girls pack the long yellow and maroon buses inward bound from Rosslyn and Arlington, filling them with new white straw hats and the hopeful scent of *Arpège*. In the evening, a visiting high-school senior from Waycross, Georgia, walks hand-in-hand with his steady under the heavy, dark trees on 16th Street, and you are charmed by their slow and graceful accents. In the afternoon, the girls from the Cathedral School turn out for softball practice near 34th Street, wearing bright yellow gym suits, and at the same moment a freshman Congressman from Indiana appears on the floor of the House sporting a new pair of perforated white shoes and carrying in his hand a speech in honor of his State Flower."

Roger Angell, in *Holiday* (May 1956)

"Some there are who profess that the Federal City of Washington is built of printed forms, questionnaires, returns, subpoenas, and similar fragments of inanimate bureaucracy. Others maintain that it is the national showcase with marbled floors malignly designed for the fallen arches of any sight-seer. Still others regard it as their personal property, supported by their taxes, and indifferently treated by its present tenants; these have a way of taking possession and giving orders whenever they land in town. All are, of course, at least partially mistaken, for Washington is, in fact, the loveliest place in the world. (As a native, I can speak with confidence.)

"For Washington is old—older far than other and more pretentious settlements. It has its customs, its traditions, its quaint folkways, its stabilities, its permanencies. Unhappily, visitors are rarely enabled to discover these charming characteristics for themselves. Instead, they are subjected to guided tours, to planned excursions, to a stereotyped round of public buildings. . . .

"Washington is the 'Seat of Government' and it is, indeed, the front seat. If a wayfarer would understand what it means to operate this greatest democratic enterprise, let him stand from eight to nine of a morning and from four-thirty to five-thirty of an afternoon at the corner of Twelfth Street and Constitution Avenue. No greater evidence of the devotion of his civil servants can be adduced in so short a time. There he will find Genesis and Exodus, but let him be careful of the frenzied and the hurried. . . .

"Few permanent residents of Washington live in the District of Columbia. Some to be sure are still discoverable in Spring Valley but, paradoxically, most now make their abode in Montgomery County, Maryland, or across a bridge in Arlington County, Virginia. There their private lives are spent; but their workadays and their diversions are in the town to which they have always a sense of belonging.

"Washington is not government, not buildings, not businesses public or private, not wrangling issues, not headlines, not even anonymity. Washington is people. Some, to be sure, are bad. Some are evil. Some are socially unadjusted. Some are prejudiced. Some are disturbing. Some are, fortunately, transients. But most are educated, sensitive, enlightened, kind. They share common interests and high purposes. They delight in the welfare of their fellows and are dedicated—passionately dedicated—to the advancement and security of the human family. They are courteous, civilized, responsive to human, gentle impulses."

David C. Mearns, in *Wilson Library Bulletin* (June 1959)

"Let me call to your attention a very special sample of what communities might consider, contained in a microscopic area in Washington that is little known to the outsider. On the Rock of Dumbarton at the northern side of Georgetown is an extraordinary complex of situations which could be called Washington's most civilized square mile, perhaps America's most civilized square mile. Here is to be found the Dumbarton Oaks house belonging to Harvard University, a center of Byzantine studies for scholars. But Dumbarton Oaks is much more than this. Dumbarton Oaks contains a neighborhood Byzantine museum, and a very lovely one. The formal gardens, among the most beautiful in North America, are open to the public. Immediately east is Montrose Park, a beautiful small public park bordering on Rock Creek Park. Immediately to the north of Dumbarton Oaks and Montrose Park, to be reached only on foot, is Dumbarton Park, America's smallest national wilderness park with its lovely stream and wild flowers, open to the public only on weekends and holidays. All of this is in the center of a great city. To Washingtonians who are in the know, this is one of the best loved places in the entire city. Here one feels, upon intimate acquaintance, that this is a suggestion of what the heart of all American residential neighborhoods could well become. Such a cross-fertilization of culture and nature within a city could well be emulated anywhere and could provide a counter-balance for the mechanized time pressures of the nuclear age."

Carl Feiss, in *A Guide to Washington Architecture* (1957)

"The graceful thing in Washington beyond any other is the so happily placed and featured White House, the late excellent extensions and embellishments of which have of course represented expenditure—but only of the refined sort imposed by some mature portionless gentlewoman on relatives who have accepted the principle of making her, at a time of life, more honourably comfortable. The whole ample precinct and margin formed by the virtual continuity of its grounds with those expanses in which the effect of the fine Washington Obelisk rather spends or wastes itself (not a little as if some loud monosyllable had been uttered, in a preoccupied company, without a due production of sympathy or sense)—the fortunate isolation of the White House, I say, intensifies its power to appeal to that musing and mooning visitor whose perceptions alone, in all the conditions, I hold worthy of account. Hereabouts, beyond doubt, history had from of old seemed to me insistently seated, and I remember a short spring-time of years ago when Lafayette Square itself, contiguous to the Executive Mansion, could create a rich sense of the past by the use of scarce other witchcraft than its command of that pleasant perspective and its possession of the most prodigious of all Presidential effigies, Andrew Jackson, as archaic as a Ninevite king, prancing and rocking through the ages. If that atmosphere, moreover, in the fragrance of the Washington April, was even a quarter of a century since as a liquor of bitter-sweet taste, overflowing its cup, what was the ineffable mixture now, with all the elements further distilled, all the life further sacrificed, to make it potent? One circled about the place as for meeting the ghosts, and one paused, under the same impulse, before the high palings of the White House drive, as if wondering at haunted ground. There the ghosts stood in their public array, spectral enough and clarified; yet scarce making it easier to 'place' the strange, incongruous blood-drops, as one looked through the rails, on that revised and freshened page. But one fortunately has one's choice, in all these connections, as one turns away; the mixture, as I have called it, is really here so fine. General Jackson, in the center of the Square, still rocks his hobby and the earth; but the fruit of the interval, to my actual eyes, hangs nowhere brighter than in the brilliant memorials lately erected to Lafayette and to Rochambeau. Artful, genial, expressive, the tribute of French talent, these happy images supply, on the spot, the note without which even the most fantasticating sense of our national past would feel itself rub forever against mere brown homespun. Everything else gives way, for me, I confess, as I again stand before them; everything, whether as historic fact, or present *agrément*, or future possibility, yields to this one high luxury of our old friendship with France.

"The 'artistic' Federal city already announced spreads itself then before us, in plans elaborated even to the finer details, a city of palaces and monuments and gardens, symmetries and circles and far radiations, with the big Potomac for water-power and water-effect and the recurrent Maryland spring, so prompt and so full-handed, for a perpetual benediction. This imagery has, above all, the value, for the considering mind, that it presents itself as under the wide-spread wings of the general Government, which fairly make it figure to the rapt vision as the object caught up in eagle claws and lifted into fields of air that even the high brows of the municipal boss fail to sweep. The wide-spread wings affect us, in the prospect, as great fans that, by their mere tremor, will blow the work, at all steps and stages, clean and clear, disinfect it quite ideally of any germ of the job, and prepare thereby for the American voter, on the spot and in the pride of possession, quite a new kind of civic consciousness. The scheme looms largest, surely, as a demonstration of the possibilities of that service to him, and nothing about it will be more interesting than to measure—though this may take time—the nature and degree of his alleviation. Will the new pride I speak of sufficiently inflame him? Will the taste of the new consciousness, finding him so fresh to it, prove the right medicine? One can only regret that we must still rather indefinitely wait to see—and regret it all the more that there is always, in America, yet another lively source of interest involved in the execution of such designs, and closely involved just in proportion as the high intention, the formal majesty, of the thing seems assured. It comes back to what we constantly feel, throughout the country, to what the American scene everywhere depends on for half its appeal or its effect; to the fact that the social conditions, the material, pressing and pervasive, make the particular experiment or demonstration, whatever it may pretend to, practically a new and incalculable thing. This general Americanism is often the one tag of character attaching to the case after every other appears to have abandoned it. The thing is happening, or will have to happen, in the American way—that American way which is more different from all other native ways, taking country with country, than any of these latter are different from each other; and the question is of how, each time, the American way will see it through."

> Henry James, in *The American Scene* (1907)
> Reprinted in *The Art of Travel* (1958)

"Like a city in dreams, the great white capital stretches along the placid river from Georgetown on the west to Anacostia on the east. It is a city of temporaries, a city of just-arriveds and only-visitings, built on the shifting sands of politics, filled with people passing through. They may stay fifty years, they may love, marry, settle down, build homes, raise families, and die beside the Potomac, but they usually feel, and frequently they will tell you, that they are just here for a little while. Someday soon they will be going home. They do go home, but it is only for visits, or for a brief span of staying-away; and once the visits or the brief spans are over ("It's so nice to get away from Washington, it's so inbred; so nice to get out in the country and find out what people are really thinking") they hurry back to their lodestone and their star, their self-hypnotized, self-mesmerized, self-enamored, self-propelling, wonderful city they cannot live away from or, once it has claimed them, live without. Washington takes them like a lover and they are lost. Some are big names, some are little, but once they succumb it makes no difference; they always return, spoiled for the Main Streets without which Washington could not live, knowing instinctively that this is the biggest Main Street of them all, the granddaddy and grandchild of Main Streets rolled into one. They come, they stay, they make their mark, writing big or little on their times, in the strange, fantastic, fascinating city that mirrors so faithfully their strange, fantastic, fascinating land in which there are few absolute wrongs or absolute rights, few all-blacks or all-whites, few dead-certain positives that won't be changed tomorrow; their wonderful, mixed-up, blundering, stumbling, hopeful land in which evil men do good things and good men do evil in a way of life and government so complex and delicately balanced that only Americans can understand it and often they are baffled."

Allen Drury, in *Advise and Consent* (1959)

DIRECTORY

Since preparation of this book, as with any guidebook, it is only natural that there will be some changes—new locations, new rates, new policies, especially in restaurants, hotels, shops.

A

Air Transport Association of America, 1000 Connecticut Avenue, N.W.

American Association for the Advancement of Science, 1515 Massachusetts Avenue, N.W.

American Association of University Women, 2401 Virginia Avenue, N.W., 154

American Automobile Association, 1712 G Street, N.W., 21

American Federation of Labor and Congress of Industrial Organizations, 815 16th Street, N.W., 37

American Forestry Association, 919 17th Street, N.W.

American Institute of Architects, 1735 New York Avenue, N.W., 105

American Institute of Pharmacy, 2215 Constitution Avenue, N.W.

American Legion, 1608 K Street, N.W.

American National Red Cross, 17th and D Streets, N.W., 153

Chamber of Commerce of U.S.A., 1615 H. Street, N.W., 36

Daughters of The American Revolution, 1776 D Street, N.W., 153

General Federation of Women's Clubs, 1734 N Street, N.W.

International Association of Machinists, 1300 Connecticut Avenue, N.W.

International Brotherhood of Teamsters, 25 Louisiana Avenue, N.W.

National Association of Home Builders, 1625 L Street, N.W., 37

National Automobile Dealers Association, 2000 K Street, N.W.

National Education Association, 1201 16th Street, N.W., 37, 174

National Geographic Society, 16th and M Streets, N.W., 37

National Grange, 744 Jackson Place, N.W.

National Rifle Association of America, 1600 Rhode Island Avenue, N.W., 37

National Society of The Colonial Dames of America, 2715 Q Street, N.W., 108

National Trust for Historic Preservation, 2000 K Street, N.W., 35, 81

Reserve Officers' Association of United States, 2517 Connecticut Avenue, N.W.

Scottish Rite Supreme Council, 1733 16th Street, N.W.

Sons of the American Revolution, 2412 Massachusetts Avenue, N.W.

United Mine Workers of America, 900 15th Street, N.W.

Young Men's Christian Association, Central Branch, 1736 G Street, N.W., 162

Young Women's Christian Association, of D.C., 17th and K Streets, N.W., 133

Street and Thomas Circle, N.W., 123

Episcopal: St. John's Church, Georgetown Parish, 3240 O Street, N.W., 110–11

St. John's Church, Lafayette Square, 1525 H Street, N.W., 81, 119, 162

St. Paul's Episcopal Church, Rock Creek Church Road and Webster Street, N.W., 121–22

Washington Cathedral, Massachusetts and Wisconsin Avenues, N.W., 25, 114–15

Greek: St. Sophia's Greek Orthodox Cathedral, Massachusetts Avenue and 36th Street, N.W., 123

Hebrew: Adas Israel Congregation, Connecticut Avenue and Porter Street, N.W., 123

B'Nai B'rith, 1640 Rhode Island Avenue, N.W., 124

Temple Sinai, 3100 Military Road, N.W.

Washington Hebrew Congregation, Massachusetts Avenue and Macomb Street, N.W., 123

Lutheran: Luther Place Memorial Church, 1226 Vermont Avenue, N.W., 123

Methodist: Foundry Methodist Church, 16th and P Streets, N.W., 119

Methodist Commission on Chaplains and Board of Temperance, 100 Maryland Avenue, N.E., 124

Metropolitan Memorial Church, Nebraska and New Mexico Avenues, N.W., 123

Mormon: Church of Jesus Christ of Latter-day Saints, 2810 16th Street, N.W., 119–20

Moslem: The Washington Mosque (Islamic Center), 2551 Massachusetts Avenue, N.W., 113, 117–18

Presbyterian: National Presbyterian Church, Connecticut Avenue and N Street, N.W., 121

New York Avenue Presbyterian Church, 1313 New York Avenue, N.W., 121, 179–80

Quaker: Friends Meeting House, 21st and Florida Avenue, N.W., 120–21

Unitarian: All Souls Unitarian Church, 16th and Harvard Streets, N.W., 120

Interdenominational: Prayer Room, U. S. Capitol, 48, 113

National Council of Churches, 122 Maryland Avenue, N.E., 124

In Maryland: Seventh Day Adventist Church, Carroll Avenue, Takoma Park, 123

In Virginia: Bruton Parish Church, Colonial Williamsburg, 202

Christ Church, 118 N. Washington Street, Alexandria, 113, 193

Old Presbyterian Meeting House, 321 S. Fairfax Street, Alexandria, 193

and 19th Streets, N.W., REpublic 7-1820, 88

Justice, Constitution Avenue and Tenth Street, N.W., REpublic 7-8200, 86

Federal Bureau of Investigation, Pennsylvania Avenue at 9th Street, N.W., EXecutive 3-7100, 25, 86–87

Labor, 14th Street and Constitution Avenue, N.W., EXecutive 3-2420

Post Office, 12th Street and Pennsylvania Avenue, N.W., STerling 3-3100, 87

State, 21st Street & Virginia Avenue, N.W., REpublic 7-5600, 89, 174

Treasury, 15th and Pennsylvania Avenue, N.W., EXecutive 3-6400, 80

Bureau of Engraving and Printing, 14th and C Streets, S.W., EXecutive 3-6400, 25, 88

Internal Revenue Service, 12th and Constitution Avenue, N.W., STerling 3-8400

Atomic Energy Commission, Germantown, Md., HAzelwood 7-7831, 215

Bureau of the Budget, 17th St. and Pennsylvania Avenue, N.W., EXecutive 3-3300

Civil Aeronautics Board, 1825 Connecticut Avenue, N.W., EXecutive 3-3111

Office of Civil and Defense Mobilization, 17th St. and Pennsylvania Avenue, N.W., EXecutive 3-3300

Commission on Civil Rights, 726 Jackson Place, N.W., STerling 3-0860

Federal Aviation Agency, 1711 New York Avenue, N.W., STerling 3-2100

Federal Communications Commission, New Post Office Building, 12th Street and Pennsylvania Avenue, N.W., EXecutive 3-3620

Federal Power Commission, General Accounting Office Building, 441 G Street, N.W., EXecutive 3-0100

Federal Reserve System, 20th Street and Constitution Avenue, N.W., REpublic 7-1100

Federal Trade Commission, Pennsylvania Avenue at 6th Street, N.W., EXecutive 3-6800, 85

General Accounting Office, 441 G Street, N.W., EXecutive 3-4621

General Services Administration, 18th and F Streets. N.W., EXecutive 3-4900

International Cooperation Administration, 806 Connecticut Avenue, N.W., STerling 3-6400

Interstate Commerce Commission, 12th Street and Constitution Avenue, N.W., NAtional 8-7460

National Aeronautics and Space Administration, 1520 H Street, N.W., EXecutive 3-3260

National Labor Relations Board,

For additional information, write

sponsoring organization or American Automobile Association, 1712 G Street, N.W.

Capitol Hill House Tour, Saturday in mid-May. Capitol Hill Restoration Society, 320 Second Street, S.E.

Embassy Garden Party and Tour, Saturday in May, held at a different embassy each year; sales at booths of dolls, flowers, hats, baked goods. Salvation Army Auxiliary, 503 E Street, N.W.

Embassy Tour, Saturday in April, six or seven embassies with tea served at one. Goodwill Industries Guild, 1218 New Hampshire Avenue, N.W.

Georgetown Garden Tour, usually third weekend in April. Georgetown Children's House, 3224 N Street, N.W.

Georgetown House Tour, first weekend in April. St. John's Church Georgetown Parish, 3240 O Street, N.W.

House and Embassy Tour, usually second Saturday in in May, six embassies, with refreshments at one, and six private town houses. Home for Incurables, 3720 Upton Street, N.W.

Maryland—House and Garden Pilgrimage, Sheraton-Belvedere Hotel, Baltimore, late April or early May, 220

Heritage Week, Historic Annapolis, Inc., 25 State Circle, Annapolis, mid-October, 220

Virginia—Historic Garden Week, headquarters Hotel Jefferson, Richmond, mid-April, 191

West Virginia—Jefferson County Historic Homes and Garden Tour, Box 430, Charles Town (Harpers Ferry, Charles Town area) late April, 212

Holmes, Oliver Wendell, 53–54, 179

Hotels and Motels. *See* Accommodations

I

Information, Sources of additional

American Automobile Association, 1712 G Street, N.W., 21

Appalachian Trail Conference, 1916 Sunderland Place, N.W., 206, 215

Esso Touring Service, 261 Constitution Avenue, N.W., 23

Greater National Capital Committee, 1616 K Street, N.W., 23, 87, 174

Supt. of Documents, U. S. Government Printing Office, Washington 25, D.C., 96

National Capital Parks System folder, 15¢

ern border of Arlington National Cemetery, 69

Sheridan, General Philip H., Sheridan Circle, Massachusetts Avenue and 23rd Street, N.W., 35

Sherman, General William T., Treasury Place, 15th and E Streets, N.W., 183

Straus, Oscar A., Memorial, Grand Plaza, Commerce Bldg., 14th Street between Constitution Avenue and E Street, N.W.

Taft, Robert A., northwestern slope of Capitol grounds, 45

Van Ness Mausoleum, Oak Hill Cemetery, Georgetown, 109

Washington, George (equestrian), Washington Circle, Pennsylvania Avenue and 23rd Street, N.W.

Washington Monument, The Mall, 23-24, 57-58, 66-67

Women's Titanic Memorial, West Potomac Park, foot of New Hampshire Avenue at E Street, N.W.

Zero Milestone, Ellipse, just south of Executive Drive and the White House

In Pennsylvania: Gettysburg National Military Park, 216-17

In Virginia: Jackson, Stonewall, Manassas, 206

Lee, Robert E., Lexington, 208

Monument Avenue, Richmond, 204

Washington, George, State Capitol, Richmond, 204

Washington, George, National Masonic Memorial, Alexandria, 194

Museums and Libraries

Armed Forces Medical Museum, 9th and Independence Avenue, S.W., 66

D.A.R. Museum, 17th and C Streets, N.W., 153-54

District of Columbia Public Library, Main Building, K and 8th Streets, N.W.

Dumbarton Oaks, 1703 31st Street, N.W., 25, 109-10, 228

Folger Shakespeare Library, 201 E. Capitol Street, 56

Interior Department Museum, 18th Street between C and E Streets, N.W., 88

Library of Congress, 1st Street and Independence Avenue, S.E., 24, 52, 54-56

Lincoln Museum, and Petersen House, Tenth Street between E and F Streets, N.W., 22, 182

Military displays, The Pentagon, Fourth Floor, 90

Museum of Currency, Bureau of Engraving and Printing, 14th Street at C, N.W., 88

National Rifle Association Musuem, 1600 Rhode Island, N.W., 38

National Historical Wax Museum, 500 26th Street, N.W., 169

Philatelic Agency and Exhibit Room, Post Office Depart-

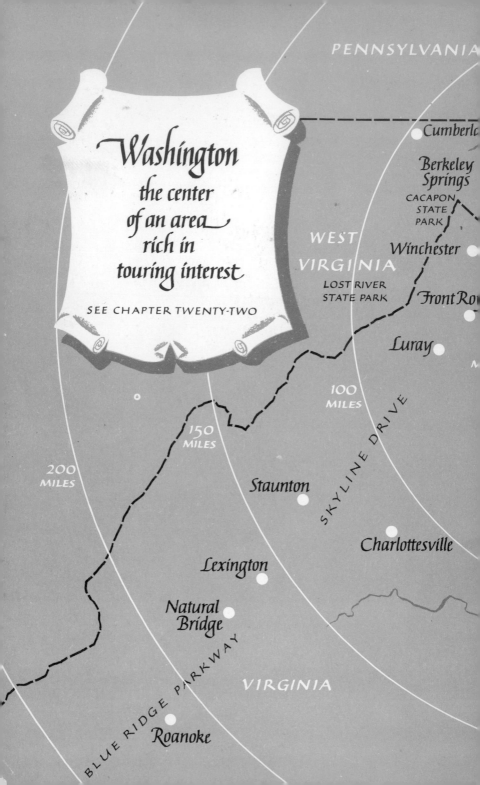

PENNSYLVANIA

Washington
the center
of an area
rich in
touring interest

SEE CHAPTER TWENTY-TWO

Cumberla

Berkeley Springs

CACAPON
STATE
PARK

WEST
VIRGINIA

LOST RIVER
STATE PARK

Winchester

Front Ro

Luray

100
MILES

150
MILES

SKYLINE DRIVE

200
MILES

Staunton

Charlottesville

Lexington

Natural Bridge

BLUE RIDGE PARKWAY

VIRGINIA

Roanoke

WASHINGTON
A Modern Guide to the Nation's Capital